RECOVERING
FROM RAPE

RECOVERING FROM RAPE

LINDA E. LEDRAY, R.N., PH.D.

HENRY HOLT AND COMPANY • NEW YORK

Published by Henry Holt and Company,
521 Fifth Avenue, New York, New York 10175.
Published simultaneously in Canada.

Library of Congress Cataloging in Publication Data
Ledray, Linda E.
Recovering from rape.
Bibliography: p.
Includes index.
1. Rape victims—United States—Life skills guides.
2. Rape victims—United States—Psychology.   I. Title.
HV6250.4.W65L42   1986   362.8′83   84–9138
ISBN Hardbound: 0-03-064002-4
ISBN Paperback: 0-03-064001-6

First Edition

Designer: Helene Berinsky
Printed in the United States of America
10 9 8 7 6 5 4 3 2 1

ISBN 0-03-064002-4 HARDBOUND
ISBN 0-03-064001-6 PAPERBACK

ACKNOWLEDGMENTS

I have been able to write this book not only as a result of the support and efforts of the individuals who helped me but, even more important, because of the people who throughout my life have allowed me to step outside the usual roles for women and have encouraged me to try to do what others have not yet done. They have been tolerant of my impatience with the way things are and they have accepted my need to try to make them different. They have defended me against many an attack by those resistant to change or disapproving of my methods. They have been friends when it would have been easier not to be. To these people I am truly indebted and always will be. I wish to thank Mr. and Mrs. J. A. Majeski (my mom and dad), Teresa Ledray, Patrick Ledray, Tom Kiresuk, Susan Voosen, Jane Phillips, Steve Hollon, Ida Martinson, and Zig Stelmachers.

I am also grateful to the National Center for the Prevention and Control of Rape for awarding me a grant to evaluate the impact of rape and the effectiveness of various treatment approaches.

I wish to thank my staff at the Sexual Assault Resource Service (SARS) in Minneapolis—Nettie Andrews, Maureen Cullen, Diane Ehrman, Carole La Favor, Chris Lewis, Michael Luxenberg, Young Pearl, Barbara Rolland-Martinek, DeAnn Rice—as well as Barbara Chester, director of the Sexual Violence Center of Hennepin County. I greatly appreciate not only their suggestions and encouragement during the writing of this book but also their dedication and belief in the work that we are doing with survivors of rape.

CONTENTS

RECOVERING
FROM RAPE

WHAT IS RAPE, AND WHAT CAN WE DO ABOUT IT?

> I was a gifted girl. I was meant to live up to a high standard, to expect much of myself, and to do great things. I could have played a great part. I could have been the wife of a king, the beloved of a revolutionary, the sister of a genius, the mother of a martyr.
>
> —Herman Hesse, *Steppenwolf*

For generations women have been socialized to defer their worth, power, and authority to men, to play a secondary, supportive role in a male-dominated world. Rape represents the ultimate surrender of any remaining power, autonomy, and control. The surrender is not by choice but usually necessary to ensure survival, or in the hope of survival. Through this destruction of a woman's feelings of personal power and self-worth, the rapist hopes to gain a sense of his own power and worth, to take from the woman what he does not already feel in himself.

Sex in our culture is often used by both men and women to exert power or control over each other—by offering it, withholding it, or even having it. However, rape is the taking of sex without consent, the violation of one person by another. Rather than an act of sexual gratification, rape is an angry and violent

1

expression of the rapist's desire to dominate someone else. Sex becomes a weapon. Unfortunately, many people, including those in decision-making positions in this country, still do not understand that rape is a crime of violence, the expression of anger, not a crime of passion motivated by sexual desire.

In the fall of 1983, in Anderson, South Carolina, three men who pleaded guilty to raping and torturing a woman for over six hours were given the choice of thirty years in jail or surgical castration. An emotional debate followed. The logic of the option of castration for rape depends to a great extent on what we consider the purpose of our criminal justice system, as well as our belief in the motives for rape. If the purpose of our courts is to ensure revenge, or to see that an eye-for-an-eye, tooth-for-a-tooth justice is carried out, then castration could be just punishment for rape. Does this mean that thieves should have the option of having a hand cut off instead of going to jail?

If, on the other hand, the purpose of our criminal-justice system is to ensure our safety from criminals and to prevent further crime, then there is no logic whatsoever to castrating rapists, except in the minds of those who believe the myth that sex is the primary motivation for rape. In the South Carolina case, intimidation was an obvious motive. The woman knew one of the three men and had threatened to name him in a paternity suit. Castration will not keep this woman safe from this man. It may even increase his anger and his violence toward her and other women and make him want revenge. However, if these men are imprisoned, the survivor and other women will be safe from them at least until they are paroled.

The decision of the judge in this case demonstrates a very serious misunderstanding of why men commit rape. Rapists will not be stopped or controlled because their testicles have been removed. This may prevent them from having sexual intercourse in the future, but rape and torture have nothing to do with their ability to have intercourse or to procreate. In fact, with testosterone injections or a prosthetic implant, some will be able to resume having intercourse, and they will be able to rape again. They all probably will be even more angry and a greater threat to society.

Nor will rapists be stopped by giving them Depo-Provera, a female hormone. Inaccurately called "chemical castration," this drug treatment is another choice that recently has been presented to rapists as an option to jail. Some men choosing Depo-Provera still will be able to have erections. Like those who are surgically castrated, they certainly will be able to torture and kill. Some believe that the threat of castration or drug treatment will act as a deterrent to rape. However, it will not protect women from being victims of other forms of violence, anger, and the desire to dominate, which are the bases of rape.

The most this kind of "punishment" will do is change the weapon used against women. In place of sex and a penis, they instead may more often use a knife, a gun, or a lead pipe. Rape will not be stopped until the myths about it are recognized as myths, until we, and people in positions of power and influence, understand the real meaning and motives of rape, until we all work toward true equality and respect for women and their value in our society.

Once a rape has ended and the woman has survived, an intensely personal second struggle begins for her: to recover, to take back control of her body and her life, and even to forge a stronger identity as a result of what has happened. This is a time for her to evaluate her vulnerabilities and weaknesses, to set new goals that maximize her strengths, and to develop strategies that utilize her abilities to attain these goals. She has been victimized, yes, but she is also a survivor who can turn the outrage of her assault into an opportunity for recovery, change, and growth.

This book is first and foremost a self-help manual designed not only to provide further support for women who report being raped but also for the 60 to 90 percent of survivors who do not report. Too many women do not seek help because they fear involvement with "the system," because they lack available resources in their area, or because they are attempting to deny the severity of the crime. Those who decide not to report need somewhere to turn so that they can understand what they are going through and what their choices are.

There is a great need for information to help survivors resolve the initial fears and anxieties that most survivors experience, and to help them avoid the development of many of the long-term problems associated with rape. Survivors must learn to identify their inner strengths and resources and to mobilize themselves to guide their own lives and more fully recognize their potential. They do not need to remain victims, immobilized by the trauma, resigned to a life of quiet desperation. They must decide if they want to get professional help in working through the often painful stages of emotional and physical recovery. *If you've been raped, you're not alone, and you don't need to suffer alone.*

Only recently has any thought been given to the impact of rape on the family and friends of the survivor. These people often also experience a significant emotional response to the assault. They too must often deal with feelings of vulnerability, fear, and guilt for somehow not having protected the survivor or prevented the rape. They are, however, much more likely to deal with these traumatic and difficult events in isolation, not knowing that these feelings are shared by others and are a normal response to the situation, and not knowing where to turn for help in understanding and dealing with their feelings, or being reticent to do so.

These people—lovers, husbands, parents, siblings, children, friends, co-workers, roommates—are referred to in this book as "significant others." Their responses to the survivor are crucial to how she copes with negative feelings resulting from the rape and the length of time it takes her to recover. *If you know someone who has been raped, you can help pull her through, and you can learn to understand better your own response to rape.*

This book should also be useful to the many volunteer rape crisis counselors across the country. Although a few professionally staffed programs have become available since the development of the first crisis center for rape survivors in the early 1970s, by far the largest group of rape survivors seen in the numerous centers that have sprung up across the nation are seen by dedicated volunteers.

The volunteers, often rape survivors themselves, have given unlimited amounts of their time, energy, and personal resources to see that survivors of rape have someone to turn to who understands, cares, and believes them. Volunteers recognized and responded to the needs of this vast population long before the professional human-services community even acknowledged the extent of the problem.

The professional community has given little information to these volunteers that would help them to accomplish their goals. There are few training manuals for rape crisis counselors. Many counselors have expressed a desire to learn more about rape. *If you want to help someone who has been raped, you can learn more.*

Considerable research data have been generated since the development in 1976 of the National Center for the Prevention and Control of Rape in Washington, D.C. Professional counselors and researchers have taken major strides in the understanding of the issues involved in rape, its impact, and the treatment needs of survivors and those involved with them. The information in this book is based in part on the research findings that have been gathered in work with rape survivors in centers across the United States. However, it is to a great extent also based on my experiences in treating survivors and their families and doing research with this group for more than eight years at the Sexual Assault Resource Service (SARS) in Minneapolis, Minnesota.

Information from national and local studies is provided here for survivors and their significant others to allow them to understand better their responses and to begin to rebuild their lives. Numerous personal accounts and case presentations are included. Although the names in these accounts have been changed, the cases presented all involve real events or feelings that have been expressed by real survivors and significant others.

The first parts of the first eight chapters are especially for the rape survivor. By having more information, by knowing that other rape survivors have felt the same way, and by knowing how these other women have dealt successfully with the same problems, the survivor will find that the process of recovery can be less traumatic and more easily resolved than if she tries to cope alone.

The second parts of these chapters are for her family, friends, and associates, the other people affected by the rape. This second portion deals with the things they need to know to understand their own feelings about rape and what they can do to resolve these feelings. They too are victims of the assault—secondary victims.

Most of the information in this book is based on the experiences and needs of female rape survivors, and feminine pronouns are used throughout to refer to survivors. However, male rape survivors will also benefit from the information provided. Although there are unique aspects of the rape of men by other men (see chapter 9, "Men and Rape"), much of what the male rape survivor experiences is similar to the experiences of the female rape survivor.

It was not long ago that we did not recognize rape as a real problem. There were no rape crisis centers or other services for survivors. Having intercourse with a woman, whether she wanted to or not, was seen as a man's right, particularly if he was married to the woman. Today we are becoming conscious of the fact that a woman has the right to give her body when she decides. We are, therefore, in a better position to help rape survivors resolve the problems that result from rape. Unfortunately, we have not yet reached the point where we have learned to prevent the crime.

PART I

1

IT'S NOT
YOUR FAULT

*Our identity is a dream. We are process,
not reality, for reality is an illusion of the
daylight, the light of our particular day.*

—Loren Eiseley, *The Star Thrower*

To the Survivor

Whatever you did—accepted a ride from a stranger, wore a low-cut blouse, had too much to drink with someone you met in a bar, invited a man you didn't know well to your home, forgot to lock a door, were out late, took a walk alone—*you did not deserve to be raped.* In retrospect, we are all aware of things we would not have done if we could have known the results ahead of time. But we cannot always know the results of our actions in advance, and we do not usually get hurt. Yes, you were hurt this time, but that does not mean you should have known better and done things differently. You are not to blame. You were the *victim* of a violent crime, not the person responsible.

Unfortunately, rape is not something that happens to only a few women. On the average of once every minute of every day, a woman is being raped somewhere in the United States. One out of every four girls born in this country will be raped at some point in her life. According to FBI statistics, in the United States alone, more than 82,000 women report being raped each year, and an estimated additional 250,000 to 730,000 women are raped but do not report the crime. Because most rapes go unreported, most rapists are still out walking the streets, free to rape again, having suffered no negative consequences as a result of their crimes.

Rape occurs anytime a person is forced or coerced, physically or verbally, into any type of sexual contact with another person, whether the assailant is a friend, an acquaintance, an employer or fellow employee, a husband, or a stranger. Although we may not be aware of it, each of us probably knows at least one other person who has been raped. Like many of these women, you may feel as if you should or could have done something to avoid being raped. But no matter what you did or didn't do, you should not feel foolish or stupid. You should not chastise yourself with thoughts like, "I shouldn't have walked down that street" or "I shouldn't have trusted him." The rape is over now and you survived. It's time to move ahead.

At first you may find it difficult not to blame yourself, especially since other people may blame you, too, or not believe you were raped. Often, unintentionally upsetting comments come from boyfriends, roommates, friends, parents—those closest to you and whose opinions you value the most. People may say things without considering the implications of their words. You should be prepared for this. You must understand the dynamics involved and know not to accept the myths about rape that you hear from others.

Janet, an eighteen-year-old woman, was out for a late-afternoon walk in the early spring.

He came out of nowhere and grabbed me from behind. I froze. He had a gun. I didn't know what to do or what he wanted. It was early, but at that moment there was no one else around. He grabbed my hair and stuck the gun in my ribs, jerking me sideways into the alley. He was holding me up by my hair as I stumbled sideways. It all happened so quickly. He raped me in back of some garbage cans. It was so dirty and so humiliating. I can still smell that terrible odor. The police brought me into the hospital and called my parents. My father came down to the emergency room. The first thing he asked me was, "Can you defend yourself against a man with a gun?" I told him I couldn't and that he had been much bigger than I am. So my father said, "That's right, so you should know better than to go out of the house alone. If you can't defend yourself, you should never go out alone, day or night."

Janet felt completely deflated and helpless. She did not know how to respond. She knew somehow that what her father said was illogical, but how could it be? She *had* been unable to defend herself, and in a similar situation in the future she would also be unlikely to be able to do so. Did that mean that she should become a prisoner in her home or to the "protection" of a man who could defend her? Was her father suggesting that the rape was her fault because she was "foolish" enough to go out of the house alone?

Her father, a large man himself, had not been there to "protect" Janet and "prevent" the rape. Nor had anyone else been there to protect her. But few women or men can protect themselves from someone with a gun, and it is unrealistic to become prisoners in our own homes, afraid to go out alone, day or night, for fear of being raped. Besides, women are also raped when they are out with their friends and when they are home with their families. In fact, more women are raped in their own homes than any other single place. In a study I conducted in Minneapolis on the impact and treatment of rape victims and their families, 29 percent of the women were raped in their own homes.* The next most frequent place was in a car, where 28 percent of the women were raped. While only 2 percent of the women were actually raped on the street, another 34 percent were first approached by the rapist while they were on the street, coming and going to work, visiting friends, or waiting for a bus.

According to these statistics, if you stay off the streets, out of cars, and out of your home, you may reduce your chance of being raped by more than 90 percent. Unfortunately, even being with a man "for protection" does not always prevent rape.

* Funded by the National Institute of Mental Health.

My boyfriend and I decided to see a late movie after having dinner downtown. I always thought I was safe out with him. I still can't believe it really happened. We were in the parking lot when all of a sudden two men were forcing us into a car. A third guy got into the backseat. They drove us to a deserted lot, somewhere on the edge of town, all the while saying that if we were just quiet and cooperated they wouldn't hurt us. The only thing worse they could have done was to kill us both. I thought they might. They made my boyfriend watch while one raped me and they forced me to have oral sex with one of the others. Then he urinated on me. When they were done with me, they raped my boyfriend.

Should Peggy and her boyfriend have known better than to stay out so late, or to park in the restaurant parking lot? Does the fact that they parked there mean that they deserved to be raped, or that they were asking for it? The initial response of one of Peggy's friends was "You should have known better than to have parked there."

Gloria, the mother of two teenage sons, was spending a quiet evening at her suburban home with her family. She went to answer the door and was overpowered by three men with a gun. They tied up her husband and eighteen-year-old son, and dragged her around the house looking for valuables, then raped her before they left.

Should Gloria have known better than to answer the door? Does the fact that she answered the door and that these men then got in make her responsible? Her neighbor told her, "You should never have opened your front door without knowing who was there."

No matter what you could have done differently, the rapist— not you—is to blame for the assault. So, why do so many otherwise-intelligent, rational people blame the survivor? Why do survivors blame themselves? Why have the many myths about rape been kept alive for so long? In order to put these detrimental myths to rest, we must first understand why certain beliefs are accepted.

THE FUNCTION OF RAPE MYTHS

Myths about rape have survived in our culture so tenaciously for so long because they have a number of social functions. The belief in rape myths allows people to feel safe by believing that rape does not really happen or at least not often, or that if it does, it is because the woman secretly wanted to be raped. The myths enable us to maintain our belief that we live in a just world. They allow us to believe we can prevent future rapes. They keep women unequal to men, living under their control and in need of their protection, and they maintain the Adam-and-Eve tradition of our culture, in which man is believed to be the innocent victim of the evil temptress—woman.

Myths Provide False Security

When we are confronted with the story of a rape, the easiest way to maintain our feelings of safety and invulnerability to rape is to believe that what we are hearing is indeed a work of fiction, not a true story. If we believe that "many rape reports are false," then we significantly lower our perceived chance of becoming a victim too. In 1978, a survey evaluating the acceptance of rape myths was conducted at the University of Minnesota School for Social Research. Most participants believed that more than half the women who claim to be raped lie about being raped because they are "angry at the man and want to get even," or "they are pregnant and want to protect their reputations." More than 40 percent reported believing that women who say they were raped are "lying to call attention to themselves."

There have been a few cases where women have recanted their stories, as happened in the well-publicized 1985 Gary Dotson/Cathleen Webb case in Illinois. However, the vast majority of women who report being raped are telling the truth. Even a woman who recants may not have lied about being raped; she may have decided to change her story for a variety of other reasons, such as to end threats from a rapist's family or because of her conversion to a religion that urges her to forgive and forget.

The implication behind many myths is that there may have

been sexual intercourse, but it was not rape. For example, the myth that "a woman can run faster with her skirt up than a man can with his pants down" is simple enough. People who believe this myth think that a woman should be able to run away from the rapist, and if she does not, then she really must not have wanted to get away. This does not, however, take into consideration the immobility that results when you are faced with a threatening, angry man, with or without a weapon, and are afraid of being killed or hurt if you don't do what he tells you.

Many people, especially men, are unwilling to believe that a rape occurred unless the woman fights to the point of exhaustion and sustains physical signs of injury, such as cuts and bruises or torn clothing, as proof of her resistance. A 1979 study done at Iowa State University found an interesting difference between male and female students' attitudes toward rape survivors who did and did not fight back. In cases in which the survivor resisted more forcefully, male students believed that the woman was *more* intelligent and *less* at fault for the rape. Female students, on the other hand, believed survivors who had resisted more forcefully were *less* intelligent and *more* at fault. According to researchers, the findings supported established societal norms. The students interpreted the survivors' behavior according to norms for their own sex: men are taught to fight back and defend themselves, and see this as the intelligent, responsible thing to do; women are taught that men will be good to them and not hurt them if they do what the men tell them to do. The result is that many women believe that if a woman is foolish enough not to follow a man's directions, she "deserves what she gets." The Iowa State University study also found that, because men expect women to resist physical aggression, they were less likely to believe a crime—a rape—had really been committed when the woman did not fight back. They were more likely to blame the woman in the nonresistant situation and to believe that the rape was her fault. After all, if she had really wanted to get away, she would have fought back—as these men felt they would do—when attacked.

Pauline met a very attractive man in one of the classier bars in town while out one Friday night. The man bought her a couple of drinks then suggested they go to another bar just a short distance away. His car was in the parking lot, so he said he would drive. As soon as she got into his car he grabbed her hair and forced her down on the seat. Then he took out a pair of handcuffs and put them on her. He drove to a deserted street not far away, raped her both vaginally and anally, and forced her to perform oral sex.

The police would not charge the case because they did not think it would hold up in court. Pauline had been seen drinking with this man and she had willingly left the bar with him. She had not fought back, and she had no cuts, bruises, or torn clothing to indicate there had been a struggle. Too many people still believe the old myths, so this man went free. This is not an unusual situation.

In reality, less than 20 percent of all rape survivors are cut or bruised as a result of the rape. Only 23 percent of the women interviewed in a 1981 Minneapolis study I completed used physical means such as hitting, biting, kicking, or pushing to resist the assailant. An additional group, 24 percent, did scream, however. More than half of the women were too frightened or intimidated to use any physical means of resistance. But they did *not* consent. It was still rape.

Women, for the most part, are not taught to resist physical attacks. We are taught to submit to physical force, and we usually do. In fact, we usually submit even before we are confronted with threats of physical harm. While aggressiveness is an expected and approved trait in boys, it is strongly discouraged in girls.

Women are expected to respond with fear to the same situations in which men are expected to respond with anger, and this expectation begins in infancy. In a 1976 study done at Cornell University, a group of subjects was shown a videotape of a small baby seeing a jack-in-the-box for the first time and were asked to describe the baby's reaction. When the group of people were told that the baby was a girl, they interpreted her response as being frightened. When another group saw the same tape of the same baby but were told it was a boy, they described the response as anger.

Some people concede that a man accused of rape may have used force, but they maintain that those who were raped "really wanted to be raped." There are women who may fantasize about being raped, but there is a big difference between what people want in fantasy and what they want in reality. No woman wants to be brutally raped by anyone. Both men and women fantasize about many things they would never actually want to have happen.

More than 70 percent of the general public responding in the 1978 survey carried out by the University of Minnesota Center for Social Research believed that women are raped because, out of an unconscious wish to be raped, they do things like dressing provocatively. Rapists, however, know that this is not true. *Only 6 percent of the rapists questioned in the survey said that rape was the survivors' fault.*

There are also many myths about how women are "supposed" to act after a rape, that is, if they were "really raped." One of these beliefs is that "after a woman is raped, she will be hysterical"; she will be extremely upset, crying, angry, or very sad.

Nina had been raped at knifepoint.

> He acted like a lunatic. He was real nice when I first met him, and insisted on walking me home so I would be safe, of all things. My apartment was close, only a few blocks away, but he insisted and he seemed so nice. When we got to my apartment door, he suddenly forced his way in and took out a knife and started talking about how he was going to kill me. I was so scared I couldn't move or speak. I did exactly what he wanted.

When Nina got to the emergency room, she was genuinely ecstatic. She was bright, cheerful, smiling, and joking with the staff. The doctor and nurse who were on that evening were both relatively new and had not worked with many rape survivors before. When the rape crisis counselor on call came in, they told her about Nina's behavior and said that they did not know if Nina had really been raped because "she's just too happy." How could she be so happy after being raped? But Nina had *lived* through the rape, something she had not expected to happen. As Nina told the counselor a number of times, "I'm just so happy to be alive. I truly believed he was going to kill me."

Although most rape victims are afraid of being killed during the rape, few respond to this fear as Nina did after the assault. Police, emergency-room staff, and counselors who have worked with a number of survivors recognize this variation of response as normal and do not question the validity of the rape.

Myths Maintain Our Belief in a Just World

We all would like to believe we live in a just world in which people get what they deserve. It would be nice to think that if we are good people and do the "right" things, bad things will not happen to us. However, following this line of reasoning, if a woman is raped, then it can only mean that she is bad or that she has done something wrong that makes her deserve it. Maybe she hitchhiked, was promiscuous, went around braless, or was a prostitute—in other words, she must be a "bad woman" who was asking for trouble. Many of the myths believed today are based on our need to maintain this assumption. But rapists know that women's reputations or previous sexual behavior have nothing to do with why they pick them as their victims. All women, no matter how "good," are vulnerable to rape and other bad things. It may be difficult for you to accept this, because you then must see yourself as vulnerable. Even if you are relatively careful and do nothing terribly wrong, you could be hurt.

Some women feel that if they can find what they did wrong that "caused" the rape, then if they do not do it again, they will not be vulnerable to being raped in the future. Indeed, there may be something you or someone else did that made you an easier target, such as leaving a door unlocked. However, many rapists break into houses when the doors are all locked, a situation that is out of the victim's control.

Angela dropped her keys as she reached her apartment door on her way home from work. When she bent over to pick them up, a man grabbed her, forced her into her apartment, then raped her. Ever since, she has been extremely careful about having her keys securely in her hand because, she says, "If I hadn't dropped my keys, he wouldn't have raped me, and I don't want it to happen again."

Finding "the thing" that you did wrong and not doing it again may actually provide a false sense of security. While no one is ever entirely safe from being raped, there *are* things we can do to make ourselves less vulnerable (see chapter 10, "Preventing Rape"). Recognizing and being aware that you are vulnerable is one of those things.

Myths Keep Women Unequal and Controlled by Men

We are more likely to blame women for being raped when it happens while they are engaging in activities not socially sanctioned for women—activities such as hitchhiking, being out in bars alone, or being out walking alone at night. These are acceptable activities for men, but the possibility of rape makes them dangerous for women. Fear of rape is an accepted means by which men keep women out of male-dominated areas, such as bars, and in their homes with their children "where they belong." Women have no recourse. Even other women often blame survivors when they are raped while not adhering to these restrictions.

As a result, women continue to be controlled by men, without equal freedom of activity. They live in fear of stepping outside their socially accepted roles and being punished by rape.

Myths Perpetuate the Adam-and-Eve Syndrome

According to the story of Adam and Eve, man was good until the seductive temptress came along and he succumbed to her evil powers.

The idea of the evil woman tempting the innocent man is perpetuated by many rape myths. We blame women for rape if they are not wearing a bra or if they are wearing a short skirt. We accept the myth that, much like Adam, the poor innocent

man simply cannot control his sexual desires when confronted
by a woman he finds attractive.

> Sue was waiting for a bus one hot summer afternoon when a
> van with two men in it pulled up and offered her a ride. She re-
> fused. The men got out and forced her into the van, then raped
> her. When the case went to court, the defendant's attorney held
> up Sue's white shorts to indicate that she had provoked these
> men. "Why else would she be standing on the corner, wearing
> white shorts?" the lawyer wondered. The men were found not
> guilty.

The outcome of this case was based on the premise that the
rape was the survivor's fault; that she was guilty and the rapist
innocent. We've all heard the myths that men need sex more
than women and that if a man is sexually excited but is not
allowed to ejaculate, he will get the excruciatingly painful
"blue balls."

Men do not "need" sex any more than women, and it is not
true that rape is a "crime of passion." It is a crime of violence. It
is a means of controlling women, of degrading, humiliating, and
using them. While sex is a part of rape, it is not the primary
motivation for rape. Anger is most often the primary motivation. The woman who is raped becomes the target of the rapist's
anger. It is no wonder women are afraid of being killed, even
when no weapon is used. They are sensing and responding to
this anger. Since rape is believed to be a crime of passion, provoked by young, attractive, sexually provocative women, when
an older or unattractive woman reports being raped, some people believe that she just wants attention or a free V.D. or pregnancy exam. Often the survivor was simply the first available
woman to the rapist. Availability is not dependent on age, attractiveness, or the type of clothes a woman is wearing. Sometimes rape is not even dependent on the survivor's sex. If a
woman is not available, a man will do.

Rapists are not "oversexed, strong, 'macho' men." They are
more likely to be angry men, unable to deal with their anger
effectively. They are often ineffectual in other relationships as

well. They may be married and have children, or they may be single. While a small percentage of them would be considered mentally ill because of other behavior, most of them appear to be basically "normal." They may be fat or thin, old or young, hairy or clean-shaven, employed or unemployed, rich or poor, or of any race. You cannot pick them out in a crowd. However, no matter how they appear, they are not normal, healthy men, or they would not be raping women.

DIFFERENT KINDS OF RAPE

You may have been raped, but while the experience was frightening and upsetting, you may not have labeled it rape. This is because there are many kinds of rape and many circumstances in which it occurs. Some of these are clear-cut cases of rape and others are not.

While all states and most individuals recognize that rape is indeed a crime, the definitions vary from state to state and individual to individual, leading to much confusion and ambiguity. In the past, the legal definition of rape was for the most part limited to vaginal penetration by a penis. This meant that men could not prosecute if they were raped, that forced anal and oral sex were not legally rape, and that vaginal penetration by an object or manipulation of the genitals was not legally rape. Fortunately, as a result of the women's movement and the entrance of more women into the legal profession, these limitations have been recognized and addressed. Now, everything from manual manipulation of the genitals to penetration by an object is considered legal sexual assault in most states. Men can prosecute after being raped; women raped by their husbands or lovers can press charges; and charges can be brought against an assailant even if he or she is the same sex as the survivor.

Today *criminal sexual conduct*, *sexual assault*, and *rape* are often used interchangeably. These terms all refer to any type of sexual contact without consent between two or more people, regardless of their sex or marital status. The sexual contact may involve the sex organs of one or both, including any penetration, however slight, of the vagina or anus by a penis, hand, or other object.

Stranger Rape

By far the easiest situation to identify is rape by the absolute stranger who "jumps out of the bushes." This is sometimes referred to as the "blitz rape" because the rapist seems to come from nowhere and, after the rape, is quickly gone. These are the situations in which other people, such as friends, the police, and medical personnel, are unlikely to blame you, and you are less likely to blame yourself. When most people think of rape, it is the stranger rape that they usually picture and are the most comfortable with as "really being rape." Although as many as 60 percent of rape survivors report being raped by a stranger, these figures vary greatly from area to area.

Date Rape

A type of sexual abuse that has emerged recently as a widespread phenomenon is date rape. At some point during a planned meeting, the male becomes interested in sex and starts attempting to "seduce" his date. When she resists, he becomes verbally and/or physically threatening. The amount of physical force or coercion the date rapist uses varies, although with each new victim, the violence usually escalates. Victims of date rape are often less able to resist because their reflexes are impaired by drug or alcohol intoxication, making them easier targets.

In a 1982 study done at Kent State University, one in four of more than two thousand female students reported experiencing sexual aggression in the form of threats, physical coercion, or violence, although they often had not labeled the experience rape. An additional one in eight stated that they had been raped. In the same study, more than 30 percent of the male students admitted to using physical force or threats and coercion to get sex when the woman they were with was unwilling to consent, and 4 percent more actually admitted to using violence. This 4 percent thought that violence was normal and acceptable. They neither labeled it rape nor considered themselves rapists.

Often other people, as well as the woman herself, will blame the survivor of a date rape because she was with the man willingly. But even if you choose to go out with a man, agree to go to his apartment or invite him to yours, and even if you have had sex with him in the past, it's still rape if he forces you to have sex when you don't want to. Whether or not he uses physical force, he may try to make you feel as though you led him on—by inviting him home or wearing an attractive dress—and that you therefore "owe" him sex. But it's still rape.

Acquaintance Rape

This includes all situations in which you have met the assailant prior to the assault or seen him on several occasions but do not know him well. He may live in your building or be the friend of a friend or you may ride the same bus to work every day.

Acquaintance rape often involves men who survivors meet by chance at local bars or parties. At the end of the evening the man offers to drive the woman home. She accepts, eager to save the cab fare. Then he either rapes her in his car, in his apartment, or when he gets to her house he insists on coming in for "a minute for a drink" and rapes her in her own home. Regardless of how or where the assault occurs, if you are coerced or physically forced to have sex with someone against your will, it is rape, no matter how "foolish" you may feel for having trusted him. How many times before did you really just get a ride home when one was offered? You couldn't have known what would happen.

Marital Rape

Until recently, most state rape statutes included a spousal exception, making rape by a husband legal. Unfortunately, many still do. Some states (Oregon and Colorado, for example) even exclude individuals in common-law marriages from the rape statutes. The laws that made rape by a husband illegal did not begin to change until 1975, the year the reform on rape laws began. Some states (such as Wisconsin, Nevada, North Dakota,

New Mexico) have gone halfway and consider rape legal in the case of a couple still married, but illegal for those who are separated and not living together, or in the process of separating or divorcing.

The belief by men and the legal system that the wife and children are the man's "property," that they belong to him and that he essentially can do as he pleases with them, appears to die hard. This is not only evident in rape laws but in enforcement of wife-battering and child-abuse laws as well.

Sexual Harassment

There is still another form of sexual abuse that occurs to many of us on almost a daily basis. This category of "small rapes" includes the verbal, sexual comments you hear from men you pass while walking down the street, and the looks that undress. It also includes the so-called compliments from men you know ("You have a great body";"Nice ass") that make you feel uncomfortable. The unwanted, unappreciated arm around your shoulder or waist is another example.

It doesn't matter if the things these men do or say might be appreciated in another context or situation, or if they had come from another person. The important thing to note and respond to is the way these words and actions make you feel. Even though we are taught to be polite, women must also learn that it's okay and even important to be aware of the double messages men give us.

These small rapes are more important than they seem. In many cases they are the way potential rapists size you up, see how easily you can be controlled and how close they can get to you. Your response will determine what happens next (see chapter 10, "Preventing Rape").

Office Rape

Another form of rape that is seldom reported is office rape. The assailant in this case may be the woman's boss, co-workers, clients, or any combination of these. It is an especially upsetting situation for most women. It carries the most implications of guilt, shame, self-blame and is the most blatant abuse of power by men in positions of authority. Also, unfortunately, many women who are raped by their bosses are so intimidated that they don't label it rape, or if they do they are too afraid to do anything about it. Because of the often-subtle intimidation used, people may find it difficult to believe that a woman could have been in a situation like this.

Mary was twenty-six at the time of the incident and had been working as a secretary for the small sales company a little less than a year. It had really begun weeks earlier with her boss, an older, conservative-looking man of fifty-seven, when he told her how attractive she was. At first she liked the extra attention he gave her, and she was especially pleased to have been selected over two other women to be his private secretary. A small salary increase resulted as well. Then he began putting his arm around her shoulder—in a "fatherly" way at first. A few days later when he called her into his office, he put his hand on her knee and up her leg a little while he talked about routine matters. She felt uncomfortable, but wasn't sure what to do. This was her boss and she had always trusted him and done what he told her. She was convinced that she must be misinterpreting a simple friendly gesture. This occurred on a couple of occasions until one day he began rubbing her crotch. When she tried to stop him he insisted she take her clothes off and have sex with him. He promised it would be "just this once." Mary was frightened and confused. All she could think about was how much she needed the job. He forced her to the floor and had sex with her. She went home and said nothing to anyone.

About a week later, toward the end of the day, her boss called her into his office. As he introduced her to the client he had with him, he put his arm around her shoulder and began to tell the client what a good secretary she was, how she always tried to please him and do her job well. As he talked he began to unbutton her blouse. When she resisted, he said he wouldn't want to have to tell anyone about the good time she'd "willingly" had with him the week before. He said he wanted to share her with his friend "just this once." He undressed her and forced her to have oral and vaginal sex with both of them. Before she left that day he reminded her how good she was and told her to remember that she had been a willing participant and had not resisted. "You probably enjoyed it, too," he added.

When she got home that night she was so distraught that she finally told her husband what had happened. She had always been told that being "good" meant obeying people in positions of authority and doing as she was told. She had done this. She had submitted under coercion the first time, hoping it would end his behavior. He had promised her it would. Now she was certain it would happen again. She had no idea what to do. Quitting her job was not even an option, as far as she was concerned, because her husband had been laid off recently.

Mary's husband called the local rape crisis center, even though he and Mary were not sure that this was rape. No force had been used, and she had not fought to get away; she had only resisted verbally, and he had only coerced her verbally. She could have screamed or run out of the office, but she had not. Surprisingly her husband was not blaming her. He knew she had not wanted to have sex with her boss and client. He was supportive, although confused and fearful himself.

Both occasions were clearly rape. The Florida rape laws specifically state that consent shall not be construed to include coerced submission. Physical force or violence need not occur. Coerced submission is rape, not consenting sex.

While a few women will report office rape themselves when they can no longer deal with the emotional trauma, they often wait until long after the incident or until they have been raped several times. This is because they usually do not think of it as rape. They have been verbally coerced, not physically forced, to have sex, and they feel that they are to blame.

In some ways it may feel like an extension of the "favors" you are asked to perform, such as being "asked" to make and get coffee for the boss, or buy cards and gifts for his wife, and the numerous other "favors" that aren't really part of the job. Perhaps the boss sees sex too as an extra bonus of being the boss and having a woman secretary around to take care of him and do what he tells her to do.

Some women quit without telling anyone what happened. They feel they were to blame and carry the guilt and shame for years. Few prosecute. More must do so if such abuse of women by men in positions of power is ever to be stopped. These cases most typically come to the attention of professionals after the woman tells someone close, who in turn gets help.

. . .

To the Significant Other

DON'T BLAME HER

There are times when it is difficult for family and friends not to blame the survivor. This is especially true when she was raped doing something you told her not to do, or when she was raped doing something you and perhaps others "know" is quite risky; thus, you feel "she should have known better." The more adamantly you tried to keep her from doing something, the more difficult these infractions are to deal with, and the more likely you will be to fall into the "I told you so" position.

> Debbie's boyfriend didn't want her to go out drinking with "the girls." Before she left their apartment, he told her, "You can get raped doing that," but she had gone out with her friends a number of times before and had had a good time. She knew her boyfriend didn't really like it, but she went anyway. While walking over to one friend's house a man forced Debbie into a car and raped her. The first thing Debbie's boyfriend said when he came into the emergency room to take her home was, "I told you you'd get raped."

There are a number of situations that appear to be quite risky and often do result in rape. Some women engage in these activities frequently and do not want to believe that they are as risky as everyone says, because they don't want to give them up. Some of these risky situations are convenient, others are simply fun. Hitchhiking is a good example of a risky activity that women and men continue to engage in because it is a convenience.

Terri often hitchhiked to her university, about a mile from her home. She did not like walking or riding her bike when it was cold out, and did not want to spend money for taxis. One morning she was raped at gunpoint and beat up by a man who had picked her up.

No matter how often you may have warned someone in Terri's situation not to hitchhike, it won't help her now for you to berate her with comments like "How could you have been so foolish?" or "What did you expect?" Terri had hitchhiked twice a day, four days a week, for three years during cold weather and had never been raped before. The risk had seemed minimal. Instead of blaming her, you can be supportive while she recovers from the attack. For instance, you might want to help her figure out a safer way to get to school. Terri now says that if she had known beforehand the fear and trauma associated with rape, she never would have taken the chance.

In a 1978 study done at the University of Illinois in Chicago, both male and female college students indicated that they thought women who were raped after hitchhiking were responsible for the assault. These students believed that by accepting a ride from a stranger, they had "provoked" the crime and should have foreseen the possibility of an attack. The students felt that because the victims should have foreseen the consequences of their actions they were to a significant extent deserving of the outcome.

That women are raped by men they meet at bars, amusement parks, or parties does not mean that they should be prisoners in their own homes or that they are responsible for an assault that occurs. It does not mean that they deserve to be raped when they do frequent such places.

DON'T BLAME YOURSELF

One of the most important things for you to remember is that whatever you did or did not do, you are not to blame for someone else's rape. It is not her fault, and it is not your fault. The rapist is the one who committed the crime. However, families and friends of survivors often spend time blaming themselves or the survivor instead of concentrating on the positive things they can do to help her cope with the effects of rape.

There are essentially three types of situations in which families and friends of survivors tend to blame themselves. These include situations in which something they did or did not do directly contributed to the assault, situations in which their actions were tangentially related to the assault, and situations in which they had no involvement.

The first type of situation, in which the assault was directly related to an action of a family member or friend, is often the most guilt producing.

Cindy and her husband had spent the past five years without incident living in neighborhoods that were considered high-crime areas. Then they moved to the quiet suburbs, where they felt quite safe. One day, at about one o'clock in the afternoon, while Cindy was home ironing her clothes before going to work, a man walked into their home through an unlocked door and raped and robbed her. When her husband had left earlier that day, he had not thought it necessary to lock the door behind him.

On her way to her friend's house, Barbara gave her mother a ride to the bank. Her mother did not lock the door when she got out. At a stoplight down the road, a man got in the car, abducted Barbara, then raped her at knifepoint.

Martha was in her bedroom just starting to get dressed for work, when a man appeared at her bedroom door. He had a gun. He wanted to know if she had a car. She told him, "It's in the garage, and the keys are on the kitchen table. Take it." Instead of leaving, he threw Martha her robe, which was beside the bed, and said, "You're coming with me." He drove to the other side of town, then raped her brutally before letting her go. When she asked why he had picked her out, he told her that he and a friend had robbed a small store in the neighborhood. In an attempt to evade the police, they had separated, and his friend had left with the car. He was planning to escape on foot until he saw her front door wide open. She later learned that her eight-year-old son had let the dog out and had left the door open.

In these instances, the husband, mother, and son expressed considerable guilt and blamed themselves for the rape. While it is true that each played a role in making the woman more vulnerable to the assault, they did not know nor could they have known that a rapist would be out there on that particular day and that he would rape their wife, daughter, or mother. We cannot live our lives in fear of a rapist being outside our doors.

In the second type of situation, the actions of family and friends are less directly related to the assault. In some of these cases, the self-blame is also less evident and may be more difficult to deal with and dispell.

> Judy's boyfriend borrowed her car one evening while she was at work. She often took the bus and did so that evening. When she got home at one o'clock in the morning, her boyfriend called to tell her he'd had a minor accident with the car. She was somewhat concerned and decided that, rather than wait until morning, she would walk the short distance to his house to see him and her car. On the way, she was attacked and raped by two men.

Judy's boyfriend was confused by his feelings of guilt and responsibility for what happened. Granted, his actions were one link in the chain of events that led up to the assault, but that does not make him responsible for the crime.

WHAT IF SHE BLAMES YOU?

If a survivor becomes angry at you or blames you for the rape, it is important for you to understand what she is going through before you react.

> LuAnn was sleeping in her upper-middle-class suburban condominium when a man climbed through her bedroom window. She had left it open for the first time that summer because it was a hot night and the breeze was refreshing. Her two roommates were asleep in their bedrooms. She awoke when the man was on top of her with a gun to her head. He told her to cover her face and not look at him. She was afraid to scream. He raped her, then left. When she woke her roommates, they called the police.

In the emergency room, LuAnn let everyone she came in contact with know how angry she was that she had been raped. The rape counselor tried to calm her down by commenting that it was nice that she had such supportive roommates who were concerned enough to come to the hospital with her. She shouted angrily, "They only came down here because they were afraid to stay in the condo alone. They don't really want to help."

LuAnn had generalized her anger to include everyone who expressed concern for her. Very often, rape survivors initially will generalize their anger at the rapist and be very angry at all men. If the rapist was black, they will be angry at all black men. If he was young they will be angry at all young men. This may include male physicians, nurses, or friends. The more similar a man is to the rapist in race, age, appearance, or mannerisms, the more likely he will incur the survivor's anger.

Betty was grabbed by a man in her garage just as she was coming home from work. He made her bend over and hold on to a dirty shelf while he raped her from behind. When he was finished, he carefully wiped between her legs and said, "You're a nice lady." The next day, after Betty had made a police report, a sympathetic officer told her, "I'm really sorry you were raped. You're such a nice lady." Betty became livid. She immediately flashed back to the rape and to her anger at the rapist's audacity to try to be nice to her after committing such a degrading crime. She was also furious at the insinuation that if she hadn't been "a nice lady," she would have deserved to be raped.

Fortunately, the police officer had worked with many survivors during their initial crisis phase and understood Betty's generalized anger toward other men. When the rapist had been present, Betty was too afraid to show any anger. The officer was a safe target for her to express some of her anger and fear.

You, too, may become "safe targets" of the generalized anger and fear of a rape survivor. It is extremely important for you to understand this and not take what she is saying personally. It will only aggravate the situation if you become defensive and angry. It often works best to respond as the officer did. Just sit quietly until she is finished, then tell her you understand that she is angry she was raped, that you are angry at the rapist, too, but that you are not the rapist. You are on her side.

As time passes, the generalization of anger may diminish. Typically, a woman such as LuAnn would move from her anger at everyone for anything to anger at all men, to anger at all men who resemble the rapist, to more appropriately focused anger at the rapist. Sometimes women need help in this process of resolution of their unrealistic, generalized anger. We all have trouble, at times, focusing our anger at the appropriate target. We do, however, need to focus this anger, so that we can deal more effectively with our feelings and their results (See chapter 2, "Your Next Move Makes a Difference").

WHY BLAME YOURSELF OR THE SURVIVOR?

There are four common reasons you may blame yourself or the survivor for the rape: a desire to maintain your belief in a just world; a desire to maintain future control; your socially expected role as protector; or to avoid self-blame. There are also personal issues that rape touches off in many of us. It is important for you too to understand why you may blame yourself or the survivor, so that you can choose not to.

To Continue Believing the World is Just

You have even more at stake in maintaining the belief that people get what they deserve than the survivor does. She was already raped, and may have faced her vulnerability. You still need to find a way to protect your sense of invulnerability. You need to find ways that you are different from the survivor, so that you can feel safe and invulnerable to rape. There are two ways for you to maintain your belief that this is a just world. The first is to find something wrong with the survivor's behavior, something she did that you think you would never even *consider* doing. If you, like the college students in the hitchhiking survey, really believe that the survivor deserved to be raped because she could or should have foreseen the consequences of her actions, then you're safe. *You* would never hitchhike, you tell yourself. This allows you to distance yourself from the survivor and the events that led to her rape.

Another way to maintain your belief in a just world is to find something wrong with the survivor's character. If you cannot find something she did that led directly to her being raped, then maybe you can find something wrong with her personality. Maybe she is extremely naïve, or not too smart. Even worse, perhaps she has done something terribly wrong in the past that makes her a "bad" person who "deserves" to be raped. However, no one—not even women who have done things they or others regret—deserves to be raped.

To Avoid Self-Blame

You may blame the survivor to avoid feeling guilty yourself. If it was her fault, then it cannot be your fault. If she is responsible, then you cannot be responsible for the assault. It is true that you are not responsible, but neither is she. The rapist is the only one to blame. You must keep your anger focused on him. Since he is not available, you may tend to take your anger out on yourself or other people, but it is not helpful to you or the survivor to do so.

To Maintain Future Control

There is another reason you may attempt to find "the thing" the survivor did wrong, or "the thing" you did that "caused" the rape. Finding it may make you feel as though you are in control. If you do not do that particular thing again, you may feel that you can prevent a rape in the future. Barbara's mother now always locks the car door when she gets out and leaves her daughter waiting in the car. She keeps the doors locked when she is in the car alone, as well, so that she will be safe, and she has her daughter do the same. As was mentioned in the portion of this chapter addressed to the survivor, while these actions may indeed lower our vulnerability and the vulnerability of others, it is important to keep them in perspective. They will not keep us entirely safe from rape. Believing that they will can only result in a false sense of security and possibly even a higher vulnerability.

Because You're Supposed to Protect Her

You may blame yourself because you think it was your duty to protect her, especially if you are the survivor's parent, husband, boyfriend, or brother. While parents do indeed have a responsibility to try to protect their children, there are limits to this responsibility. It is unrealistic for you or other people to expect that you can always be there to protect your daughter, wife, girlfriend, or sister. It is unrealistic to expect husbands, brothers, or boyfriends to be parentlike to women or to be available all the time to be strong and able to stop bad things from happening. It may even be harmful for you and the survivor if you try to do so. If she is an adult, she must be allowed to be responsible for her own life.

Your response to the survivor and the things that you do now can make a significant difference to both of you. You must respond to her in positive ways that not only help her alleviate her anxiety temporarily, but also help her take back control over her feelings and actions in the future.

2

YOUR NEXT MOVE
CAN MAKE A DIFFERENCE

*Experience is not what happens to a
[woman]. It is what [she] does with
what happens to [her].*

—Aldous Huxley *(1933)*

To the Survivor

It was dark and cold and I was alone again—finally. I wasn't
sure where I was. I had tried to see where he was taking me, until
he grabbed my hair and forced my head down onto the front seat. I
was freezing. He had driven away with my coat still in his car, and
my shirt was ripped. A car pulled up. I was terrified that it was
him again. But I saw it was another man, and he was offering me a
ride. I called out, "No. No, leave me alone," and started walking
faster. He shrugged his shoulders and drove off. I knew I'd never be
able to get into a car with a strange man again.

While Ann is still confused and disoriented, a normal response after such a serious life crisis, her primary need and concern at this point is finding out where she is and getting to a safe
place with people she can trust. She will then need to make
some important decisions about getting medical attention and
contacting her local rape crisis center.

You may or may not have considered and made your decisions about these matters already. You may or may not be satis-

fied with the results. This chapter should answer any remaining questions as well as help you understand what your own experience was all about. It will be especially helpful to those who may not have taken the initial steps yet.

DEALING WITH THE POLICE

One of the most important decisions you still may be struggling with is whether or not to report the crime to the police. While the number of reports is rising, unfortunately only about one out of four women who have been raped decide to make a police report.

Why You Should Report

FOR YOUR SAFETY. The police can get you to a safe place and will know the resources available in the community to help you, and they will know the best place to take you for treatment and for the evidentiary exam. They will also provide transportation.

While some survivors do get to the hospital on their own, are brought by friends, and on rare occasions are even dropped off by the rapist, most are brought by the police. They play a key role in getting you to where there are people specifically trained to provide the emotional and medical care you need. In most communities this is the emergency room of a major medical center. The police will know which hospitals have established a protocol for dealing with rape survivors. If a private physician completes a sexual-assault evidentiary exam, he or she might be subpoenaed as a witness, though it is unlikely, if the case goes to court.

In one case the Minneapolis street police spent several additional hours with a rape survivor getting her home and seeing that a locksmith changed her locks before they left her alone. If the rapist has your keys and knows your address, you must have your locks changed immediately. Even if the rapist doesn't use your keys himself, he may sell them on the streets to others who might.

FOR THE SAFETY OF OTHER WOMEN. Even if a substantial amount of time has passed and little evidence is available that could lead to an arrest and conviction in your case alone, reporting may provide useful information to aid the police in finding a man who has raped other women. You even may be asked to serve as a witness in another case. Your testimony could make the crucial difference in the court's finding the man who raped you guilty of another rape.

> The county attorney had decided not to take Arlene's case to court. It was her word against the two men who raped her, until Hazel decided to call and report her rape to the police. Arlene had met the men at a neighborhood bar and had had a few drinks with them. They offered her a ride home. She accepted and was raped by both of them in their car. It turned out that Hazel had been raped by the same two men, in much the same manner, after meeting them at the same bar one week earlier. They pled guilty.

IT'S YOUR RIGHT AND RESPONSIBILITY. It's both a right and a responsibility to report the crime of rape. There are many treatment programs for survivors of rape today (see the listing of rape crisis centers at the end of the book). These programs did not exist before the early 1970s, when women were willing to demand that something be done about rape. Federal and local governments began allocating money to develop these programs only after large numbers of women who had been raped were brave enough to come forward and be identified as survivors whose lives had been dramatically altered as a result of the anger of men.

While we have indeed made progress during the past fifteen years, we are still a long way from having a just or objective legal system. As women, we must continue to play a role in defining rape by reporting rape. If we don't report coercive sex, rape by an acquaintance, date rape, or marital rape, we are buying into the male interpretation and definitions. We are allowing others to decide what is and is not rape. We are sitting back and choosing to remain victims instead of standing up and being heard and taking the risk necessary to effect change.

It is true that today only a small percentage of all rapists go to prison. However, reporting is the *only* way rapists can be caught and prosecuted. If you chose not to report the crime, you will be reinforcing the impression that rape is less common than it is. Deceptively low statistics on rape give us all a false sense of security. Little will be done to improve the legal system so that more rapists go to prison. And the person who raped you will be free to rape again.

YOU MAY BE ELIGIBLE FOR COMPENSATION. Many states and counties have recently passed legislation that allows the county or state to pay the cost of the medical exam if you report the rape to the police within thirty-six hours. The reason they do this is that the exam is necessary for the collection of evidence that the state or county needs in order to prosecute the case. Most of the medical evidence is only present for the first thirty-six hours, so under this program the exam is not done after that time. In many areas you need only to report the crime to the police for the exam expense to be covered. You need not agree to proceed with prosecution. Payment of medical fees is contingent only on reporting in these areas. This may include all aspects of evidence collection, pregnancy testing, V.D. testing, and care of injuries. Your local rape center would be able to give you the most up-to-date information about the policy in your area.

Many areas now also have crime victim compensation programs. These programs provide a variety of types of compensation, depending on their resources and philosophies. They range from compensation for medical costs resulting from violent crimes, such as rape, to compensation for material loss or theft, to compensation for the cost of crisis counseling for the psychological turmoil that often results when you have been victimized. Once again, your local rape crisis center or your county attorney's office is a good resource for further information about such programs in your area.

Why You May Not Have Reported

THE RAPIST THREATENED YOU. You may have decided not to report because the rapist threatened you with retaliation if you told anyone. In an estimated 75 percent of all rapes, threats are the rapists' parting words: "If you tell anyone I'll kill you"; "If you report this to the police I'll come back and get you again"; "If you tell, next time it will be your daughter." In some cases, the wife of the rapist, one of his friends, or the rapist himself will go to the home of a survivor or call her repeatedly and threaten her so that she won't press charges. This is the rapist's way of trying to keep you his victim and exert control over you even after he has gone. Too often it works. However, rapists rarely carry out these threats or retaliate physically against survivors who report to the police.

Women who are threatened by a rapist but report the crime anyway may be even safer against retaliation because the police know. There have been reports of a rapist returning several times and repeatedly raping the same woman—someone he did not otherwise know. However, when the woman finally decided to report to the police despite the threats, the rapist did not return. If he sees the police cars outside your home, he will know that the police have a description of him and, even more important, that you were not as easily intimidated and controlled as he had counted on. Even if the assailant is not apprehended right away, he knows that there is a record of the assault and a description of him with the police. He will be more easily caught if he tries to do further harm to you or your family. No matter how frightening his words are, his presence was even worse. In deciding whether or not to call the police, you have the choice of doing what is best for the rapist or what is best for you. Most likely, your silence will hurt you, benefit him, and allow him to rape other women. You are probably not even the first woman he has raped.

YOU FEARED BLAME OR INSENSITIVITY FROM THE POLICE. In addition to a fear of retaliation by the rapist, you may have decided not to call the police because you were afraid of being blamed for the rape or of the police being insensitive to your fears and concerns. Maybe you have even had a bad experience with the police in the past. Just as there are still hospitals that don't know how to care for rape survivors, there are still some police who are insensitive to the issues of rape. Police officers, mostly men, are simply a cross section of the general population, many of whom still believe myths about rape.

If you don't report the crime, you may avoid unpleasant reactions to what happened to you; however, this denies you your rights under the law. It precludes any possibility of catching the rapist, and it may place more women in danger.

A police officer's accusatory or insensitive comments say more about him than they do about you or your situation. This is his problem, not yours. His name and badge number will be on the record with your case. One option that might be very helpful to him and other survivors he may encounter is to write him a letter (with a copy to the chief of police) describing how the things he said and did felt to you and affected you.

Fortunately, police training programs are slowly changing the attitudes of police toward survivors. While more training is certainly essential, you are less likely today to encounter insensitive police than you might have been five years ago. More police today will be supportive, understanding, and knowledgeable about where you need to go for what type of help.

YOU JUST WANT TO FORGET ABOUT IT. Some survivors try to go on with life as if the rape never happened, but at some point, every survivor needs to deal to some degree with the emotional impact of the rape. You may not be ready to do that now. That's okay, and it's up to you to decide when you are ready.

Telling the police does mean that you must describe the whole event verbally in detail, which will be hard to do. Survivors often find that talking about it helps desensitize them to the horrors. While it was bad, perhaps the worst thing you've ever been through, it's not so bad that another person can't hear the details, and it doesn't make you an "untouchable" or "unclean" person whom no one will accept or respect. Some women report feeling much better after telling someone all the details and still being accepted by that person as a worthwhile human being. The fact that you have been raped need not become part of your personal identity forever.

YOU DON'T WANT OTHER PEOPLE TO FIND OUT. You may not have reported to the police because you were afraid police cars in front of your house or newspaper articles would allow other people to find out about the assault. You have the right to maintain your anonymity, but the vast majority of survivors say they feel much better if they at least talk about the rape with a friend or relative.

YOU DON'T PLAN TO GO TO COURT ANYWAY. You may have decided not to report because you don't plan to prosecute and go through the whole court process. Just remember, reporting and prosecuting are separate procedures and separate decisions. Deciding to report keeps your options open. You still don't have to go through with the prosecution, but you can. A few days after the rape, once the shock and initial fear have passed, survivors often change their minds about wanting to prosecute. If you report to the police, the evidence will be collected and you'll be able to prosecute later if you choose to do so. If you do *not* report right away, valuable evidence will be lost and the chances of the case being charged and successfully prosecuted will be substantially reduced.

You Can Still Report

No matter how long it has been since your rape, if you want to make a police report you still can. With immediate reports, the police are able to question people in the vicinity of the assault. Someone may have seen something they remember as being unusual, which may provide the police with important information.

After the rapist had gone, I flagged down a cab and the driver radioed the police. I told the police that the rapist had dragged me from a jogging path through the woods down near the lake. One of the policemen went back to the lake with me. They found the piece of masking tape the man had used to cover my mouth, and a footprint of a tennis shoe in the sand. His fingerprints were on the tape. The other policeman questioned an older couple sitting on a bench nearby. They said they had seen a man park his car, go into the woods, and come back with his shirt off. They remembered what the car looked like, its make, approximate year, and the last three numbers of the license plate. One officer spent more than four hours trying to identify the car, but wasn't able to at the time. Then, eight months later, the same couple saw the car again. They got a complete license number this time and called the police. When the police went to the man's home with a warrant, they found a tennis shoe whose print matched the picture of the one in the sand, and he was arrested.

The circumstantial evidence—the couple's seeing the rapist come and go—would not have been sufficient for his arrest without the crime site evidence also available. He never would have been caught without all components of the investigation. Had this woman not reported immediately, he would be free today instead of in jail.

While immediate reporting is important, if you report within the first thirty-six to forty-eight hours, sufficient evidence will probably still be available (see the section on the medical evidentiary exam later in this chapter). You must realize that the longer you wait, the lower your chances of obtaining a successful prosecution. Every hour and certainly every day you delay significantly lowers the chance of an arrest and prosecution.

Not only is evidence lost with delayed reports, but unfortunately, your credibility as a witness is also more likely to be questioned. As a result of undispelled myths, some police continue to believe that women who say they were raped days or weeks earlier are lying. While these attitudes are changing as police departments institute training programs, change is always slow.

It wasn't really anything he said when we talked. He just seemed anxious to take my statement and get rid of me. He must have asked me three times why I waited a week before coming to the police. I told him again and again that I was afraid of the guy. I knew him. He even called and threatened me the next day. I finally got angry. I knew the cop didn't believe me, and I knew he did not plan to pick up this guy. I told him how awful it felt to have been raped, and then when I finally got the nerve to stand up for myself by reporting it, to have him look down his nose at me and not believe me. His attitude changed then. He actually apologized and said he did believe me now. It made me feel good for the first time since the rape. I had really stood up for myself. Somehow, I felt like I had won.

If you feel that the police don't believe that you were raped, ask them why. It is best to do so before you get angry, but it is important to confront them whenever you can and to let them know exactly how you feel.

Regardless of the problems inherent in late reports, many women who were raped months or years ago reach a point where they want to report their rape to the police. One of the most common reasons women give for this is the need to acknowledge that what they experienced was indeed rape, a crime. Additional reasons are the desire for others to know that rape really happens and to be counted as a survivor. If you decide to make a late police report, it is important that you make your reasons clear to the police. A full-scale investigation will probably not be helpful at this point. Let the police know you understand this, but that you want them and whoever reads the local and national statistics on rape to know the extent of the problem.

What the Police Will Want to Know

Should you decide to report, the police will ask you some very basic questions, such as your name, age, address, and place of employment, in addition to questions about the assault. It is very important that you give them complete and accurate information. If you misrepresent any piece of the information, it will make your whole account less credible. Be sure to give your current address and phone number. They will need to contact you later. Unless there is a specific reason for the police to contact your employer as a part of the investigation, they will not do so, so don't be afraid to give them the correct name. If you're unemployed, don't be afraid to tell them that either. This information is not going to be used to judge you.

The police will also ask you specific information about the assault, such as the date, time, location, and description of the assailant(s). If you are unsure of any details, say so. This may prevent them from following incorrect leads instead of good ones, which would discredit the part of your story of which you are sure. The most difficult part is usually telling them the details of the assault. They do need to know exactly what happened, the sequence of events, and what everyone involved did, including the most intimate sexual acts, and what the assailant(s) said to you. Be sure to repeat it to the police, quoting him as directly as you can remember. They are his words, not yours. The more exact the statement, the more likely it will hold up, should you go to court, and the more helpful it will be in identifying the assailant.

They may also ask you about your activities before and after the assault. It is very important for you to tell them the whole truth. You should not be afraid to report to the police because of the circumstances leading up to the rape or because you have a number of outstanding parking tickets, for instance. They're not going to check your record and arrest you. The police are not there to judge you. Their concern now will be the rape and getting the information that will allow them to find, arrest, and prosecute the rapist. Some survivors hesitate to admit such things as their own use of drugs or alcohol or particularly unpleasant circumstances surrounding the assault. When these facts are omitted, the story as a whole may not quite fit together properly. The police may sense something is amiss and not believe the story at all. Rape survivors have won rape cases in court in which they went somewhere with the assailant to purchase stolen property or illegal drugs and were then raped. A prostitute even won a case against a man with whom she had agreed to have vaginal sex; he raped her anally. If there are circumstances or information that you're afraid may be incriminating, it's best to know from the very beginning the effect of telling them, instead of taking the chance that the defense attorney will bring them up in court.

If you like, you have the right to have a friend, relative, or counselor with you while you answer the police officer's questions. You also have the right to refuse to answer any inappropriate questions, such as, "Well, what did you expect to happen?" or "Why were you out alone anyway?" You need not answer any question that feels accusatory or inappropriate. It's the officer's job to get the facts, not suggest that it's your fault or that you should have known better.

You will probably need to go to the police station to make your statement. The detective you see will most likely not be wearing a uniform; he or she will be in street clothes. Most police officers will understand how difficult it is to tell anyone, especially a man, the intimate details of a rape. It's also normal for you to feel embarrassed, sad, angry, or even nothing at all during the interview. Don't worry if you cry or have a difficult time. Those trained to help you will understand.

If you don't hear from the police in a day or two after reporting, call them. Ask who has been assigned to your case and what the current status of it is. You have a right and responsibility to keep in contact with the police and to be aware of the progress of your case. This is especially important if a suspect has been apprehended. He can be held for only thirty-six hours without your making a formal statement (see chapter 8, Convicting the Rapist).

While reporting to the police is one way to help stop rape, the decision to report can be made only by you. You may have good reasons why you decided not to report or why you have not yet made a report. Whatever you do, it is important to make an informed decision, not one based on fear or lack of information.

GETTING MEDICAL CARE

Another important decision is whether or not you get medical attention, and if so, what type of attention, and from where.

Why You Need Medical Attention

While many survivors do not get medical help after being raped and suffer no ill affects, others have serious problems that could have been avoided. In order to avoid potential problems, even if you were raped some time ago, you need to go to a hospital, clinic, or doctor's office for a pregnancy test, to see if you contracted a sexually transmitted disease such as gonorrhea or syphilis, to make contact with other community support services, and for the care of any injuries that may have resulted. As previously mentioned, the evidentiary exam usually will not be done after the thirty-six hour time limit has elapsed. Since VD and pregnancy testing are generally included as part of the evidentiary exam, and are then paid for by the county or state, you can avoid extra expense as well as the loss of evidence by getting medical attention early. Contact the rape crisis center closest to you for information on the policy in your area for payment for the evidentiary exam.

Where You Can Go for Help

There are a number of options available, some of which will provide you with more complete services than others. The choice depends upon your needs, desires, and the services available in your area (see listing of rape crisis centers in the back of the book).

The most comprehensive and complete care after a rape will usually be obtained through the emergency department of a major hospital with an established protocol for a sexual-assault evidentiary exam. Your local rape crisis center and/or the police will know which hospitals in your area provide this service. At such a facility you can expect to receive a wide range of services from a well-trained, sensitive staff. By getting treatment at such a facility it is less likely that you will encounter individuals insensitive to the needs of rape survivors.

If you don't want to go to a hospital emergency department, there are a number of other choices. If nothing else, you need V.D. and pregnancy tests. You don't have to give any specific reason for requesting these exams. The important thing is to have the testing done. Early diagnosis and preventive treatment are essential to reducing risks and complications. Some of the tests can be done as early as five days following the rape, though others won't be valid until four to six weeks after the assault. If more time has passed, you should *still* be tested. This can be done at any private physician's office or neighborhood women's health clinic. Planned Parenthood is an excellent resource, and their fees are minimal.

While you may expect that a private physician or clinic will be able to collect evidence for you, many are not set up to accommodate this. If you called or went to your doctor and she or he suggested another clinic or hospital, don't feel rejected. They may just want to ensure you get the best care available. There are specific requirements regarding the "chain of evidence" that must be followed in order for the evidence to be valid in a courtroom. The requirements are so specific that without experience and the proper specimen containers, it is unlikely that the specifications will be met. While it may not seem important to you at first that the necessary evidence be obtained, like many survivors, you may change your mind in a few days or weeks, especially if a suspect is apprehended. If the evidence is collected immediately, you can always choose not to use it. If it's not collected, it can never be retrieved.

The Evidentiary Exam

The actual procedure for the collection of evidence may also vary from hospital to hospital but will include the same basic components. There are three primary purposes and uses of the evidence collected. The first purpose is to show that recent sexual intercourse occurred. The second is to document signs of force, so as to corroborate that the sexual intercourse was *not* consentual. The third is for use in identifying who the assailant was.

EVIDENCE OF RECENT SEXUAL INTERCOURSE. The occurrence of recent sexual intercourse is confirmed by the positive identification and collection of seminal fluid, sperm, and elevated acid phosphatase levels in vaginal secretions. Gauze squares are usually used to collect samples of the secretions in the areas involved in the rape—the vagina, rectum, and/or mouth. The nurse needs to know all the areas involved so she can do a complete exam. Matted pubic hair may be cut off and sent to the lab for analysis and to look for sperm, seminal fluid, and for blood.

While there is some variance, for the most part, acid phosphatase levels in the vagina will remain elevated for approximately eighteen hours after sexual intercourse. Sperm may be found for thirty-six to forty-eight hours. The effectiveness of these tests is thus limited, and that is why they are not done after the thirty-six hours have gone by. It is important to note that the absence of sperm does not mean intercourse did not occur. Studies show laboratory results only establish proof of recent sexual activity in about two-thirds of the cases. This may be due to the considerably high number of cases in which the rapist is sexually dysfunctional or simply does not have an orgasm.

EVIDENCE OF FORCE. Any trauma, including bruises, is carefully noted, and pictures are taken to be used as evidence of force, if the case goes to court. One picture is worth a thousand words when dealing with a jury. Since bruises often don't appear for twenty-four to forty-eight hours, if you have already had the exam, you may want to ask to have additional pictures taken at a follow-up appointment. Any torn or otherwise soiled clothing is also retained by the hospital staff, with your permission, to be used as evidence. You will get this back later, either after court or when it appears there is no chance of going to court. In either case you may need to ask to have your clothing returned.

Just as the absence of seminal fluid and sperm may not indicate the absence of intercourse, the lack of physical trauma does not mean force was not used, or that sexual relations occurred by consent. My research has indicated that only about 20 percent of rape victims sustain even minor physical injuries during the assault. A very small percentage, however, are hurt so badly that they must be hospitalized as a result. Your emotional state and pertinent comments may also have been recorded as evidence. You can ask to see what is written on your hospital chart.

Blood samples are sometimes drawn for drug and alcohol screens. These may be used for various purposes. If you were drugged by the assailant, this will identify the drug. When there is no physical trauma, blood alcohol levels may also be used to show that you were unable to give consent because you were legally intoxicated.

IDENTIFICATION OF THE ASSAILANT. Seminal fluid, when found, can also be used to help determine the identity of the rapist by identifying his blood type. Approximately 80 percent of men are "secretors." This means that their seminal fluid will contain a substance (ABO antigen) that identifies their blood group. While this can eliminate a man or include one as the actual rapist, it cannot be used as conclusive evidence because many people have the same blood type. Blood group substances are also found in saliva; however, they are ten times as potent in semen. A gauze square moistened with your saliva is also collected for comparative purposes.

Any other foreign matter on your body that may have originated from someone or something other than you, such as leaves, fibers, hairs, et cetera, is collected and sent to the lab for examination. This includes a combing of the pubic hair for loose hairs possibly belonging to the assailant. Pubic and head hairs are also taken from you for comparison purposes. Blood and sperm stains on your clothing, acid phosphatase, ABO antigens, and sperm remain identifiable for months and thus will be helpful in identification of the assailant.

This type of evidence has had a significant effect on prosecutions. In one case in Minneapolis an assailant was positively identified and convicted on the basis of one of his pubic hairs found on the survivor. The police reported that this additional evidence, along with other circumstantial evidence, was decisive in obtaining a conviction. Each piece of evidence alone would not have been sufficient.

Pregnancy Testing and Prevention

If you went to a hospital directly after the rape, you were probably asked to give the nursing staff a urine specimen, which was to determine if you were pregnant at the time of the rape. It is extremely important that you understand that this test will only tell if you were pregnant *before* the rape. It will *not* show if you got pregnant as a result of the rape. In most cases you will be able to call for the results in the next day or two or you will be given the results at your next visit. Ask the nurse about their policy. It is essential that you be retested to see if you got pregnant as a result of the rape. The emergency-room staff will either make an OB-GYN (obstetrics and gynecology) clinic appointment for you or give you a phone number so you can make an appointment. In most facilities, follow-up visits are paid for by the state or county as part of the evidentiary exam if you reported within thirty-six hours of the rape.

Serum (blood) tests can be done at the clinic in ten days to determine if you are pregnant as a result of the rape. The results are available in twenty-four hours. Urine tests are not valid until six weeks after your last menstrual period. There are also urine pregnancy tests available in most drugstores at a minimal cost. They can be used nine days after you miss an expected period. They appear to be quite accurate as long as you test them at about that time. Although you may be pregnant even when the urine test indicates that you are not, these tests are especially accurate when positive.

It is important that you be aware that a missed period does not necessarily mean that you are pregnant. Many women miss a period when they are under stress. It should be regarded as serious and investigated to rule out pregnancy or other problems. Though it is unlikely, it is also possible that you could have a light period and still be pregnant. If you are at all concerned, be sure to be tested. There is no reason to worry unnecessarily.

DETERMINING THE RISK OF PREGNANCY. It is especially important to determine if you were at a high risk of becoming pregnant at the time of the assault. If you were not on the pill or using an IUD (intrauterine device), you may be at risk. If your menstrual cycle is fairly regular and you know the usual number of days from the end of one cycle to the end of another, then you can determine your risk of pregnancy with some accuracy. If, however, your cycle is irregular, as is quite common, then such a determination of when you may be at risk will be less reliable. You ovulate fourteen days before your period begins. If you are on a twenty-eight-day cycle, you determine your risk period by counting fourteen days from the first day of your last period. Because sperm usually remain alive for two to three days, you are at a higher risk of getting pregnant during the two to three days before and after ovulation, or for a seven-day period.

1   2   3   4   5   6   7   8   9   10   11   12   13   14   15   16   17   18   19

Date
last   *high risk for pregnancy*
period
began

20   21   22   23   24   25   26   27   28

Ask your doctor or nurse to help you determine your risk if you are uncertain of your calculations.

PREVENTION OF PREGNANCY. If the rape occurred during that time in which you are at a very high risk for pregnancy, or if you are irregular or uncertain about exactly when your last period was, you too may be at risk. If so, you may want to consider one of the methods of prevention available.

Unfortunately, there are some physicians who feel, often because of their own religious beliefs, that they have a right to withhold this information from women. They may even refuse to discuss this and/or inform you that you are at risk of becoming pregnant because from their moral vantage point it is immoral even to consider the prevention or termination of a pregnancy. This is a moral judgment that only you can make. Fortunately, the majority of medical personnel realize that they in fact have a moral and ethical obligation to tell a woman if she is at risk of pregnancy. Only by being provided with the medical information and options can you make a decision about what is right for you and your body. Neither the doctor nor anyone else has the right to make those decisions for you.

It is important for you to know that there are options for preventing pregnancy and that they must be initiated early. These include the use of diethylstilbestrol; high doses of a natural estrogen, such as Ovral; menstrual extraction; or IUD insertion. All of these have side effects and need a doctor's prescription. You should discuss them with a physician.

Diethylstilbestrol (DES) is a synthetic estrogen commonly known as the "morning after" pill. With this method you will typically receive 25 mg. twice a day for five days. It must be begun within seventy-two hours of the first sexual contact. Most women experience some nausea and vomiting with this method. The most serious side effect is correlation with vaginal cancer in an exposed female fetus if termination of the pregnancy does not occur. While no causal link has yet been firmly established, there appears to be a higher than normal association. Because of this association, although DES was at one time used extensively, it is usually not the preventive method of choice today.

Oral Estrogen (Ovral) is a female hormone that is produced by our bodies naturally. Ovral is a brand of estrogen. It is also commonly used as a method of routine birth control in low doses. Higher doses of estrogen (Ovral) are now being used, much like DES has been, to prevent a pregnancy. It too must be begun within seventy-two hours and preferably within twenty-four hours. About one-third of the women report nausea and vomiting with this method. If you vomit within an hour of taking a pill, be sure to call your doctor immediately to determine if you need to take extra pills to make up for the ones lost in vomiting. You may also choose to ask your doctor for medication, such as Compazine or Tigan or suppositories, to prevent nausea.

This method is almost always effective in preventing pregnancy if used as directed. However, if you do *not* have a normal menstrual period within four weeks after taking the last tablet, you should contact your physician to determine if you are pregnant. You may want to do this at an earlier time, approximately ten days after the assault, just to be sure.

A major advantage of this method is that it will not cause an abortion if you were previously pregnant. If you are uncertain if you were pregnant before the rape, oral estrogen is a good method of preventing a pregnancy from the rape without terminating a possible previous pregnancy in its early stages. No medication, however, is totally without potential risk.

Menstrual extraction is a method by which the contents of

the uterus, including the lining that builds up prior to menstruation and the fertilized egg, if one is present, are removed by a suction device. If the egg is still in the tube, the lack of a lining will prevent its implantation and development. This procedure is usually done in the out-patient department or emergency room of a hospital and takes only a few minutes. Most women report feeling a sensation of cramping or burning in the lower abdomen during the procedure.

IUD insertion, while acknowledged as being a very effective method of preventing a pregnancy, does carry a high risk of perforation of the uterus, as well as infection. Ineffectively treated, an infection may cause sterility. As a result of the seriousness of these possible complications, many physicians no longer recommend IUD insertion to prevent pregnancy. While experts are uncertain of exactly how the IUD works, essentially while this plastic or copper-and-plastic device is in the uterus, it prevents any egg from attaching itself to the wall of the uterus.

In addition, not everyone is able to tolerate the stretching of the cervix and insertion of an IUD. Women who have not previously been pregnant have a very small cervical opening and are much more likely to experience extreme pain and considerable cramping, and may expel the IUD or need to have it removed to stop the pain.

It is important that you be tested for pregnancy as early as possible. If it has been six weeks since your last period began (you are about two weeks overdue), get a pregnancy test. Early prevention is quite safe and easily accomplished by a variety of methods.

What If You Become Pregnant?

Some survivors are so afraid that they have become pregnant that they don't hear when they are told pregnancy is unlikely. With these women the fear and anxiety may reach phobic proportions.

When the rape counselor went to visit Loretta, all she could talk about was her fear that she was pregnant. She had taken Ovral in the emergency room and had had a period since the assault two weeks earlier, so it was highly improbable that she could be pregnant. She was from a strict religious background, and sex outside of marriage was prohibited. While she had been a virgin prior to the rape, she was feeling considerable guilt because she had felt sexually attracted to men. She believed that the rape was punishment for this unacceptable lust, and becoming pregnant would be the ultimate punishment. Her fear was so strong that she told the counselor she continually had visions of going to work pregnant. If that happened, she would be forced to tell people about the rape. Everyone would know she was no longer a virgin, and her punishment would be complete.

While Loretta was certainly dealing with many difficult sexual issues, the possibility of her being pregnant—however unlikely—became the focus of her concern.

As studies reported by the National Center for the Prevention and Control of Rape indicate, women rarely become pregnant as a result of a rape. However, those who do may have an especially difficult time recovering from the rape, whether or not they terminate the pregnancy.

At the age of twelve, Nora became pregnant during a gang rape. When she was thirteen, she was charged with child neglect and her eight-month-old baby was placed in a foster home. Nora had not wanted to have the baby, but her mother did not believe in abortion.

One option the rape survivor has, upon confirmation of a pregnancy, is abortion. An abortion should be performed before the twelfth week of the pregnancy when the medical risk is minimal. While abortions can be performed even after sixteen weeks, the process involves inducing labor at a point when the fetus will not be able to sustain life outside the womb. Between twelve and sixteen weeks there is a much greater chance of perforating the uterus as well as the likelihood of more bleeding.

The type of advice you receive regarding an abortion depends upon the philosophy of the staff at the hospital or clinic you choose. If they are not open with you about their biases, ask them how they feel about recommending abortion and then decide, based on your needs and desires, if you want to get care at that facility or elsewhere.

Some women who become pregnant from rape do have babies they choose to keep. Others give them up for adoption. Elizabeth, now thirty-six, has a twenty-five-year-old son, the child of a rape. While she loves him, she admits, "I am reminded even now, every day, of the rape. He is my constant reminder. I still have nightmares and have not been able to put the rape aside."

Since you are the one who will have to carry the baby nine months and then take care of it for the next twenty-one or more years, you are the only one who can decide what is really best for you. Abortion is legal in the United States. You must make the moral decision for yourself. Should you need to make a decision of this nature, do find someone with whom you can talk who can rationally discuss both sides of the issue and who will allow you to decide for yourself without pressure. It's an important decision, and it's your decision. Don't let anyone else make it for you.

The Fear of Sexually Transmitted Diseases

After a sexual assault many women experience an overwhelming fear of contracting a sexually transmitted disease (STD). This fear, which may be more debilitating than the disease itself, has been magnified recently with the epidemic spread of herpes and AIDS, for which there are currently no cures. While more women do contract sexually transmitted diseases than become pregnant, the number is still very small, typically less than five survivors in one hundred.

Since some diseases may not show symptoms for some time after the assault, you may want to abstain from sex for a week or two after being raped, to see if any symptoms appear. As long as you get the suggested tests and are alert for symptoms, there is no reason for further concern. It is unnecessary to remain overly cautious for months.

Syphilis and gonorrhea are the most frequently discussed sexually transmitted diseases. Other STDs that survivors risk contracting are venereal warts, herpes, trichomoniasis, and yeast infections. Crabs (pubic lice) may also be contracted as a result of the sexual assault. In addition, if the rapist has NSU (non-specific urethritis) caused by an organism called chlamydia, then the woman may get a serious infection that can lead to Pelvic Inflammatory Disease (PID). Although chlamydia is now the most widespread sexually transmitted disease, unfortunately, there are few if any early symptoms other than an unusual discharge, so the disease may easily go undetected until later stages when severe abdominal pain occurs. Sterility may then result. While it is always best to consult your doctor or clinic if you have any concerns, the following chart will tell you what symptoms you should look for.

STD Treatment

You need not have all the symptoms of an STD to have the disease. If you have any of the symptoms, see your physician immediately. Except for herpes, for which there is not yet any effective cure, all the others can be treated. Herpes can be treated symptomatically, sometimes quite effectively, although it is likely to recur. Warts may also reappear. When vaginal infections are not treated, they can become more serious. In rare cases they may even become life threatening. Don't take the chance. A home remedy for yeast and trich. infections that can be quite helpful, though not as effective as prescription medication, is douching with two tablespoons of vinegar in one quart of water. If this does not help, be sure to see your doctor. A soaplike substance that will kill lice can be purchased in most drugstores. This is effective in killing crabs when used as directed before a shower or bath.

GONORRHEA. Gonorrhea is not limited to the vaginal area. If rectal or oral sex was a part of the rape, it is also possible that you contracted rectal or oral gonorrhea as well. During the exam, a vaginal, rectal, and/or oral culture will be taken, depending on the areas involved in the assault. A drop of fluid, such as a vaginal secretion, is taken, put on a culture plate, and

DISEASE	SYMPTOMS IN WOMEN
Gonorrhea	Symptoms may not be present. If present, symptoms may include vaginal odor or discharge, vaginal or rectal itching or soreness, mucus in stools, sore throat, swollen glands.
Syphilis	Symptoms may not be present. If present, symptoms may include crusted or open sores (chancres); rash on palms, soles of feet, or general body rash; loss of hair; flulike symptoms; internal-organ involvement.
Venereal warts	Symptoms are usually not present until one to three months after contact. Appear as a bump or growth in the genital area. In moist areas may be pinkish red, soft, and look like cauliflower. May be itchy.
Crabs (pubic lice)	Symptoms present in four to five weeks. Small bugs about the size of a freckle. Lay eggs that also may be seen. Itching in pubic area. Crusty rash may develop.
Herpes	Symptoms may not appear immediately. Painful blister usually in vaginal, rectal, or oral area.
Trichomoniasis	Symptoms present in one to four weeks. Smelly green, yellow, or white discharge. Itching in the vagina. Burning during urination.
Yeast infection	Onset varies. Vaginal discharge that looks like cottage cheese. Itching and redness of vaginal area. Painful intercourse.
Chlamydia	Unusual vaginal discharge if any symptoms present at all. May lead to Pelvic Inflammatory Disease.

let grow in a warm environment for two days. It is then examined under a microscope to determine if the gonorrhea organisms are present.

Just as with the pregnancy tests, it's important that you understand that these initial tests in the emergency room may not indicate that you contracted gonorrhea from the rapist. In a few cases, gonorrhea contracted from the rapist will be identified from the specimen taken during these initial tests; however, it generally takes some time for the gonorrhea to be detectable, so when you return for your first Ob-Gyn clinic appointment in five to seven days, you should be retested.

Untreated gonorrhea can spread to your ovaries and fallopian tubes and cause a serious and painful infection. The scarring from the infection can result in sterility or tubal pregnancy.

SYPHILIS. As with gonorrhea, syphilis can also be contracted through vaginal, oral, or anal sexual contact. During the exam, a blood specimen will be taken to determine if you had syphilis *prior* to the assault, but this will not tell you if you contracted syphilis from the rapist. You can have syphilis and have no symptoms. You also can have it and not have a positive blood test for it for up to ninety days. It is therefore extremely important that you be rechecked at the four-to-six-week clinic visit and again at the end of three months. If left untreated, syphilis can eventually lead to serious heart disease, blindness, insanity, and death.

Syphilis can be treated effectively with medication. If you are in an area where the initial exam is paid for by the county or state if you report a rape, these clinic visits and treatments usually will be paid for, too.

HERPES. Herpes is more formally referred to as Herpes Simplex Type 1 when it affects the oral area and Type 2 when it affects the genital area. While the symptoms are similar, most experts believe there are two different organisms involved. Type 1 is believed to also affect the genitalia but Type 2 does not appear to affect the oral area. There is still no cure for this virus, which may remain dormant, without symptoms, for months at a time. Symptoms may periodically reoccur, especially at times of stress, though some people never have a second outbreak. The most serious problems result when a woman has an active case while pregnant, near the time of delivery. Herpes may be life-threatening to the fetus, but only if sores are present during delivery. A Caesarean birth will be necessary in these cases to prevent exposure of the newborn. Medication that provides symptomatic treatment of herpes is available from your local clinic or physician. Because herpes is such a devastating disease, affecting so many people, considerable effort is currently going into biochemical research, and it is likely that in the years to come more effective treatments and preventive methods will be available.

Care of Injuries

If you were injured and have not yet seen a doctor, you should do so, unless of course your injuries were minimal and they are healing well. The philosophies vary somewhat as to the best means of assessing your physical injuries. Some hospitals will ask you specifically about the assault; the areas involved—vagina, anus, mouth—and the types and places of additional trauma; based on this assault history, an exam limited to the involved areas of trauma is done. In other facilities you may receive a complete physical. Regardless of whether a complete or partial physical exam is done, you will need to tell the hospital staff what happened in some detail. It is important that you tell them what sexual acts occurred so that you get proper treatment. It is normal for you to feel uncomfortable, embarrassed, even frightened or scared. Retelling the story may seem like reliving the events. Don't feel bad if you start to cry or get angry. Hospital personnel usually understand these feelings.

If necessary, X rays may be taken to determine if you have any broken bones. If there was sufficient trauma to the head, it may be necessary for you to spend some additional time in the hospital under observation to ensure there is no bleeding within the brain. If not dealt with early this could lead to a life-threatening situation. In cases of severe physical trauma, hospital admission may be necessary.

During the days after the attack, you may feel a general muscle soreness. If you struggled, you may have overtaxed muscles you seldom use. Bruises can become especially painful a couple of days after the assault.

If you were choked or strangled, you may develop little red spots on the skin around your eyes in the next day or so. These are broken blood vessels and will heal much like a bruise.

YOUR SAFETY AND SECURITY

Safety will probably be much more important to you now than ever before. You may want to make environmental changes so that it is more difficult for a rapist or a burglar to get into your home. But more important, you'll need to rebuild your internal, personal sense of security so that you can feel comfortable once again walking down the street without the fear that someone will come out of nowhere and rape you.

During the first few days or weeks you will probably find that you need to rely more on external signs of safety while you rebuild your internal sense of security. This is quite normal. Making yourself feel physically safe may actually facilitate the restructuring of your sense of personal security, but expect that to take longer.

Your safety concerns now will vary depending on the circumstances of the assault. If you were raped at home, you may not want to stay there for a while. Whatever the circumstances of the rape, related places and situations may be very frightening to you at first and make you feel quite anxious and worried about your safety. You need to feel safe so that you can relax. You will probably not want to be alone for the first few days or more. Many women find it helpful, and in some cases necessary, to take time off from work or school. Many actually go stay with friends and relatives, away from the environment in which the assault occurred. You may need to go to a place where you'll have few responsibilities and little pressure, where you can feel safe around people you know and trust, someplace where all of your energy can be directed toward dealing with the trauma and in regaining a sense of personal security and control.

If you decide you do not want to leave home for a while, or are unable to do so, there are other measures you may take to increase your sense of safety. This will be especially important if the assault occurred in your home or in your neighborhood. This is a good time to evaluate realistically the security of your home. Most police departments are willing to help you do this. If you do not have dead-bolt locks on your doors—all of them—

this may be a good time to make the investment. You can purchase them at a local hardware store and install them yourself. This is not a difficult job, and there are a number of good products on the market. If you don't feel capable, perhaps a friend or handyman could do so. Locksmiths do good work, but they are expensive. There are also a number of security systems available at discount stores, which, if you install them yourself, provide excellent security at a reasonable cost.

Women who have had a rapist get in their front door often feel better at first with just a two-by-four board or chair propped up against the door at a forty-five-degree angle while they are inside. Others feel safer with the window shades down and with all the lights on so there are no dark corners. There are even lights available, which turn on automatically if any noise occurs near them, that you can install by your doors. Try anything that will lessen your anxiety and tension and allow you to feel safer and more relaxed. Don't worry that it seems "strange" or "paranoid" to have a board against your door. You don't need to tell your friends. They might not understand, but then they weren't just raped. Although nothing guarantees complete invulnerability, practical home-security measures can make you less vulnerable.

RAPE CRISIS CENTERS

If you do not go to a hospital or call the police directly after the assault, another option is to call your local rape crisis center. Safety is such an important concern that the police are often the first called. Many other women who do not want to report the rape to the police or go to a hospital, those who try to deal with the assault alone, may finally call a rape crisis center when they realize that they *do* need to talk with someone who understands. Some of these calls have been made as late as twenty years after a rape. No matter how long ago you were raped, if you have not yet resolved your concerns, it is not too late to talk about them. A list of rape crisis centers throughout the country is included at the back of the book. They will either be hospital based or community based.

Hospital-Based Programs

While hospital-based rape centers may be called directly, they are usually set up to make contact with rape survivors who come to the hospital emergency department. Many years before rape crisis centers began, hospital emergency-department staff were dealing with and trying to meet the needs of survivors of rape. In some hospitals psychiatric nurses became involved; in others social workers or trained volunteer groups. All worked toward meeting the emotional needs of survivors while in the hospital and for various lengths of time after the assault, depending on philosophy and resources available. In many medical centers these efforts resulted in the establishment of rape crisis centers at the hospital.

The Sexual Assault Resource Service (SARS) in Minneapolis is an example of a hospital-based center. Trained professional nurses with counseling expertise are available twenty-four hours a day, seven days a week. Whenever a survivor of rape arrives at the medical center the special SARS nurse is called and comes into the hospital to be with the woman and her family or friends. Services available at centers such as SARS may vary, but usually they include short-term and sometimes long-term individual counseling, family therapy, and group therapy for the survivor. Services are often available for the friends and family of the survivor as well, to help them deal with their own concerns and thus better help her.

Community-Based Programs

More rape crisis centers are community based than hospital based. They offer essentially the same services as the hospital-based programs described above. These programs are more likely to be run primarily by volunteers, many of whom are rape survivors themselves.

Why Call for Help?

In some medical facilities, you will need to ask to have a rape crisis counselor called. In others, a counselor will come automatically. Don't be afraid to ask for one or to talk to one who is there. It may be difficult to ask for help when you really don't know what it is you need and when you don't know the person you're asking. It may be even more difficult when your self-esteem is at an all-time low. You may be blaming yourself, feeling dirty, and it may be two in the morning and minus 20 degrees outside. However, the job of an advocate or counselor is to help you. That's why she went through weeks or months of training, and your life will be much easier if you do meet with her.

This person is available to provide you with sensitive understanding, caring support, and to act as your advocate throughout the medical and legal process if you report and prosecute. She knows the procedures and the system and can help you anticipate what will happen and explain to you why it's necessary. She knows the options you will have, the decisions you will need to make, and will provide you with the information necessary for you to make informed choices while you learn to regain or maintain control of your body and life. She can help you and your family understand what happened so you can decide what to do next.

Your rape crisis counselor will help you with whatever your immediate crisis needs are, no matter how unusual. She will also help you with your very practical needs, such as deciding who you want to tell. She can help you anticipate their response and be better prepared to deal with it. She may be able to help you find a safe place to stay if you don't feel safe at your home. She will know where you can get your locks changed. If you live in a rental unit, in many areas your landlord will be expected to pay the cost of having new locks installed.

During the first few hours or days after an assault you may still be in a state of shock, dismay, disbelief, and numbness. Few women recognize the full extent of the impact the assault will have on their lives in the weeks to come or in the long term. You may really believe you can go home, forget about it, and it will go away. It won't. Keep the door open for support from the rape crisis-center counselor. Take her card and keep her name and number, so that even if you don't need help now, you will know where to find help if you change your mind later, even in the middle of the night. You don't need to think that because you refused help initially you can't ask for help later. If not tonight or tomorrow, at some point you are going to need to deal with your feelings.

Crises such as rape are important points of change and adaptation. During the crisis period, typically the first few days and weeks afterward, you learn new ways to adapt and integrate this experience into your life. Some ways of coping are effective. Others are maladaptive, ineffective, and only lead to further, perhaps more serious, problems in the future. A trained counselor, familiar with the pitfalls that lead to further problems, can help you avoid them. She can help you identify more effective coping strategies so that you can move on.

■ ■ ■

To the Significant Other

You, too, may have felt confused, angry, in shock, and disbelieving when you first heard that someone you care about was raped. The hours and days immediately following the assault are a time when, in addition to dealing with your own and the survivor's emotional responses, you have a number of important medical, legal, and safety concerns. Decisions must be made right away. Unfortunately some of these decisions won't wait until the emotional crisis is resolved. While most are decisions the survivor must make, there are some matters you will need to decide too, and there are things you can do to make her decisions easier for her.

DON'T TAKE THE LAW INTO YOUR OWN HANDS

When Denise told her fiancé she had been raped, he was livid. Not trusting the police or legal system, he convinced her not to report. "They don't do anything anyway. I'll take care of him myself. I'll give him a good scare." After calling two friends, he got his shotgun and left. A few hours later Denise got a call from the police. Her fiancé and his friends were in jail, charged with attempted murder. The rapist was still free. *He* had called the police for protection. Six weeks later her fiancé was still in jail. The rapist was out on bail and later cleared of the assault charges.

After a rape, the first reaction of friends and family often is to want to get revenge. Husbands, lovers, parents, brothers, and sisters may feel the need to do something to "make up" for not having protected the survivor and prevented the rape, however unrealistic that may be. Your judgment may be less than optimal at this time. Like the survivor, you are reacting to the confusion and disorientation of a serious life crisis.

Stephanie's father's response was to fight back.

> Stephanie had been picked up on her way to school by two men in a blue van. They both raped her before letting her go. Just as Stephanie's family returned home from the hospital, with Stephanie safe inside, a not-so-uncommon event occurred. Her father had put the car into the garage and was picking up the paper when a blue van stopped at a stoplight in front of their house. The two men in the front seat were in their early twenties and white, just like the rapists. Before anyone knew what was happening Stephanie's father jumped on the van, thinking it must be the rapists, and was trying to open the door and drag the driver out. The men inside had no idea what was happening. Why was this "madman" attacking them? The light changed, and with the door partially open they hit him to break his grip and sped off. Stephanie's father fell off the van, fortunately unhurt.

While the description of the rapists was quite vague and general, Stephanie's father wanted desperately to catch the men who had raped his daughter. Still somewhat in a state of shock, he wasn't thinking clearly, and his usual good judgment was not operating. He didn't realize at the time how illogical and uncontrolled his behavior was.

While these initial impulses to strike out at someone are really quite common, when they go unchecked they can end up getting you hurt or in jail, as happened with Denise's fiancé. That may mean that you're not only unavailable to help the survivor through the crisis, but that she now has something else to worry about.

CONTACTING THE POLICE

You can best help catch the criminal by encouraging the survivor to contact the police as soon as possible. More than one-third of the time it is a friend, roommate, or family member who first suggests that the police be called. Doing so is a rational way of dealing with your need and desire to get even, to catch the rapist, and to see that the survivor gets the protection she needs and deserves. However, you should not call the police without her consent. She has just been in a situation, in being raped, where she was controlled by someone else. Don't take more control from her. Encourage her to call the police, or call with her permission. In the confusion that results from her experience, it may even be difficult for her to remember her own phone number let alone how to get in touch with the police.

If the survivor doesn't want the police called because she doesn't think she wants to prosecute, you can reassure her that reporting and prosecuting are two separate procedures. Many survivors who initially don't think they want to report change their minds later. However, it is important to remember that *if the survivor doesn't report now, it may be too late later.*

It may be helpful to find the clothes she was wearing during the assault, especially her pants, panties, and any torn or soiled clothes that have not been washed. Put these into a bag, with her name on it, and set them aside to give to the police. When the police arrive they will take a brief statement. If the rape occurred within the previous thirty-six hours, they may then take her to the hospital for an evidentiary exam. You can go, too. If the rape occurred where they meet you, the police may also take pictures there and gather other evidence. They may need a description of the assailant and some details of the assault. This may be hard for her to say in front of you and the police. It may be hard for you to hear. This is not something with which you should expect to feel comfortable.

It may be that she's afraid you will feel different about her if you know the terrible things the rapist did to her. Some people do react this way. Men who consider women as property may see them as "damaged property" after a rape. With others, being with the survivor during this initial period, being able to know and accept what happened to her and still accept and respect her, can create an even stronger bond. This bonding during a crisis can even occur with strangers, or rape crisis counselors, who become significant others for survivors of a rape.

You know what you can and cannot handle. If you aren't ready to hear the details, it may be a good time to excuse yourself to see that the house is secured, or attend to another task while she answers the police's questions.

If you can handle the details, this is an excellent time to sit beside her, to hold her hand, and to tell her how all of this makes you feel. If you want to cry, do so. Don't be afraid to express your feelings to her. That will give her permission to express hers to you as well.

It will usually be necessary for her to go down to the police station to see a police detective and give a complete statement. This can be a frightening and intimidating experience. She may still be afraid to go out of the house alone. You can help her by offering to go with her or seeing that she has transportation with which she feels comfortable. If you can't go with her, and she would like someone else to be there for support, perhaps you can help her decide who might be available. Don't forget to consider a rape crisis counselor. They are usually willing to accompany survivors during the police statement. They know the system and her rights under the law as well. They can be excellent advocates for her and for you. In some cases, the police will decide not to issue a warrant. This can be devastating to the rape survivor. Both of you may feel helpless and victimized once again. A rape crisis counselor can help you understand the decision of the police. The most important thing is to remember that it does not mean she was not really raped (see chapter 8, "Convicting the Rapist").

What If She Doesn't Report?

It's extremely important for you to realize that just because she may not have reported the rape to the police, and perhaps still does not want to, it does not mean she wasn't really raped. The first portion of this chapter, "To the Survivor," reviews some of the reasons she may be hesitant to report. It may be helpful for the two of you to consider them together so that her decision will be an informed decision, whatever it is. You may not want her to report for some of the same reasons. Talk about them with her and let her know your feelings, but remember she is the one who was raped and the final decision is hers.

MEDICAL CONCERNS FOR YOU AND HER

It is also important that rape survivors receive medical care as soon as possible. The evidentiary exam described earlier is only helpful during the first thirty-six hours after the assault. Even if it has been longer, she still should get medical attention. Medication to prevent pregnancy can be taken up to seventy-two hours after sexual intercourse, though the sooner the better.

Testing for pregnancy and a sexually transmitted disease (STD) can also be done at a later time. Call your doctor or clinic and ask their policy. *This testing is essential. She may have an active STD and have no symptoms.* If you are sexually involved with her, you could also be at risk. While some sexually transmitted diseases can have very serious consequences, they are all curable with the proper care and medication, with the exception of AIDS and herpes. Herpes can be treated symptomatically, sometimes quite effectively.

If She Won't Get Treatment, What Can You Do?

If she refuses to be tested for STDs and you are concerned about your own exposure, you can be tested regardless of her decision. The symptoms of STDs for women are in the first section of this chapter (see page 56). They are quite similar for men.

What If She Becomes Pregnant?

You too may experience a fear that the survivor will become pregnant. If she does become pregnant, what rights do you have in influencing her decision if you are her husband, her parents?

DISEASE	SYMPTOMS IN MEN
Gonorrhea	Burning on urination, puslike discharge from penis ("the drip"); sore throat or swollen neck glands; mucus in stools, rectal itching or soreness and discharge from rectum.
Syphilis	Chancre (crusted or open sore) where the germ entered the body. Usually the penis. Later symptoms include: rash on palms and soles of feet; general body rash; inflammation of joints; flu-like symptoms; internal organ involvement.
Venereal warts	Symptoms are usually not present until one to three months after contact. Appears as a bump or growth in the genital area, most often on the penis. In moist areas may be pinkish red, soft, and look like cauliflower. May be itchy.
Crabs (pubic lice)	Symptoms present in four to five weeks. Small bugs about the size of a freckle. Lay eggs that also may be seen. Itching in pubic area. Crusty rash may develop.
Herpes	Symptoms may not appear immediately. Painful blister on the penis head or shaft or in the rectal or oral areas.
Trichomoniasis	While itching in the penis is possible, there are usually *no symptoms* in men.
Yeast infection	Usually *no symptoms* in men.
Non-specific urethritis (NSU)	Itching or burning on urination, possibly discharge from penis.

The fetus is not really any part of you, yet it will certainly affect your life. What if she insists on maintaining a pregnancy resulting from the rape and you disagree? What are her rights if she is a minor? What are your rights? What can you do?

One couple, who had been trying unsuccessfully to have a baby, actually hoped a pregnancy would result. It did not, but they saw this as one way they could have the child they wanted regardless of how it was conceived.

These concerns are of grave consequence. If there is any

doubt or disagreement between you on how to resolve these issues, by all means seek professional counseling. Shop around for a counselor who will be open-minded enough to help you objectively consider all sides of the issue rather than persuade you toward any particular decision.

It is essential that you communicate your fears and concerns to each other. Even with open, honest communication, these are trying, difficult issues. They are issues with every possibility of being disruptive to even a strong relationship. Your relationship may or may not survive.

How You Can Help

She's the one who must have the exam, so only she can make the decision to do so. You can best help her decide by gathering information for her, finding out where she can have the tests and exams completed, and how much they will cost. You can find out the policy for payment in your area by calling your local rape center listed in the back of the book.

You can reassure her that she's important to you, that her health is important to you, and that she deserves good care. She deserves to take care of herself. She doesn't need to hide and be ashamed of what happened. She was the victim of a crime; she's not the criminal. Part of surviving is taking care of her body now that she has control of it again. Honesty and openness with each other will do the most to improve your likelihood of pulling through this crisis together.

RAPE CRISIS CENTERS AND YOU

Rape is traumatic for all involved. In many ways you too have been victimized. You may experience the same crisis response. You are to some extent a secondary victim. Most rape centers recognize this and provide services for family, friends, or roommates, who may need help resolving their concerns as well. Even if she decides to try and "go it alone," you can call and get help for yourself. By doing so you may be able to help her to adapt more effectively. (See the list of rape crisis centers at the end of the book.)

3

SORTING OUT YOUR FEELINGS AND RESPONSES

My last salutations are to them who knew me imperfect and loved me.
— Rabindranath Tagore

To the Survivor

For most of you, rape is the most serious life crisis you will have to face, with few exceptions. It is a time of overwhelming turmoil, confusion, and disorganization. You may be concerned about the way you are feeling in response to the rape. You've probably never felt the extreme and conflicting emotions you do now—the fears, the rage, the panic attacks, or the worthlessness. You may even be afraid that you are "going crazy," or that you will never recover and be able to go on with life again. But you will. What you are experiencing is normal after a very serious life crisis. Dealing with the pain is the first step in the process of recovery. The worst is over.

There are four general phases of response after a rape. The first phase, shock and disbelief, and the second phase, confusion, fear, depression, and anger, are discussed in this chapter, along with typical emotional reactions to each of these phases. While the time periods vary considerably depending on individual circumstances, the first phase typically lasts a few days and

70

the second phase lasts six to twelve weeks. The third phase, resolution and coping, is addressed in chapter 4, "Your Recovery: Taking Back Control." The final phase, long-term adjustment, is discussed in chapter 6, "The First Anniversary and Beyond."

There is really no such thing as a "normal" response to rape. "Normal" only means the way most people react, the average response of a large group of people. There is a wide range of reactions on both sides of the average. However, it can be helpful to use the term *normal* because it gives us an idea of what to expect. There are many reasons for the way you are feeling right now. You should not judge your response as right or wrong, good or bad. It is important for you to understand why you feel as you do.

The things we do, how we act at home, at work, or at school, are all based on how we really feel about ourselves, other people, and what we have experienced. Unfortunately, many people have not learned to be in touch with their true feelings. How we respond to others is not based solely on what they say to us, but also on these inner feelings that color our interpretation of what they say. When Betty (chapter 1) blew up at the policeman who told her she was a nice lady, she wasn't reacting to what he said, she was reacting to her feelings of rage at the rapist.

Learning to be more introspective will give you more control over your emotions and your response to people and situations. It will allow you to sort out feelings that may have nothing to do with the rape from those directly related to the rape. Once you are able to separate the two you can choose to identify but not act on that part of your response that is based on feelings about things that happened in the past. You will then be reacting more appropriately to present events. Had Betty been more aware of her feelings, she might have identified her anger at the policeman's words as anger at the rapist and might not have exploded at the officer. You will feel much better about yourself as a result. Remember, getting to this point is a process, like any physical healing process, and it will take time. While survivor's reactions do vary, most people have the following feelings to some degree at some point after being raped.

SHOCK AND DISBELIEF

During the first few hours or days after being assaulted, almost all survivors will struggle with the question "Why me?" Women who cannot face the fact that rape actually happens or who believe the myths that the assaulted woman really wanted to be raped or did something to provoke the attack and therefore deserved it, will probably be the least prepared and the hardest hit if they or a loved one is raped. As Joyce, a fragile housewife of fifty-three said, "No one could rape me. I would fight to the death."

Women who know intellectually that rape can happen at any time, even to them, will also feel shock and disbelief and may not be as emotionally prepared as they might have expected.

It was about three o'clock in the morning. There was no moon that night and it was very dark in my room. I couldn't get back to sleep and I was alone. I remembered gasping for breath, a man choking me—but it could have been a dream. And I remembered a familiar voice, like a friend of my brother's. But it couldn't have been. I looked around. No one was there. The room looked the same. I was home in my own bed where I'd slept every night for over eighteen years. I had had nightmares before, but never like this. In the morning, I heard my mother and brother downstairs. I got up, though I hadn't slept at all. I felt tense, afraid. I kept telling myself it couldn't really have happened. Then as I stepped out of my room, I started at the sight of my reflection in the mirror at the end of the hallway. There were bruises all over my neck. It was true . . . I'd really been raped.

Were it not for the bruises, Jane did not think she would have mentioned the experience to anyone, not even as a horrible nightmare. She just would have tried to forget about it and hope she could convince herself it had not happened.

The rapist had come and gone within a fifteen-minute period. Jane could not see him and, having been awakened, was some-what disoriented. In addition, the assailant did indeed turn out to be a friend of her brother, someone she knew and trusted. How could she possibly believe he would assault and rape any-one, let alone her?

The extreme response in situations where reality is too difficult to face is to blank out the memory of the assault. Although it is rare, some rape survivors do indeed blank out the time period between when they are first approached by the rapist and when they are finally free of him and at a safe place again. This happens when the events surrounding the assault are so terrifying that a survivor cannot even maintain the memory in her consciousness. This happens with people in combat situations and in other very traumatic events.

At first, most of these survivors remember or dream about only small portions of the episode—a room that strikes terror, a face that awakens them to tears and being stiff with fright. As the conscious mind develops the strength and resources to deal with the memories of the event, they return. Flashbacks or nightmares are a positive sign that your subconscious is dealing with events that your conscious mind may not be ready to handle yet. Some women never reach this point. The memories remain buried, affecting their lives, behavior, and relationships in ways they don't understand.

Your Body's Response

For some people this initial crisis can even be physiologically invigorating, giving them more energy and drive than they had previously had. When faced with danger, your adrenal glands release adrenaline into your bloodstream. This protective mechanism helps you remain alert, ready to fight or run. Your body is preparing you to deal with danger. Part of this "fight or flight" response involves chemical change that results in your body retaining more fluids. Seven to ten days after the rape, sometimes even sooner, the body's biochemical balance returns to normal. When this happens you will find that you need to urinate more frequently as previously stored body fluid is released. You also may feel physically weak, with little energy, as a result of this fluid loss. This is a normal biochemical response to stress experienced by many survivors.

In addition to conditions resulting from actual injuries, it is likely that physical symptoms of distress will also be present during this initial phase. The reaction will depend on the individual. Many people are prone to certain physical symptoms during times of stress, such as headaches, perhaps even as severe as migraines; others experience gastric distress such as nausea and vomiting. Skin rashes are particularly common following a sexual assault. These physical symptoms come about as a result of the manner with which your body responds to the stress you have endured and the overwhelming distress you feel. It is important to remember that these very real physical symptoms have been brought on as a result of the crisis and that they will pass with time. Measures to lessen the discomfort, such as aspirin for headaches and a special cream for a rash, may be helpful. Diagnostic tests, which can be expensive, are probably not necessary unless symptoms persist.

Denial

It is during this initial stage that you are most likely to come into contact with others who will want to do something to help you. It is also a time when you may not yet realize the full extent of the impact. You may still expect you will simply be able to continue life as usual. Some women try to do this. If raped on the way to work or school, they may simply change their clothes and continue to work or classes, saying nothing to anyone, convinced they can handle it. While they may recognize the reality of the assault, they deny that it will affect them.

Denial is a primary defense mechanism of many survivors, even some with extensive psychological training. Some women are able to deny the effect of the assault for a while, to put it aside and continue with other activities, but not many, and usually not for long. Naomi was raped just before a big final her senior year of college. She somehow managed to put the rape aside until after the final, then the full impact hit. Maxine was raped two days before a scheduled biopsy to determine if she had cancer. She too put the rape aside until after dealing with a more threatening and more pressing situation.

When strong emotions are denied by our conscious minds, they remain buried within us at the cost of a considerable amount of energy. If not dealt with consciously, they will still affect our lives, only we may not connect the things we are feeling with the rape. Without making the connection you cannot resolve the problems.

I was raped by a student at the school where I worked just before my last vacation to see my family. I was looking forward to the trip and decided nothing was going to spoil it. I drove home, telling no one. I guess I was in a state of shock. During the vacation I decided I couldn't return, but then I had never really liked my job as a school social worker, so I blamed the decision on my dislike of my job. I was still denying any effect of the rape. I quit my job and moved home. A month after returning home I realized I had lost interest in everything. I was bored all the time. I blamed that on the move. I had a lot of job interviews but no offers. Finally a friend who is a psychologist told me I looked terribly depressed and asked what had happened. It wasn't until then that I realized what was going on. I told her about the rape. It was such a relief.

You may not be ready for help at first, because you have not yet accepted what has happened, let alone what will result and how it will affect your life. Most rape counselors know this. You will probably feel the need for help later as you move through the next three phases of response.

CONFUSION, FEAR, DEPRESSION, AND ANGER

While the initial phase of shock and disbelief will probably last a day or two, some women essentially pass through it during the assault and immediately after experience the resulting confusion and disorganization. Many women bounce back and forth between these two responses, one moment saying, "I don't believe this. It could not have happened," and the next moment, having accepted the reality, experiencing turmoil.

Some of the problems women must deal with during this time are special fears, such as the fear of death, of seeing the rapist again, and of situations that bring to mind the rape, as well as depression, anxiety, thoughts of suicide, anger, guilt, and loss of self-esteem.

The Fear of Death

The most widespread fear that rape survivors experience is the fear of death. Research I conducted at Minnesota's Hennepin County Medical Center indicated that well over half of all survivors did not expect to live through the rape. This feeling may be experienced whether or not weapons were used and whether the rapist was six feet five inches tall and 210 pounds or five feet six and 120 pounds. Rape is a crime of violence and aggression against women. It is not a crime of passion. For rapists, sex is a weapon used to humiliate, control, and degrade women. We have all heard stories of women who are raped and then murdered. It is the anger and aggression you are sensing and responding to when you fear for your life.

This realization that you were suddenly, unexpectedly vulnerable to death—perhaps in a location where you felt the safest, such as your own bed—may have a significant impact on how you view the moments thereafter. The dirty dishes in the sink or the unfinished report for work may seem much less pressing. New priorities may surface, and more basic needs and desires may be realized.

While you may respond to this life-threatening situation with fear and panic, you may also respond with genuine elation. You may be so happy to have survived the experience that you are just glad to be alive. Nothing else may seem to matter as much as your survival. Don't be alarmed if other people are surprised by this type of response. They probably don't understand why you are happy. You may want to explain to them what it is you are feeling. It may be important to make it clear to them, even though it may seem obvious, that you are not happy about the rape or blocking out the trauma, but rather that you are happy to be alive.

Fear of Seeing the Rapist Again

Fear is a universal response to rape. All women report being afraid at some point. The things you fear, however, may be very different from what other women fear. More than half of rape survivors express the fear of accidentally seeing the rapist again.

He appeared from nowhere once, so he could well do so again, and if he does, what will you do this time? Some women have actually seen the rapist again when least expected, but the second time they were a little better prepared.

> I walked into a neighborhood restaurant for a late dinner. They were busy, so they asked my girlfriend and me to wait in the bar. As I turned to walk into the bar, I froze, unable to move. It was him, there was no doubt in my mind. The man who had raped me was sitting at the bar. He looked so relaxed. I felt so tense. I was afraid he had seen me. I didn't know what to do—yell, run? I turned around after what seemed like an eternity and went to the lobby phone. I called the police. When they arrived he was still there drinking. They arrested him. I felt an intense sense of pleasure as the officers put handcuffs on him and everyone watched them take him from the room. He didn't look so relaxed anymore.

Fear of Similar Sounds, Smells, Places

For the most part you are likely to fear those situations that remind you of the rape or the rapist. You have learned to associate any number of places, sounds, or smells with danger. You may react with fear when you smell the same after-shave the rapist wore. If you were raped in the parking lot, you may be afraid to walk to your car alone. If you were raped by a man of another race, you may develop a phobic fear of men of that race. Your fears may be more general. You may be afraid to go out of the house alone or not feel safe even at home. As mentioned earlier, these result from feelings of vulnerability because you have lost your inner sense of security. This is especially common if the rapist seemed to appear from nowhere. You are now more fearful because you know such events are not impossible.

It's normal to feel fearful for a few days or weeks. This may be a good time to stay with friends or family. Do whatever you need to feel more safe. These feelings will eventually pass, but you may want to resolve them with the help of an experienced counselor.

Depression

It is during the first few days after the shock has passed that you may experience the most severe and the largest number of symptoms of depression. Research completed in Pittsburgh in 1979 indicates that approximately half of the women who report being raped experience moderate to severe depression. More experience some major symptoms of depression. You may feel discouraged about the future, as though you have nothing to look forward to. You may feel as though you'll never get over your troubles, as though things are hopeless and can never improve.

You may exaggerate your faults and feel as though you have failed as a parent, wife, or even as a person. A common problem of depression, and one of the ways it perpetuates itself, is that when you are depressed, there is a tendency to see only the bad. Somehow when depressed, you don't remember the periods in the day when things were going well and you felt good. You may misinterpret what people say to you as negative when it is not. Your perception of the world is altered in a self-destructive fashion.

The things you once enjoyed may no longer provide you with any sense of satisfaction, leaving you bored most of the time. Feelings of guilt and worthlessness, self-disgust or self-disappointment, may result in the belief that you are being punished, though you're not sure for what. You may even feel as though you deserve and want to be punished.

You may cry all the time or not be able to cry even though you want to. Small incidents may irritate you more easily than they once did, and decisions about even the smallest matters may seem impossible for you to make. This may affect your work and motivation, making it difficult to get started or continue a task once begun. You may be so completely absorbed in thoughts about the assault that you can't think of anything else. You may feel tired all the time, have difficulty sleeping, or wake up earlier than usual, still tired, but find it hard to return to sleep. Nightmares are also common.

Your appetite may be poor or you may have none at all. Some women lose weight and others gain fifty to sixty pounds within the year. You may feel as though you look older or less attractive. You may even try to look less attractive to keep other people away, making it easier to withdraw socially.

If these symptoms are severe, you may want to see a counselor to help you resolve them. They can be extremely painful, incapacitating, and disruptive, affecting all areas of your life. Just when you really need other people the most, symptoms of depression and the accompanying low self-esteem may result in your pushing away those who want to help. You may feel unworthy of their help and concern or just not have the energy or motivation to interact with them.

With proper help, the milder forms of depression will be resolved within six to twelve weeks. Without help it may take much longer. Even six weeks, however, may seem like an eternity, and may result in other significant losses, such as damaged relationships, drops in school grades, and even the loss of a job you no longer feel able to perform. The effects may then continue long after the depression lifts.

The amount of depression you're feeling may vary greatly from one day to the next. You may have a number of good days, and then for no apparent reason you may have a very bad day again. If you have too many bad days, you might want to consider counseling, if you're not yet seeing someone. Having someone to help you sort out your feelings can make a significant difference.

Anxiety

Anxiety, much like depression and often associated with mild depression, is one of the predominant responses to rape, both initially and during the first few months. Symptoms can take many forms, from generalized anxiety to phobic responses (persistent, irrational fear of a specific situation, activity, or object) and panic attacks that may occur at unpredicted times or during specific situations. These are all normal responses after a rape, but when the symptoms persist they are considered by mental health professionals to be disorders.

Symptoms generally include trembling, shakiness, restlessness, being easily startled, jitteriness, twitching muscles, and an inability to relax. You may also experience profuse sweating;

a pounding heart; cold, clammy hands and a dry mouth; light-headedness and feelings of faintness; diarrhea; hot or cold flashes; nausea; and a rapid pulse.

If you are experiencing severe anxiety you may have the foreboding feeling that something terrible will happen to you or a loved one. This may result in considerable worry, apprehension, and difficulty concentrating on other matters.

The symptoms may be less intense, but constantly present, only mildly impairing your normal routine, or you may experience panic attacks that significantly impair your activities. Panic attacks are most often brought on by a specific situation or activity that brings back memories of the rape. During these usually brief attacks you may feel intense terror, apprehension, doom, inability to move, trembling, shakiness, or fear of losing control.

To some extent the resulting anticipatory fear of the possibility of another panic attack may be more incapacitating than the panic attack itself. Some women become extremely dependent and afraid to be alone or to engage in normal activities for fear of a panic attack. This avoidance of activities or situations may have a significant impact on your adjustment.

When this type of anxiety persists, it is important to evaluate the rationality of your response in relation to the actual dangerousness of a situation. If you experience either generalized anxiety or panic attacks when walking alone at night down a dark alley, you may indeed be reacting appropriately, even if this persists years after the assault. It's an easy enough situation to avoid. On the other hand, if you experience the same feelings every time you wait for a bus, even in the daylight, it is an excessive and unreasonable response. If the anxiety continues, you may want to seek professional counseling to help you resolve your fears. In reality, you are not reacting to a current danger but rather to unresolved fears from the rape.

The Loss of Self-Esteem

A survivor often experiences a significant, immediate loss of self-esteem that may continue for a long period of time. Many rape survivors report feeling soiled, dirty, used, useless, and worthless and are afraid they will always feel that way. The events that occurred and the memory of them are so degrading that they feel shame and humiliation and fear rejection by others if they even know the terrible acts they were forced to perform and endure. The concomitant depression, anxiety, and fears make them feel helpless and unable to regain their feelings of self-worth.

Self-criticism may result from low self-esteem. This may be an indirect attempt to have needs met when you do not feel worthwhile enough to ask. However, self-criticism often does not elicit the desired response, and without realizing it, you may become the perpetuator of your own distress.

You may be self-critical in an attempt to seek reassurance from those around you. You may feel bad about yourself as a result of your lowered self-esteem and feelings of worthlessness and helplessness, and be unable to ask directly for reassurance that you're still cared about and loved.

It may be that your self-criticism is an attempt to ward off what you feel is an imminent attack by others. You may think that if you're critical of yourself, other people are less likely to be critical of you. It may also be a way of keeping others from making additional demands on you that you don't feel able to handle. Self-criticism can be a protective device so that others know better than to expect more from you and won't ask you to take on additional responsibility.

Self-criticism can also be very hostile. You may say things like, "I never do anything right," criticizing yourself so that others will feel responsible for and guilty about your pain. Other people will quickly tire of reassuring you that you're not such a terrible person when it becomes a futile "Yes I am," "No you're not" exchange. Being hostile to those around you may just drive them away in anger. You need to tell them, "I just feel so terrible about everything," and then deal with the pain, which they did not cause but may be able to help you resolve. However, it is also possible for self-criticism to help you change for the better and grow. Take the time to evaluate what you want to achieve, and how you might get your needs met in a better, more direct way.

Guilt

Feelings of guilt often accompany the loss of self-esteem. Guilt results when you turn blame inward instead of focusing it toward the rapist, where it belongs. Feelings of guilt may result whenever you feel that something you did—such as hitchhiking, talking with the rapist before the rape, being dressed in something that may be considered sexy—makes the assault your fault. You may have done something that resulted in your being where you were and with the person who raped you, but this does not mean that the rape was your fault.

Survivors who became sexually aroused during the rape commonly feel quite guilty. Your body may respond physiologically to the sexual contact, but it is still rape. Women—and men— can become physically aroused even when they do not want to have sex. It's a normal response, just like laughing when someone tickles you. It is not always something you can control or prevent. Although infrequent, it does happen to some rape victims.

Withdrawing Socially

While some survivors will become very dependent on social contact to feel safe, they usually rely on one or two people—a husband, boyfriend, brother, mother, or father. Others withdraw from social contact. You may feel more comfortable alone because you feel as though everyone thinks the rape was your fault, even though they may not even know you were raped. Because of the depression and anxiety, your perceptions are changed. One survivor felt that everyone knew and was looking at her as though she had *Raped* written on her forehead.

You may find yourself withdrawing not because of a loss of interest in other people but simply because your fears make it so much more difficult to get out to your usual places of entertainment and socialization. You're literally afraid to leave home.

Many survivors want to be less attractive so they will be able to withdraw socially. This can be attributed to depression and loss of self-esteem as well as the immediate cause of both.

Dressing asexually in baggy clothing is a common attempt to blend in with the crowd. Women often do this because they continue to believe the myth that they were at fault because of the way they looked or dressed. They think that by looking less attractive or dressing differently they can prevent it from happening again.

Withdrawal into yourself, away from others, may be a healthy response for a few days. Time alone to evaluate your feelings, contemplate your current situation, and to decide where you want to go from here may be very healthy and helpful. However, if you or others who care about you feel that this is becoming a problem, you may want to seek counseling.

Thoughts of Suicide

You may have thoughts of killing yourself, because you feel you, your family, and friends would be better off if you were dead. While this is not a common response, some survivors do indeed feel so badly about themselves after being raped that they consider suicide.

In many instances, suicidal thoughts or attempts may be a way of expressing your most intense feelings of despair when other means of communication have been unsuccessful. If you ever consider suicide, you owe it to yourself and to those who care about you to see a qualified counselor. Even though you may not believe that seeing a counselor will help, in many cases it does. As long as you are alive, you have another chance. Don't think of punishing yourself or those who love you. You survived the rape. You can survive the crisis too, but you may need professional help.

Most areas in this country have a suicide-prevention crisis center you can call twenty-four hours a day. No matter how badly you may feel about yourself, no matter how those around you respond, your life is worth the effort of one phone call.

Anger

While often experienced immediately after the rape, anger may also occur after a period of overwhelming depression and anxiety. In many cases depression is anger turned inward, and like anxiety, it can be immobilizing. Anger, on the other hand, is directed outward and when properly focused is a more functional, less destructive response than depression. Anger, much like fear, is expressed by nearly all rape survivors, although the forms of expression and targets of the anger may vary. Most often the initial anger expressed is generalized. In the most extreme cases, the survivor will express anger at everyone for anything.

The initial feelings of anger will usually be directed toward all men. This is why hospitals, rape crisis centers, and police investigative forces have found it helpful to have women available whenever possible to work with rape survivors directly after the assault. The anger is directed at individuals with characteristics most like the rapist's. The sex difference is the most obvious distinction to make. The next most obvious distinction and one often made is race. If you were raped by a man of a different race, you will probably generalize your anger toward all men of that race. If he was the same race as you are, you may focus on his age and experience anger toward, for example, all nineteen- or twenty-year-old males.

This type of generalization and the gradual ability to focus your anger more specifically is a natural process. Prejudices develop when we do not recognize what is happening and allow the anger to remain generalized to a larger group. All nineteen-year-old white males are not rapists, even though the one who attacked you may have been. It is irrational to blame and distrust all members of this group or to be angry at all of them. The more specifically you focus your anger, the more in control you will be, and the less the assault will affect and change your life.

Anger also can be directed inappropriately when you focus your anger at the rapist on specific people in your environment who then become scapegoats. You may get angry at your husband, father, or at God for letting this happen to you. It is easy to blame other people for your problems, but in doing so you also give them a lot of control over your life. You may have the notion that if others are responsible, you cannot be. It may be that they are just safe targets for your anger, especially if they are your husband or parents. You may feel that even if you get angry with them, they won't desert you. However, this misdirected anger is not fair to others, no matter how much they love or care about you.

You may also become angry and blame yourself for the assault. Anger turned against yourself can be especially disruptive and destructive. It is the rapist who deserves to be punished, not you, and not anyone else.

SEXUAL DYSFUNCTION AND PROMISCUITY

Although most survivors report that the sexual aspects of rape are of far less concern than the fear of being killed, rape often has a significant impact on your feelings about sex. Sex is no longer solely something for pleasure. It now has become a weapon to be used against you as a means to intimidate, humiliate, and control you—while you fear for your life. Your response is to a great extent dependent on your past sexual experiences and feelings as well as those of your current or future sexual partner. Survivors' responses include both frigidity and promiscuity, with a wide range in between.

At first most women express at least some apprehension and discomfort when faced with any physical closeness after the assault. Physical pain from injuries may occur as well, and sex may be out of the question for a few days or weeks. Many survivors experience less interest in sex, diminished sexual arousal, difficulty relaxing with their sexual partner, a loss of pleasure and enjoyment from sex, fewer orgasms, and a general discomfort with sex. "I feel so cold inside," one survivor said. Many women also experience an intense disgust and repulsion to specific sexual acts they were forced to perform during the rape. This is especially true of sexual acts in which they did not routinely engage.

My research indicated that approximately one-fourth of rape survivors decide to completely abstain from sex after the assault. Others, a much smaller group, may abstain from sex with men only and experiment with homosexual relationships. They may indeed find another female less threatening and more acceptable sexually. This seems to be more likely to result if they are assaulted when young, before experiencing any satisfactory heterosexual relationships or close friendships with men. Trust of men in general may be very low, and anger at the rapist may, as a result, be directed toward all men. Rape survivors who were previously incest victims are especially distrustful of men and may have more difficulty relating to them in the future.

The other extreme occurs as well, though less frequently.

Kim, a slender fourteen-year-old virgin, was walking home from her suburban school when two men forced her into their car. They took her some distance to their apartment where they both raped her. She quickly learned that they were pimps and had no intention of letting her go. Throughout the night and the next morning she was raped orally, anally, and vaginally by many men who came and went. The next evening one of the men put her in his car and left Minneapolis for California. She was beaten regularly and raped repeatedly along the way. Once in California the pimp hid in the bathroom of a hotel while she performed sexual acts with Johns. One became suspicious and reported her to the police. She was arrested as a prostitute, then the whole story was revealed, the pimp confessed, and Kim returned home.

Once home, things appeared to be going well at first, though Kim found out she had contracted gonorrhea. Concerned about her safety, her parents insisted on driving her to and from school and did not allow her out alone. She became angry and started staying out late and going to parties with older boys. Her school grades dropped. By now her mother knew she was sexually active and tried to impose further restrictions. Only more rebellion resulted.

When Kim finally ran away from home she left her mother a note saying "I'm gone for good. Don't look for me, and don't worry, I'm not selling my body." One month later, she was picked up working in a "massage" parlor.

Teenage girls around ages sixteen or seventeen who have been virgins before a rape seem the most likely to become very sexually active after a rape. Sometimes they express a curiosity to see what "real, normal" sex is like. At other times their sexual activities seem more of an attempt to deny the importance of sex or of remaining a virgin until marriage. They now engage in sex frequently because they need to lower the value of abstinence and the virginity that has been taken from them. If they continue to value virginity as essential before marriage they can only feel bad about themselves. However, one sixteen-year-old survivor who highly valued being a virgin before the rape was able to distinguish rape from sex in her mind and consider herself still a virgin. She said, "Virginity isn't something that can be taken by a rapist any more than by a speculum. It must be freely given."

At other times promiscuity may be the result of feelings of worthlessness and a lack of self-esteem, of no longer valuing yourself or your sexuality, of feeling used and useless. A common practice among pimps is to rape young girls repeatedly, often runaways they pick up on the streets, as a prelude to coercing the girls into working for them.

Treatment programs for teenage prostitutes and studies of prostitutes estimate that the first sexual experience of more than two-thirds of all teenage prostitutes is rape or incest—sexual relations forced by an adult.

While the frequency of sexual activity usually returns to normal after three to six months, it often takes longer for women to enjoy sex again.

FACTORS AFFECTING YOUR RESPONSE

There are a number of factors that may affect your response to the rape. These include specifics about the rape situation, factors within your external environment, and variables within yourself.

Circumstances Surrounding the Rape

Studies indicate that if you feel as though you have little control over your life, you are more likely to become depressed. A number of rape situations that take away more control have been shown to result in greater depression and more difficulty readjusting after a rape. These include the sudden, unanticipated rape, where the assailant jumps out of the bushes or from behind a car. Your sense of control is also less when weapons are used, when threats of physical harm or death are made, when there are multiple assailants, and when there are witnesses who do nothing to help. These situations too may result in more depression and anxiety, more safety concerns, and especially more difficulty in later social adjustment. If you were beaten or tortured you will most likely have significant problems with later social relationships and with your self-image. Sexual dysfunction is also more likely.

However, despite the pain and depression, at least black eyes, neck bruises, and cuts and scratches in visible places, especially the face, elicit more support and less blame. Even though the rape was more traumatic, the social support may help counteract this and facilitate your recovery.

Sexual dysfunction as well as a loss of self-respect are more likely to result when you were raped by a husband or ex-husband, a lover or date—someone you knew and trusted. It may be more difficult for some time to be close to another man and feel intimate without wondering when the rules will change and rape will result. It may be difficult for you to trust men.

If you were raped in your own home, especially in your bedroom, you may experience considerable anxiety and fear, especially for your safety. This type of situation has been found to have the most profound effect on recovery. Many survivors decide to move to a new location for fear of never feeling safe in their homes again.

There is also more general disruption associated with prior victimization. If this was not the first time you were raped, you may experience a greater disruption in general social functioning. Women who are especially prone to victimization often have many other long-term problems with which they are dealing that make them both more vulnerable and less able to cope effectively with rape.

The Effect of Other Stress

Your recovery is somewhat dependent on other events occurring in your life, some related to the rape and some not. It may be that at this point in your life you are not dealing solely with the rape. You may also be dealing with chronic, long-term stresses, difficulties that are present over a span of years, things that don't go away but continually drain your energy reserves. These chronic stresses include such things as ongoing unemployment or underemployment in low-paying, uninteresting jobs with little sense of accomplishment and resulting economic hardship and strain. These stresses include chronic substance abuse (drugs, alcohol), long-term personal illness or the illness of a close family member, as well as continual conflicts and disruption in close relationships (especially marital relationships). Other difficulties include crowded living situations that result in frequent interactions with other people and do not provide adequate privacy, space, or time to be alone to deal uninterrupted with your own concerns. The other extreme, social isolation with a lack of family and friends with whom you interact, is also a chronic stress.

We all have a certain amount of energy available for dealing with events in our lives. Dealing with rape uses up a lot of that energy, so we don't have much left over. As a result, we are likely to be more upset by other smaller problems that at another time would not seem important at all. For example, Jane had a flat tire one month after the rape. She became very upset, tearful, unable to decide what to do or where to turn for help. The friend who was with her really didn't understand her reaction. This same overreaction typically occurs in relations with other people. If you can anticipate feeling easily irritated and annoyed, and remind yourself it's not your friends or children to whom you are reacting, you may be better able to avoid overreacting to the minor irritants. Excusing yourself and removing yourself from the situation before it gets out of hand is an effective technique.

Rape cases that go to court usually do so approximately three months after the assault. This experience can also be traumatic and the process often results in more severe symptoms of stress, including depression, anxiety, and fear.

How You Affect Your Response

You, your background, past life experiences, and your current sense of who you are and what you want out of life are the most important variables in determining your response to the rape. Your willingness to face and deal with reality and to recognize when you need help, as well as your willingness to ask for help, will be important factors.

Your past experiences with stressful events are significant. Typically, rape has the greatest traumatic effect on those who have had few past life traumas. Past experience in dealing with difficult situations prepares you to recognize your strengths and draw on your resources. If you have not identified your resources in the past you will need to do so now. You will need to learn that you can take back control, and that you do have the resilience necessary to do so.

If you have dealt with a serious crisis in the past, you probably already know on whom you can rely, with whom you can talk when you need to talk, where to turn for help. You also may know which of the strategies that other people use to cope do not work for you and are not worth trying. You are on your way toward resolution of the crisis.

The Effect of Those in Your Environment

Numerous reports, books, and articles resulting from years of study and research in all types of crises, including rape, show that next to you, the key figures in your recovery are supportive family and friends, those significant people in your environment. Their support and understanding is important in helping you better deal with the emotional trauma and resolve the fears, anxiety, and depression. It's much easier to take risks and face dangerous, uncomfortable, frightening situations with someone beside you. Although social support cannot make up for your feeling that you lack control over your life, social support can certainly give you the extra confidence necessary to take risks, face your fears, and overcome the immobilizing effects of anxiety and depression.

This is a time of turmoil. You may be afraid you'll never recover, but you will. With your own determination and the help of others you can speed this process and reach new heights of self-fulfillment you did not previously think possible. Be patient with yourself, however, since change takes time.

■ ■ ■

To the Significant Other

Rape is a social crisis. It affects not only the survivor but those people with whom she interacts and their relationships with her. Rape elicits an emotional response from you. Your feelings will be based not solely on the rape but also on many other factors, many other biases as well. These may be so ingrained that you are not even aware that they are altering your response. In order to deal most effectively with the rape survivor you must first deal with the dynamics of your own response. You must sort out your feelings and decide which are a result of this situation—this rape—and which are based on other factors. This process involves introspection, looking into yourself with a willingness to understand.

UNDERSTANDING YOUR INITIAL RESPONSE

Much as the survivor may respond at first with shock and disbelief, you too may need some time to accept the rape. This is especially true when she still looks the same, when there are no visible cuts or bruises, signs that she was violently attacked. If she has calmed down and is not emotionally distraught when you first see her, acceptance may be even more difficult.

Many studies of people's responses to rape survivors have found that there is less disruption in social relationships when the rape was more threatening to the survivor, such as when weapons were used, when there was actual harm done, when she struggled and tried to get away, when there was more than one assailant, and when the attack was a sudden attack by a stranger. There is less social disruption because in situations of this nature the survivor is less open to criticism and blame. It is clear to you and others that it was rape, that it was against her will, that she did nothing to cause it, and that there was nothing she could have done to escape. She was clearly the victim.

Once the shock has worn off, you may respond with many of

the same feelings she experienced, such as depression, anger, and anxiety. Many people close to survivors react in much the same way as the survivor. Review the material in the earlier part of this chapter on the phase of confusion, disorganization, and fears. Becoming familiar with the survivor's feelings may help you sort out your own feelings.

HOW YOU CAN HELP

There are a number of things you can do for her right now to help lessen the severity of the initial impact.

Believe Her

If you really want to help her, the first thing you must do is believe her—even if no weapons were used, she knew the single assailant, she didn't make a police report, and/or there is no evidence of harm. It's not necessary for you to decide if she was "really raped." She says she was raped and that's enough. She feels raped, and she needs your support.

> When Tammy's mother first got the call from the police station she was frightened. What could have happened? The police officer told her, "I don't want to upset you, but there's something very wrong with your daughter. I think she needs psychiatric help. We found her, confused and despondent, wandering in the street. She had only one shoe on. She wouldn't talk with us at first and then she told us this incredible story about a man jumping out of the bushes with a halloween mask on, dragging her into the bushes, and raping her. But it couldn't have really happened, because *that type of thing doesn't happen in Greensburg.* I hope you can find her help."
> Tammy's mother believed the police officer, who she thought would certainly know what does and does not happen in Greensburg. Tammy was still somewhat dazed and confused, and she did only have one shoe on, but her mother knew she had been fine when she left for school that morning. Her mother was confused, but on the policeman's advice, she called the county's psychiatric crisis center frantic to get help for her daughter. Since there was a rape crisis center at the same hospital, they had the mother bring Tammy in for a sexual-assault exam. She was hesitant but agreed.

Much to the mother's surprise and relief, they found sperm during the exam. Her daughter was not "crazy."

The story may have ended even more tragically had this rapist been one of the many who are sexually dysfunctional—unable to ejaculate—thus providing no proof, or had the mother taken Tammy to a therapist in Greensburg who also believed that "that type of thing doesn't happen in Greensburg."

The one thing that will make the most significant difference in how the survivor recovers from this very traumatic experience is your acceptance and support of her in these next few days and weeks. It will be extremely important to her and her recovery. You are part of her social-support network, and right now she needs support, acceptance, and reassurance that you still care. You may be a central source of her support or a tangential source, someone to whom she hasn't turned for help often in the past. Depending on the response of the other people around her, it could be that your response will be crucial, more significant than you ever will realize.

Reassure Her

This is not a time when she needs to be questioned. ("Why didn't you run away?" "Why didn't you yell for help?" "Why didn't you kick him?") It's not important now what she did or didn't do. She lived through it, so whatever she did was right. She needs reassurance that her survival is all that really matters. She acted on her instincts at the time, and that is the best anyone can do. Agonizing over the things she could have done is really a futile exercise.

She will also need reassurance that to you she is the same worthwhile person she was before the rape. She needs to know that you still value and care about her.

Accept Her Feelings

She is probably scared and angry not only because of the rape, but also because of the things she is feeling, the fears, anxiety, depression. These extreme feelings may make her afraid that she's "going crazy." She knows it's not "normal" to be afraid to go out of the house or to panic whenever she sees a man with a beard (because the man who raped her had a beard). However, after a rape this fear is very normal. It's something that many survivors experience, and it does not mean she's "going crazy" or that she will always feel this way.

If she can tell someone else, perhaps you, about the things she's feeling and you accept her feelings, then it will be easier for her to accept them herself.

Be There to Listen

Don't be afraid to talk with her about the rape. If it's painful for you to listen, imagine how painful it must have been for her to experience and how upsetting it is for her to talk about it. If you pretend that it didn't happen, you will only increase her isolation. She's going to need someone she can trust, someone who will listen without judging her on how she's feeling, someone on whom she can count when new small crises occur. She'll especially need someone who can listen to how she's feeling, not just what she's saying. She may need help sorting it all out. If she's feeling pain, but unable to say so, she'll need someone who can listen beyond the words. Statements such as "I can't do anything right," or continual self-blame and criticism about both the rape and current problems may in fact mean "I feel terrible about myself, I feel confused and upset." Instead of responding to what she said, respond to the feeling. You might say, "You must be feeling really bad again," or "You're being awfully hard on yourself." Let her know that it is safe for her to express her feelings, that you understand and can hear them without being repulsed, judgmental, or rejecting her.

Let Her Know How You Feel

If you are honest about your feelings, it will be easier for her to be, as well. If you feel angry at the rapist or upset that she's in so much pain, let her know. If it hurts you when she takes her anger at the rapist out on you, let her know that. She may not realize she's doing so. Again, you need to hear beyond the words. Don't respond to the anger that is misdirected at you. Respond to the real source of her anger. You might want to remind her, "Hey, I'm on your side. I'm angry that it happened to you, too, but it hurts me when you say those things to me."

Provide Support Without Taking Over

It's a normal response to want to rescue a rape survivor, to become overprotective of her. You weren't there to protect her and prevent the rape, but you are there now and you want to be there in the future. You don't want to let anyone hurt her again. Some parents set more strict limits on their daughters' activities after a rape. While the intent is to keep them safe, the result often seems more like punishment to the survivor. In some cases the restrictions are unreasonable and to some extent *are* punishment. If your daughter was raped when walking to or from school or some other activity in which she and her peers normally engage, restricting her from these activities or insisting that you take her and pick her up all the time is unreasonable and only limits her further. On the other hand, if she was at a girlfriend's house until four o'clock in the morning and was raped walking home alone, perhaps more limits are in order.

When unreasonable restrictions are imposed after a rape, even though the intentions are good, it is understandable if the survivor becomes angry and upset by these restrictions. They and the person imposing them may even become the target of much of her anger at the rapist. She may react by rebelling against the new restrictions. While it is certainly important to communicate your concern to her, restricting her freedom is unnecessary and can only be counterproductive. This is true whether she complies and becomes dependent, or rebels in order to maintain her independence. She must be allowed to continue to make her own choices and to live her own life as she sees fit. The best you can do for her is to teach her and allow her to do so, even though you want desperately to keep her safe.

The desire to rescue and protect the "helpless victim" is indeed a pitfall of many trained counselors as well as family, friends, and loved ones. We all need to be aware of this very well-meaning desire within us to protect the helpless, weak, and suffering. It feels good to be needed. It feels good to do things for people who are in need of help.

The survivor may look weak and helpless and be suffering. She may feel helpless and want to be protected and taken care of. We all do at some time in our life, and at such times it is appropriate to provide support, comfort, and understanding. This can be done without taking over, without taking control away from her. She is not really weak and helpless. She can take care of herself. If you take over for her she may become weak, helpless, and dependent on you. While it may feel good to be needed for a few days or weeks, as the dependence continues and grows, it won't feel so good anymore. It will become a burden. You will become her victim and she yours.

> It had been one year since Jeanette was raped. She was a social worker at a high school. She was raped by a student one night as she left work a little late. Being a strong woman, she had managed to wrestle with him, and she got the attention of a passerby. Together they held him outside with his pants down and kept him there until the police arrived.
>
> After a year had passed without resolution of her feelings, Jeanette decided to seek help. She told a counselor "I think I may retire this year. It's much earlier than I planned, but transportation is too difficult now that I've quit driving. I don't know what I'll do in the house all day while my husband is at work, though. I'm okay at the school after he drops me off, because all the other people are around, but I never go out of the building for lunch, and I'd never leave the house alone. He'd be angry if I did anyway. I guess it's hard for him too. He had to miss a meeting tonight to bring me here. I don't know what we're going to do."

Jeanette's husband was sitting outside the door during the interview. He felt he had to be there to protect her. He was a teacher at a nearby school. While they usually rode together, the night she was raped he had left early and she had stayed late for a meeting. He felt guilty, as if it were his fault that she had been raped. She felt deserted. In the first few days after the rape he "needed" to protect her to overcome his guilt, and she liked being protected and taken care of because she was still afraid and felt vulnerable. They reinforced each other's maladaptive coping needs, which then became exaggerated and imbedded. Things had gradually gotten worse until, a year later, she *never* went anywhere without him. Because of his guilt feelings, he had encouraged and held up under her complete dependence longer than most people would.

It is normal for a survivor to need support right after the rape. During the first week or two, many survivors experience anxiety and fear. A survivor may even have a panic attack when she is out alone. This is normal and something that can be expected. It does not mean she is "crazy" or helpless. It means that she is still acutely aware of her vulnerability and is reacting accordingly. She has lost her internal sense of safety and security and for the moment is relying on you to be an external source of safety. One woman who had been picked up off the street and raped hid in her house for three days. She was a chain smoker, and finally on the third day emerged with her counselor only because she had to have a cigarette. They went to the store together.

One of the most important things you can do for the survivor is to help her rebuild her own internal sense of security. It is unrealistic for you or anyone else to be there with her all the time. Even if you could, like Jeanette's husband thought he could, it is not good for either of you. She must learn to be independent again. She can rely on herself. She can regain this inner sense of security that will allow her to function alone in the world and feel in control and safe again. However, it will take time.

4

YOUR RECOVERY: TAKING BACK CONTROL

If one advances confidently, in the direction of [her] own dreams, and endeavors to lead the life [she] has imagined, [she] will meet with a success unexpected in common hours.

—Henry David Thoreau

To the Survivor

As horrible a crime as it is, rape, a physical and emotional trauma, gives the survivor an opportunity to make positive changes in her life. You may find that you are no longer willing to continue living with situations that you previously have been tolerating. The turmoil of the rape has probably disturbed old patterns of behavior and changed your perceptions of what is and what ought to be. This firsthand knowledge of your vulnerability can serve as an impetus for change. You have just faced the possibility of your own death. Your values are not likely to remain unexamined or unaltered.

By now you may have accepted the rape. The crime cannot be undone. You have experienced the pain and emotional turmoil. Now is the time to begin putting your life back in order, an order not limited by the past or by what other people expect, but instead one that fits your newly recognized goals and aspirations. You need to draw upon your resources to resolve your negative feelings and prevent long-term social and psychological maladjustments. This is an opportunity to emerge from chaos and turmoil better able to handle other crises you may face.

You do not have to remain helpless and immobilized by your anger, fear, and grief. When you are ready you can take back control over your life. You'll need to evaluate your resources, choose the coping strategies with which you feel the most comfortable, and begin the process of resolution. You may want the help of a rape crisis counselor or a professional therapist, or you may want to go it alone. It may be a smooth, easy process, or it may be a very difficult one that will take years to complete. The amount of progress you make and the speed with which you do so will depend on your situation and the resources available to facilitate your problem solving. Be sure that the coping strategies you use are really helpful. For example, having a drink or taking a sleeping pill the first few days after the assault may offer an escape from uncomfortable or frightening thoughts and feelings; however, keep in mind that if you begin to depend on drugs or alcohol, your recovery will be hindered.

You may be reluctant to begin trying to make positive changes in your life because you are not sure that things can ever be better for you. There is a certain amount of security in following routines and knowing what to expect—even when it means you can expect to continue being unhappy. That is why we so often remain in situations and relationships long after they stop being pleasurable or positive forces in our lives. We are afraid that something new and unfamiliar may be even worse.

Deciding to change always involves a risk. If one method doesn't work, don't waste time worrying that it means you are a failure as a person or that you'll never be able to manage. You simply need to try a new approach. Even if one approach doesn't help you feel better after you've given it a chance, at least you are taking action and are no longer helplessly immobilized. Whatever your experience, with continued effort you will eventually feel much better than you do now.

Avoid pressure from other people in making decisions about your life. Your goals and what you do to reach them must be based first and foremost on your own needs. For instance, if you have always wanted to take a year off from school, move to Denver, and work at a ski area, you may decide that this is the time to do so. Your friends and family may have a multitude of reasons they want you to stay home—so they can protect you and keep you safe, because students are supposed to complete a course of education without any interruptions, because they are afraid of what the neighbors will think. You may want to change jobs; perhaps you never really liked your old one anyway, there was no challenge. Your boss, however, may not want you to leave—you are a good worker and training someone new takes a long time and is expensive. While you certainly need to be responsible to other people, you are under no obligation to meet the needs of other people at the expense of your own.

EVALUATING YOUR RESOURCES

Everyone has many resources that are seldom considered because they are seldom needed. Now is the time to make a list of your assets, the resources upon which you can draw to help you move from turmoil and disorganization back to control of your life.

Resources Within Yourself

The fact that you are reading this book is an indication of your willingness to look at your responses and attempt change. This openness to change and the willingness to get information is essential. To some extent, the tension you are feeling as a result of the assault can be a motivating force and a source of strength. Your health and your body's adaptive capacities must not be overlooked. If you were physically hurt during the assault, the fact that your body is healing itself is an example of its own power.

Your past experiences, your educational background, and your experience dealing with stress can be assets. If you've dealt with serious stress in the past, regardless of the outcome, you're stronger today for having gone through that process. You know more of what to expect. If you've survived something worse, you know you can survive this.

Get in touch with your feelings. Be honest with yourself. It's easy to focus on your faults, but a positive view of yourself is much more helpful. Think of all the things you have done well, and feel good about your successes.

Resources in Your Environment

Aside from you yourself, your family and friends are your most important resources. They are often supportive by just being there to care and listen. They may provide more tangible support, suggesting a counselor they like or helping you find a safer place to live. Even more important, they can provide a sense of emotional security. Although some women have no one with whom they feel close enough to share important feelings, most have at least a few close friends.

In addition to your informal support network, you may rely on the more formal community social-support system. Most communities have a number of public and private agencies available to provide assistance with particular problems, such as rape crisis centers; victim-witness programs that assist survivors who go to court; victim-assistance programs that may provide financial assistance; employment programs for help finding a new job or making a career change; sexuality programs; counseling services; or self-help groups. Your local rape crisis center may have a list of resources other survivors have used.

If you're not aware of an agency in your community that is set up to provide information and referrals, call Directory Assistance and ask for the telephone number of a referral agency. If there is no such service in your community, your local United Way, Red Cross, or a member of the clergy may be able to help.

COPING WITH FEAR, ANGER, AND DEPRESSION

Coping with a problem involves dealing with internal or external conflicts and reducing tension to a manageable level.

Some tension is motivating and facilitates change. Too much is overwhelming and incapacitating.

Combat Negative Thoughts and Feelings

While you could not prevent the rape, you can learn to control thoughts about it and your emotional response to it. Many survivors report feeling that the rapist controlled their thoughts for weeks afterward, because the assault was all they thought about. It may be that for a few days or weeks you feel the need to go over the rape in your mind again and again.

You need to take back control. Each time you have intrusive thoughts of the assault, stop and say to yourself, "I am not being raped now. It's over and I survived. He's gone. I'm safe, comfortable, warm, and in control of my body. I'm going to think about what I'm doing now."

Count yourself lucky. Many survivors minimize their experience in an effort to feel better about what happened. They say things like, "It could have been so much worse." If they are young they will say, "I couldn't handle it if I were old." If they are old they may say, "It would be so much harder for a young person who has not seen life." These are self-protective mechanisms to help us feel better about painful situations.

Instead of telling yourself how weak, useless, or helpless you are, learn to tell yourself how well you are doing and how far you have come since the turmoil immediately following the assault. Each day that you feel less overwhelmed by negative thoughts and feelings, tell yourself, "I'm learning to take back control."

Make sure you are not misinterpreting other people's actions and their reactions to you. For example, maybe you asked a friend to go to lunch with you and she said, "I'd love to but I have to take my cat to the vet." Your response might have been to feel as though she didn't like you, was upset with you, or was embarrassed to be seen with you because you were raped. What evidence really exists that your interpretation is accurate? Were there nonverbal cues? If so, what were they? Does she even know about the rape?

You may find it helpful to write down the negative thoughts you have about yourself, what you are doing when you start to feel bad, and what people say that you believe is critical. You can then review these with someone whose opinion you trust and with whom you feel comfortable talking.

Examine Your Fear

When you are out alone, you may find yourself feeling so afraid that you think you'll never be able to walk down the street alone without feeling tense and vulnerable. But you can teach yourself to control your emotional responses to activities. Don't pretend that you are not afraid to be out alone if you are afraid. Once you acknowledge your feelings, you can determine what is causing them. Is it being out at night? Did the fear begin when you passed someone, perhaps a man with a beard like the rapist's? Did you hear or smell something that reminded you of the rape or the rapist? It is important to identify as specifically as possible the cues in your environment that elicit uncomfortable emotional responses. Then ask yourself what the likelihood is of anything bad happening where you are *now*.

Sometimes when you begin to feel tense it helps to take a deep breath. Let it out slowly. Anxiety can trigger rapid, shallow breathing. This will help you control your physiological response to anxiety while it helps you collect your thoughts and increase your awareness.

Another effective relaxation technique is referred to as systematic desensitization. Make a list of those things you are afraid of doing. Put the things you are least afraid of at the top of the list. Next imagine yourself doing the activity at the top of your list while keeping your body relaxed. Imagine yourself doing each activity in turn. You should not proceed to a more fearful situation until you feel relaxed in the least fearful situation. Because this method is best accomplished with the help of another person, it is described in greater detail in the second section of this chapter, "To the Significant Other."

The next step in overcoming your fears is to engage in the activities that make you afraid. You may want to have someone with you first, then go alone. You should assess the actual danger of each activity. If you were raped walking through a dark alley late at night, for example, you may not want to do this again. If you are having trouble separating the real from the unreal, rape-related fears, talk it over with a trusted friend or counselor. If you do not confront these situations, you will be victimizing yourself by placing unnecessary constraints and limitations on your activities.

Express Your Anger in Positive Ways

Expressing anger is one of the ways we can direct blame toward others, such as the rapist, rather than turning it inward against ourselves. There is no reason to fear anger. It need not be destructive if constructively channeled. Survivors' anger following a rape takes many forms, some appropriate, effective ways of facilitating recovery, and some ineffective, hampering or preventing return to normal activities. The manner in which you express your anger may affect the recovery process. The effective resolution of feelings such as anger can have a pervasive impact on your ability to function in all areas of your life.

Anger is an emotion many people have great difficulty expressing constructively. They either explode or keep their feelings buried inside. The initial form of your expression of anger after a rape will tend to be the same or similar to the way you express anger in other situations. Now is an important time to evaluate your usual style of dealing with anger, and perhaps to learn a more effective method.

Telling people who are willing to listen how angry you are, telling your cat or dog, or yelling at the rapist while driving alone in your car can be very effective releases. Another positive method of dealing with your anger is becoming involved in the legal process. Report the crime to the police, complete the investigative report, and provide information to be used as evidence in the prosecution of the rapist. Especially if other assaults have occurred in a particular area, talk with neighbors or distribute fliers to the neighborhood so that others are aware of the dangers. To feel less helpless, Tanya and her mother, Selena, used fantasy to deal with their anger.

Tanya, eleven years old, was raped by a neighbor's fiancé. At the time, no one knew he was out on bail for rape and had served time for rape in another state before he raped Tanya. She was too frightened and intimidated to put up much resistance. Her mother walked into her bedroom as he was zipping up his pants.

Later the mother told Tanya's counselor, "I know what it's like to be raped. I was raped when I was thirteen years old. I still wake up with nightmares, in a cold sweat. I got pregnant, but I didn't tell anyone until the pregnancy began to show, and then they thought I was lying. Tanya and I spent the night after her rape talking about how we'd post her rapist's bail ourselves, then how we'd kill him. We'd never do it, of course, but the fantasy was a helpful outlet."

You can also use fantasy to rewrite the ending of the rape. You may want to imagine the rapist approaching you as he actually did, but then visualize yourself overpowering him and preventing the rape.

Keeping a journal is another way to sort out the things you are feeling, to discharge emotions, and to see the progress you make over time. You need not write in your journal every day, but rather when you feel in a more contemplative mood or when something important has happened to you. You may want to include in your journal your goals, aspirations, and strategies to attain them. You may choose to write down your dreams. They can give you important insights into your subconscious fears and concerns. Be sure to include your feelings during the dreams.

Channel your angry, aggressive impulses into socially acceptable behavior, such as sports. Tennis, racketball, handball, or golf are excellent choices because you strike the ball and exert considerable energy. Walking, jogging, swimming, and bike riding are also effective. This particular form of expression of anger has an added benefit. Only recently have people become aware of the biochemical changes that occur as a result of physical activity. It is now believed that substances called endorphins are released during physical exercise. These in turn are effective in lowering the level of depression. Many long-distance runners report a "jogger's euphoria," thought to be the result of these biochemical changes. Many counseling programs now include jogging or other forms of exercise specifically for their positive impact on mood.

Humor can be another acceptable, effective method of expressing anger. Humor allows you to express unpleasant feelings, to focus on realities that may otherwise be too difficult to bear without making yourself or other people uncomfortable. One survivor quipped, "The best way to prevent rape is to castrate all men. Of course, then we would have a number of other problems to deal with."

It is not always necessary to express anger. It is also legitimate and effective to recognize that you are angry, but to choose not to take any action. At times you may decide to postpone a highly emotional reaction. However, whether or not you choose to express your feelings, it is important to recognize that you have these emotions so that you can remain in command of your feelings. If you realize that you are expressing your feelings in ineffective, detrimental ways, or not at all, you will be able to change your behavior.

The social taboo against the expression of anger by women is often so strongly ingrained that you may have learned not to recognize this unacceptable feeling. You may believe that if this feeling is even acknowledged it will mean you are unfeminine, unladylike, and thus unattractive to men. As a result, you may block it completely from your conscious awareness. Unfortunately, what is likely to result is that the anger will affect other areas of your life without your being aware of what is happening. Depression has long been described as anger turned inward. Just as anxiety and depression manifest themselves as physical symptoms, so can unrecognized anger.

It can also be helpful to identify the source of your anger. Very often people become angry because they have been hurt. In the case of a rape you may feel angry because you felt hurt and humiliated by the things that were done to you or that you were forced to do. It may feel as though every shred of your humanity was stripped away. You were not in a position to get angry at that time, but now the hurt you felt may be expressed as anger.

Talk with a Friend

Most survivors find that talking about the rape to a close friend or to someone who has been through a similar trauma is very helpful. Talking about the rape will help you accept it for what it was—a past experience that you should not allow to control your present and future life. Retelling the incident in detail, which usually occurs in the hospital or with the police, is an important part of this acceptance. If you have not told anyone all of what happened, you may find it helpful to do so now. You may have omitted the most upsetting or embarrassing parts of the assault. Verbalizing a painful experience—getting it out of your system—is often a good way to put the experience behind you.

Be selective in deciding with whom you share these most intimate details (see chapter 5, "Telling Other People"). You may choose to talk with a counselor instead of a friend or relative. A counselor may be better equipped to help you than someone with an emotional investment in you.

Spend Time Alone

It is also important to have some time set aside to spend alone, to relax and sort out your feelings, to remove yourself from the demands and expectations of everyone else for a while. Go for a walk alone, sit and listen to music, or daydream about things you enjoy doing. You may also want to use some of this time to reflect on the progress you have made.

If your rape was recent, you may need to learn to be alone again. You may still want others around to provide an external sense of safety. Many survivors, especially during the first few weeks or months, avoid being alone. But with a concerted effort, you will soon learn to be comfortable being by yourself again.

Get Involved Socially

Increasing your activities and social contact may also help. The general increase in social activity will provide you with outlets that can help block the intrusive thoughts of the assault. It is good to have new people with whom you can talk, and it can be reassuring to know that you are still a worthwhile, acceptable human being. Research studies at the University of Washington in Seattle, 1981, have shown a direct relationship between emotional health and the presence of understanding others, and even social contact, regardless of the level of intimacy. While it is certainly true that more intimate relationships are the most important social resource, contact with nonintimate friends plays an important role in helping you resolve conflicts and deal with depression and anxiety, even when you do not discuss the rape with them.

In reviewing your community resources you may have identified a number of clubs, organizations, or classes that are available. This may be a good time to utilize them. Your local university, community center, or church may be able to help you find activities that interest you.

Change Your School Routine

Some rape survivors who are students decide to quit school for a while. They find that the fears, anxieties, and intensive thoughts interfere with their ability to study. Others discover that studying more is an effective way for them to keep their minds off the rape.

Change Your Work Routine

Some survivors decide to change jobs within a year after being sexually assaulted. In many cases the jobs were uninteresting and dissatisfying to the women, and they had considered a change prior to the rape. In these instances the turmoil of the assault provided the impetus to make a needed change.

In other cases the rape was related to their job. For example, women who work evenings and were raped while going to or from work are often uncomfortable with the high vulnerability and look for day work. In other cases, high levels of customer contact becomes uncomfortable and the survivor chooses to find another job, perhaps in the same company, where she does not have the same level of public exposure.

Other women are just uncomfortable working where people

know about their rape. This may happen regardless of whether or not the response of their co-workers was helpful. They just want to begin anew elsewhere.

Many survivors change jobs not because they want to but rather because the fears and anxieties resulting from the rape are so incapacitating that they are unable to continue to perform their duties. It may be that you no longer can deal with job-related stress that was manageable before the rape. While the first few weeks are the most difficult, if the case goes to court, the demands of time and energy may continue for months. A change to a less-demanding job may be an effective short-term coping strategy, especially if you were considering making a job change prior to the assault. Some time off between positions may also be helpful, if this is financially feasible.

Should you want to maintain your current job, however, you should be given the same considerations as someone dealing with the stress of illness or childbirth. This should include time off, possibly sick time, or you may want to take a vacation or a leave of absence without pay. These options should be negotiated with your employer. You will better represent yourself if you decide what arrangements you would like to make before speaking with her or him, then present your ideas. You may not be able to afford leave without pay, or you may not have much sick leave accrued. Decide what will be best for you and then present the reasons for your proposal. Even if it has been three months and you're just now going to trial, you may need more time off to deal with and recover from the courtroom experience.

Change Your Place of Residence

If the assault occurred in or near your home, the location may become a constant reminder. You may continue to feel vulnerable and afraid. The women who have the most difficult time during the first few months seem to be those women raped in their homes, who do not, or for financial reasons cannot, move. Women who move usually do so very soon, because the fear and anxiety can be so overwhelming. While some women do continue to feel afraid even after such a major move, by far the majority feel relieved. Although moving often helps, it is no magic cure. Other fears may remain. Emotional recovery takes time.

REBUILDING YOUR SELF-ESTEEM

Eventually, anger will dissipate, the depression will lift, the anxiety will pass, and you'll be able to resume your normal activities. You will find that you feel better about yourself in general. Positive feedback from other people is directly related to how we view ourselves. The things we value about ourselves are often the things other people value about us. The more isolated you are the less chance there is to hear good things about yourself, or do things you feel good about having done.

Unfortunately, women, more often than men, assume personal responsibility for failure and bad things happening to them and attribute success and positive happenings to chance or other circumstances beyond their control. Men do just the opposite. They take credit for their successes and attribute failure to chance or outside influences. Recognizing that we are responsible for our successes is an important component in feeling good about ourselves and building our self-esteem. It is important that you learn to accept credit for your success as you resolve this crisis. You alone are responsible, you alone are in control, and you alone deserve the credit for success.

You need not feel guilty about the assault. Don't judge your response to it as right or wrong. There is no right or wrong response. If you were aroused or wanted to hurt or kill him, that's okay too. If you have strong religious affiliations, you may want to discuss your guilt feelings with someone from your church or synagogue. Remember, however, they may not understand rape and may have some biases themselves.

LEARNING TO ENJOY SEX AGAIN

After the first six to twelve weeks, most survivors resume the same frequency of sexual contact as prior to the assault. This is especially true when women are involved in an ongoing sexual relationship. On the surface sexual activity may appear to have returned to normal, or their sexual partner may feel it has. A large portion of these women, however, report that they are not as satisfied with sex. It is no longer as enjoyable to them. This lack of interest, enjoyment, and satisfaction often is reported to continue through the first year and in some cases much longer.

Women report that physical closeness, being held, being cuddled, and feelings of warmth and caring are a very important part of sexual relations. To many women these are as important or more important than the physical act of intercourse or having an orgasm. Sexuality is much more than simply having intercourse. It's feeling comfortable, close, and intimate with another person. It involves feeling attractive and likeable and being able to feel good about yourself. Don't settle for satisfying only your partner's needs to maintain the relationship. Giving up the positive aspects of sexual intimacy usually also means giving up much of the related emotional intimacy and may reflect a loss of satisfaction in other areas of your life.

In order to be comfortable with sex, you need to be comfortable with being physically close to another person. This may involve learning to trust men or a particular man again and not feeling forced or coerced into being closer than you want to be. It also involves learning to feel good about yourself and your body. While you now know how sex can be used as a weapon, you must remember that it can bring pleasure, and it can be a way of sharing yourself with the partner of your choice.

You may need to be assertive and draw limits as to the level of physical closeness you want during the weeks and months following the rape. If you feel uncomfortable, say so. A caring partner will respect your feelings.

GETTING HELP OR GOING IT ALONE

You must also decide if you need extra help from someone skilled and experienced in dealing with issues you now face, so you need to know what asking for help means.

What Does it Mean to Ask for Help?

It's much easier for some people to ask for help than for others, because asking has a different meaning for each of us. Some people see asking for help as a sign of personal failure. To them, asking for help is admitting to a weakness, or being dishonorable. These people only ask for help as a last resort, when all else fails.

To other people, asking for help is a sign of intelligence and resourcefulness. To them, getting help is a sign of wanting to do things better than they could by themselves. These people don't feel the need to be an expert at everything. They feel good about being able to find and use the resources available, and they understand they don't need to handle everything on their own.

Don't forget, you get help with the less important things in your life without feeling that it is a sign of failure: when your television breaks, you don't expect to fix it yourself; you probably took lessons to learn to swim because you wanted to do it well. By getting help from someone who is trained to deal with a crisis such as rape, you can speed your progress toward recovery. You can accomplish much more than simply keeping your head above water.

Getting Help and Maintaining Control

Getting help does not mean that you are turning yourself or your problems completely over to someone else to solve. They are still your problems, your responsibility, and you are the one who must solve them. Each one of us sees our life and our problems a little differently from the way someone else will. The fact that someone else is a trained professional does not necessarily mean that they are better able to sort out the problems or determine a better solution than you can. Only you can decide what is a problem for you and what will be the best solution for you.

However, the people from whom you seek help can play an important role in helping you sort through your feelings. Since they are not emotionally involved with you, they can help you better understand the source of your feelings and behavior.

They can help you review coping strategies you have used in the past, suggest new strategies you may want to try, and help you recognize choices that may not be readily apparent.

Therapists, counselors, and advocates are there to facilitate your recovery. They can provide you with support and encouragement while you try new approaches to life and new ways of interacting with the world around you. They can help you see the world and yourself from a different perspective, allowing you to achieve insights that will help you change. Remember though, a therapist is not there to change you but rather to help you change yourself.

How to Choose a Therapist

You may want to check your health-insurance policy, if you have one, to see what restrictions are imposed on payment. Many policies will only pay if a medical doctor or licensed psychologist is involved. Some policies will not pay for any counseling. Most limit the number of visits. You should know this before deciding whom to see.

Psychiatrists have medical degrees and are the only counselors who can legally prescribe medication. Some, though not all, rely heavily on it. This is something you may want to avoid. It is easy to develop unrecognized dependencies after any length of time. They also usually charge the highest fees.

Psychologists usually have a Ph.D. Those with only a master's degree may be more limited. A person with a Ph.D. in counseling or clinical psychology probably will have in-depth theoretical training and may have considerable experience in a specialized area such as biofeedback or hypnosis. Their fees will be somewhat less than those of a psychiatrist. You may also see a psychiatric nurse, social worker, counselor, or paraprofessional, all of whom will be less expensive than psychiatrists and psychologists.

You may begin your search for a therapist by calling an agency or a friend and getting a recommendation. Before making an appointment to see a counselor, be sure to ask about his or her fees. Ask if they have a sliding scale, and if they meet the criteria for your insurance coverage. If they meet your payment criteria, ask for an appointment with a counselor. Be sure to specify whether you prefer to see a man or a woman. You will probably want to see someone who has experience in dealing with rape survivors. Ask if a counselor has any special training or background in this area.

When you go in to see the counselor who has been assigned to you, it does not mean that you have made any long-term commitment to see her three times a week for two years, ten times, or even for a second visit. You can only decide that after you find out more about how compatible the two of you are. Whether her services are free or very expensive, the time spent should be productive and worthwhile.

When you first see the counselor, ask about her training and background. Ask her how many rape survivors she has worked with in the past, and why she feels women get raped. Unfortunately, some counselors still believe many of the myths about rape that the general population believes, and because of this are very ineffective in dealing with rape survivors. One male therapist even asked an eighteen-year-old woman, "You've had sex before, right?" The client replied "Yes." The male therapist then said, "Well sex is sex, so what's the big deal? You weren't hurt."

You need to size up the counselor during the initial interview. If she tells you things you simply cannot accept as true for you, ignore them. Don't judge yourself on the basis of other people's truths and values. This is part of recognizing and accepting the value of your own uniqueness.

In deciding if you will return, ask yourself these questions: Did she ask me how I feel and what I see as the problem? Did she ask me what I want to accomplish by seeing her? Do I feel stronger, more in control, rather than helpless and as if she is trying to bring me in line with her expectations? If the answers to the above are positive, then you may have found a good therapist. If not, try someone else. Don't be afraid to tell the therapist that you will not be returning and don't be discouraged and give up if the first one you see is not right for you.

Do keep in mind, however, that a good therapist may also make you feel uncomfortable. Recovery is hard work and requires facing difficult issues. She may ask you questions to which you do not know the answers, or bring up topics that upset you. Trust your instincts but make sure you evaluate carefully how you feel at the end of the session. Choosing a good therapist is an important process. Her opinions and values will have an impact on your recovery process.

■ ■ ■

To the Significant Other

Just as recovering from rape can be a growth experience for the survivor, you too can learn about yourself through the way you respond to her and her pain and the way you deal with your own feelings. Expressing feelings and concerns is especially important during times of stress. By being available and open, you can give the survivor permission to talk with you and utilize you as a source of support. If you are a woman, it may be easier than if you are a man for you to share your innermost feelings with each other. Most women are used to talking freely with at least one close female friend. Men, on the other hand, tend to share activities more than feelings with lovers, friends, and relatives. If you are a man, providing the kind of emotional support the survivor needs may take more of a conscious effort.

SHOULD SHE BE OVER IT BY NOW?

The physical wounds of rape—the cuts and bruises—will heal first. The psychological and emotional wounds are much deeper and take much longer to heal. One of the most unfortunate yet frequently faced dilemmas of rape survivors is the expectation from others that in two weeks to a month, when the cuts and bruises heal, they should "be over it." Once the outward signs of the trauma are gone, which usually takes no longer than a month, it is more difficult for others to see and understand the inner turmoil. It may be hard for you. You may be tired of hearing about the assault, and be tired of telling her it's okay. You may be "over it," but then you didn't actually experience the trauma firsthand.

You may begin to feel drained by her continued need to talk about the rape, and you may want to withdraw, not be there anymore, or change the subject when she brings up the rape. These are normal responses on your part. It is a difficult time for you as well. It may be helpful for you to understand that her repeated reference to the rape and her need to talk about the incident is her way of attempting to integrate the event into her life experience. Unfortunately this may take some time, and you must see it through in order for her to be successful. As she successfully integrates the event, references will become more tangential—less direct—and will diminish in frequency. The time she needs to spend talking about the rape will be reduced once this integration occurs. Your willingness to listen, or the willingness of someone else, will be a key factor in her recovery.

Some survivors are unable to talk about the assault for weeks or months. Others have told no one even years later. They continue to deny the reality of the rape, the extent of the trauma, or the impact it is having on their lives. They are unable to face the rape. Unfortunately this denial is often supported and encouraged by the people around them who tell them how "strong" they are and how "well" they are doing. In reality they are too frightened to face the rape. By now they may be trying very hard to please other people.

Those people around them who are relieved by the denial may also be too uncomfortable or too afraid to face the terror of the rape. For the moment denial is easier for everyone—everyone except the survivor.

If you know a survivor who seems unable to talk about the assault, you may want to try some of the approaches suggested in chapter 5, "Telling Other People." Give her permission to talk about the rape without pushing her to do so. Be patient with her, and allow her to address issues as she is ready to do so.

With some counseling or crisis intervention it will probably take her six to twelve weeks to being to feel "over it." However, some women take longer.

WHAT YOU CAN DO TO HELP

During the first few days, perhaps a week, she and you just may want to relax. You will probably be exhausted from all the activity and stress. After this initial period of recuperation, however, you may want to start looking at specific problems.

Safety often continues to be an important issue to both of you. Your concerns will vary depending on the circumstances of the assault.

> John feels a cold chill when he enters their apartment. He had been out of town when Sandy was raped in their home. Ever since he has felt unsafe there. He doesn't want to come home from work at night because he knows this terrible foreboding feeling will return. The noises in the house sound so foreign now, so threatening. He can't relax. He knows he can't continue to live there. They would have to move soon.

It is usually the survivor who feels uncomfortable and unsafe, but husbands, family members, and male or female roommates sometimes experience this terror as well. If the assault occurred in your home, you too may decide it's easier to move, to start over fresh somewhere else, someplace without the terrible memories. There are precautions you and the survivor can take to increase your sense of safety. The important thing is to avoid taking over for her and making her dependent on you or anyone else in the process.

Helping Her with the Blues

It is important for you to be aware that while she is feeling sad or depressed she will be more likely to misinterpret events and see only the negative side of her current experiences. Unfortunately, this also tends to make the depression worse. You can help her evaluate her perceptions. She may feel as though everyone knows she was raped and as a result is treating her differently or looking at her "funny." She may hear only bad in whatever is said to her. Help her evaluate exactly what makes her feel this way. Is it really happening or is it her altered perception?

Physical and social activities are good ways to lessen her feelings of depression. By providing her with motivation, helping her plan activities, and encouraging her to participate, you'll be able to give her the support she needs to get started again.

Because her perceptions of herself are altered, she may not see what she does well. Point out her successes to her. Remind her of the progress she's made. Help her see more of the positive sides of events.

Helping Her Deal with Her Fears and Anxiety

Because fears and anxiety are so disabling, these may need to be dealt with prior to a major increase in activity. One of the most effective ways that you can support her is by guiding her through a process of slow and systematic desensitization to specific fears and situations. The first step is to have her write down the things she is afraid of doing and to arrange them in order, with the things she is the least afraid to do at the top and the things she is most afraid to do at the bottom. For instance, Ann made the following list:

- going out of the house with someone during the day
- going out of the house alone during the day
- going out of the house with someone after dark
- going out of the house alone after dark
- walking down an alley alone during the day
- walking down a dark alley alone at night
- seeing the rapist when with someone else
- seeing the rapist and being alone

The next step is to help her learn to reduce tension. You can do this by utilizing the following exercises.

You will want to choose a quiet, private place where you will not be interrupted and where you both feel comfortable. This may or may not be your home. You will act as her coach in helping her to relax more completely.

RELAXATION EXERCISE. Have the survivor sit comfortably. Ask her to tense and then relax her muscles, beginning with those in her forehead and around her eyes. As she tightens her muscles, she should take a deep breath and hold it, then slowly breathe out as she relaxes. Work from the head to the neck, shoulders, arms, hands, chest, abdomen, thighs, knees, calves, feet, and toes. Ask her to concentrate on feeling the tension flow away as she relaxes her muscles. With practice, the survivor will be able to feel completely relaxed in just a few minutes.

VISUALIZATION EXERCISE. While the survivor is sitting comfortably in a relaxed state with her eyes closed, ask her to picture herself doing each of the fearful activities on her list, beginning with the least frightening. Slowly talk her through each activity. In Ann's case, where the first entry on her list is "going out of the house with someone during the day," you would begin by asking her to picture herself putting on her coat, walking slowly to the door with you, standing in the open doorway, and stepping outside. The whole process should take from twenty minutes to one hour, depending on her level of comfort. You both should find the process relaxing and invigorating.

If she feels comfortable with the imaginary walk, the next day you may want to take a real walk. Do the same thing except now with your eyes open and for real. Each time she feels anxious or afraid, stop, have her concentrate on her breathing, and relax her body from her head to her toes. Then continue. If she can't relax, slowly turn around and go home. Just as with your imaginary walk, each time she should be able to go farther and do more and still be relaxed, comfortable, and feel safe.

Do the same with the next item on her list. In Ann's case, going out of the house alone during the daytime. While it's okay to imagine doing all the items, there may be some you will decide not to do in reality or even in your imagination, for instance, on Ann's list the sixth item is "walking down a dark alley alone at night." There are two good criteria to use in making this decision: (1) the necessity of the item in real life, and (2) the danger in real life. There is nothing that Ann does that makes it necessary for her to walk down a dark alley at night alone. It may be dangerous. If it is and she doesn't need to do so, it's probably not an activity in which to engage.

The last two items on Ann's list which involve seeing the rapist, are fears of many survivors. They may or may not happen. If he's caught, she probably will have to face him again, though not alone. Imagining what it may be like is a good way to prepare for situations like a lineup or courtroom. Deciding what to do ahead of time in your imagination can help make such difficult situations easier.

AVOIDING BURN-OUT

There are things you can do to avoid being worn out while she is still in need of your support. These should be initiated early. Don't wait until you just can't help anymore and then try to set some limits.

While you may initially like the feeling of having her depend solely on you, this may become overwhelming. There are probably others on whom she can rely to some extent. Don't discourage her from doing so. You may even want to help her explore others in her group of friends and acquaintances who may be good sources of support, such as a friend who was raped or a friend with whom she has felt comfortable in the past. While you may remain a central source of support, it's best if you're not her only one.

It may also be important after the first few days or weeks to set some limits on the time you're available or on the time you spend talking about the rape when together. Thirty minutes a day or an hour three times a week may be plenty. Set that time aside to talk about her concerns, when you don't expect to be interrupted.

You can provide support without spending all your time discussing the assault. Plan some leisure activities, things you both enjoy, that you can do together. Biking, hiking, going to the movies, or visiting other friends will allow you time together that's not focused on the rape. It's important to try to maintain your relationship without basing it solely on the rape.

You may decide you need some time apart as well. Wanting time alone is normal under any circumstances, but especially when you are both under additional stress. Daily time alone may work best for you, or a few days alone may be necessary. You must give yourself permission to recognize this need. Wanting to be alone does not mean you don't care, or that you are deserting each other.

Remember it's normal for you to have many of the same feelings she does as a result of the assault. You will be able to help her better if you maintain some emotional distance. You can help her sort out her feelings of anger and anxiety, rather than experiencing them for her, but first you must deal with your own reactions.

If you can't resolve your feelings you may decide together that it would be helpful for her to see a professional counselor, someone not emotionally involved. You may both want to become involved in counseling. This is something important to consider and discuss. You may both change and grow in response to this crisis.

BEING THERE WHEN THE OTHERS HAVE GONE

It may be that at first she didn't turn to you as a source of support. Perhaps she relied more on others in her network of friends. Two weeks, two months, or even longer after the assault, when the others have "burned out" and no longer feel able to provide support may be just the time when she will need your support the most. Being available for her to talk with at this later point may be more important than it would have been earlier. There are usually many more people willing to provide support during the first few weeks. It's now that she has fewer resources upon which to draw.

It is still important to safeguard your emotions. You still may need to guard against overdependence. This is especially true if her previous support system tried to take over and rescue her. That relationship may have ended because the others could no longer deal with her dependence. In this case, it will be especially important for you to set limits from the very beginning, to avoid her transferring these dependencies to you. You would be doing her no favor in supporting this dependence. The initial crisis is over. She needs to begin functioning more on her own.

WHAT IF YOU CAN'T TALK ABOUT IT?

The rape may have had such an impact on you that it has become unmentionable. You may be afraid you'll say the wrong thing and make it worse. You may not want to talk about the rape because you don't want to admit it happened. Even words may make it too real. You may not understand how it could have happened, or you blame her, or you may even feel differently toward her now, knowing she had sex with another man, even if against her will.

If she needs to talk about the rape, but you want to change the subject each time she brings it up, the first thing you should do is explain your feelings to her. Be as honest as you can. It's better to explain your true feelings than for you to keep changing the subject, or for her to keep trying in vain to talk about the rape. Both of you will become anxious, frustrated, and perhaps even angry with each other if the problem is not openly dealt with. She needs to know that at this particular time it is difficult or impossible for you to talk about the rape but that you are not rejecting her and you still want to be with her and talk about other things. Let her know you understand she's ready to talk and needs to talk, but that she will need to find someone else better able to deal with her concerns. You do not feel able to do that just now. Being direct will also make it easier for her to find someone else with whom she can express her concerns, someone who will understand and provide the support she needs.

Other people have had all the feelings you are experiencing. They can all be resolved. Try to identify your concerns and the source of your inability to discuss the rape. Remember, you are a secondary victim. You too may need help understanding your reactions to this very serious crisis. You may want to look for a counselor who has worked with friends and family of rape survivors.

5

TELLING OTHER PEOPLE

To the Survivor

He had gone. Afraid to move, Carol was still in bed gripping
the sheets tightly up around her neck. Her first thought was that
she had to hide what had happened. "If no one knows, it will be
less real. It's over, so I'll just forget about it and go on like nothing
happened." But she couldn't block it from her mind. And she discovered that she didn't need to tell her family that something had
happened. The bruises on her face made that apparent. Her teenage brother was angry. He wanted to kill the rapist. Her parents
felt guilty and responsible. They had been right there in the house,
with their daughter, but had done nothing to stop the assault. She
had screamed and they had not heard her. They didn't want to call
the police. Then everyone would know. Even the neighbors would
know about the terrible thing that had happened—know it was
her parents' fault—know they hadn't stopped this man and protected their daughter. They knew Carol needed help. They needed
help, too. They decided to call their minister. Carol showered,
changed clothes, and cleaned up while they waited for him to arrive. She felt detached as she watched herself go through the mo-
tions. The reality and the unreality of the moment seemed to
converge.

Deciding if you will tell anyone about the rape, and if so, whom you will tell, when, and how are certainly important decisions, decisions that will affect your recovery. Many survivors are afraid of telling anyone. Sometimes these fears are unfounded and sometimes they are quite reasonable. Just as the crisis is likely to facilitate an evaluation of your life in general, it is likely to precipitate an evaluation of your relationships. You will find both good and bad surprises as it becomes clear to whom you can and cannot turn for support. You will learn to know your friends—their strengths and weaknesses—better as a result. Don't judge them too harshly. There are likely to be some individuals in your circle of friends who are well-meaning and would like to help but don't have the necessary resources or skills. Perhaps they have serious problems of their own to resolve.

Even without any physical signs it is not easy to hide the emotional trauma that results from rape. People who know you well will probably notice that you seem different, especially right after the assault. You may need to offer some explanation. While there are risks involved in telling other people, these risks are outweighed by the benefits. Telling other people certainly does not guarantee a positive, helpful response. However, not telling denies you support or assistance. It is important to find at least one person whom you can tell about the rape. You'll be surprised at what you can endure if there is someone to whom you can turn and on whom you can count. People who care about you can help you overcome the low self-esteem that often results from rape. They can help rebuild your self-confidence and assist in problem solving.

THE FEARS OF TELLING

Take some time to consider the most likely response of others to the news that you were raped. If you can anticipate a lack of understanding from someone you want to tell, you will be better prepared for the response. It may be that people you expect to be supportive will not be. You need to be prepared for these unfortunate surprises as well.

You should remember that we all interpret events according to our own dispositions. Others' response say more about their personalities than about you or the rape. While it is unpleasant to deal with blame or rejection, it is important to keep these reactions separate from the way you feel about yourself.

Fear of Blame

Depending on the circumstances of your assault, you may want to be selective about the people you tell. If people ask you what you were wearing, for instance, tell them, "What I was wearing makes no difference. No matter what a woman has on, no one has the right to rape her." Confront them directly and make them deal with their biases before you provide them with the information. Try to avoid sounding defensive when responding to their question. This is a chance to educate them and to help yourself.

You may want to respond in a similar way to other questions, such as "Did he have a knife?" "Did he threaten to injure you?" "Did you know him?" "Had you ever dated him before the rape?" "Did you struggle or resist?" "Was there more than one?" "Are you divorced, married, or single?" These questions are, in many instances, attempts on the part of others to determine how much consolation they think you "deserve" and how much you should be blamed.

Fear of Being Looked Down On

To some women, rape is a great disgrace. They want to keep it a secret because they are afraid that people will view them differently and be curious about the details. While these feelings are certainly uncomfortable and at first may result in low self-esteem, they are usually short-lived. Your feelings of self-worth must come from your own inner strength and competence. Don't elevate the opinions of others above your own. There are often as many different opinions about a single issue as there are different people. You are a worthwhile human being. You must learn to reject negative labels from other people, even those people who are important to you. If the people in your community or religious organization do not understand rape and you believe that their knowing about your assault will stigmatize you, don't tell them. This is probably not the time to educate them about the realities of rape. Get confidential emotional support from someone outside your community.

The Fear of Being Overprotected

You may be afraid that if you tell people who care about you, they'll overprotect you and take away your freedom and independence. While the intentions may be good, overprotection can be destructive. If it happens to you and you are unable to talk effectively with others about it, an uninvolved third party—a friend, neighbor, rape counselor, minister, or anyone else whose opinion you value—may be able to help. Whoever is being overprotective needs to see that instead of helping, his or her behavior is hampering your adjustment and recovery.

WHOM TO TELL

If people are helpful, supportive, and make you feel better about yourself, spend more time with them. If being with them makes you feel worse about yourself, avoid them. There is no reason to subject yourself to these bad feelings. Set your own boundaries. Make new friends if necessary. Join new organizations. Choose to be with people and engage in activities that encourage a positive self-esteem, growth, and feelings of self-worth. You deserve and need to feel good about yourself.

You should remember that some people, even close friends, may withdraw because of their own fears. Don't judge other people in terms of your experiences and values. They may not be as strong or understanding as you expected. A negative response does not necessarily indicate a lack of concern about you. You may want to try being with them again later, when you feel stronger.

It is also important not to expect whomever you tell to fix everything. Telling someone else is not a magic cure, no matter how understanding and supportive that person may be. Such unrealistic expectations will only result in disappointment and frustration. Although the rape cannot be undone, you will recover from it. You may move far beyond the point where you were before the rape, but that will take time, effort, and the desire to change on your part. Giving someone else the sole power to make you feel better will only delay the recovery process.

People Who Need to Know

You may decide to tell only those people who need to know. They may include police, hospital personnel, your parents, your husband, or your roommate. Your relationships to them and your anticipation of their responses will influence this decision. The circumstances of the rape may be such that you need not tell them. Even if you have cuts and bruises, you may tell some people you were attacked without mentioning the sexual assault. You should not feel guilty not telling the whole story.

> Cheryl decided not to tell her employer after she was raped. She chose to try to continue her job as a waitress. Her attitude and behavior toward the customers had changed. She was no longer friendly, and easily became irritated. Her boss didn't understand why she was acting so differently and was on the verge of firing her.

Cheryl's boss may have been more accommodating and understanding if she had known about the rape. She might have switched Cheryl to a position with less direct public contact. Cheryl did not even take any time off from work after the rape. She worked the next evening, though her adjustment may have been much easier had she not done so. It may be helpful to take time off, perhaps to take sick leave. However, you will need to provide some explanation in order to do so. Survivors in school who have told their instructors about the rape have been able to delay taking exams for which they were not able to prepare.

People You Want to Know

There are other people you may decide to tell, because these are the people on whom you rely for support and understanding during good and bad times. They are the sounding boards for your anger and the people who help you make order out of chaos. You trust them to accept you and be there for you.

Members of the clergy are often the first people to whom families will turn for help. They are familiar people and can be trusted to maintain confidentiality. They usually won't judge you. Fortunately, they also do not attempt to deal in isolation with all the issues brought to their attention. Rather, they act as entries into the larger community support system. This was the case with Carol and her family. Their minister recognized the need for immediate medical, legal, and emotional support for the family, and with his reassurance, the decision was made to call the police and a rape crisis center.

It may be that with this crisis you will rely on people in addition to or other than your usual support system. Your best friend, your mother, your husband—the people who usually provide support for you during crises—may be so upset by the rape that they are unable to help you. Some survivors even find themselves with the extra difficulty of needing to allay the anger, fear, and anxiety of those closest to them. They must become caretakers of their "support system."

A co-worker, with less emotional attachment than a friend or relative, may be in a better position to provide objective support without experiencing all the terrors herself. She may be better able to maintain the emotional distance necessary to help you through the crisis.

The need to talk with someone who can maintain the objectivity of this emotional distance is one of the reasons survivors decide to talk with counselors. You may find a support group helpful, too. Many rape crisis centers offer these on an ongoing basis. You need someone who can care without becoming part of your pain.

WHEN TO TELL

Unlike the police and medical personnel, other people will not necessarily need to know immediately. When to tell may be a function of external factors. You may decide to tell other people before your case goes to court, because you're afraid they will find out from someone else and you want to tell them first. If there's a big family event, you may not tell anyone until afterward, to avoid curiosity. On the other hand, you may want them to know so they understand if you act differently, or so they can be supportive. These are decisions only you can make. They should be based on your own needs and desires.

Nancy knew her parents would become overprotective and want her to move back home. She wanted to stay in her apartment. This was her first time living alone. She knew she was still on shaky ground and it would be too easy to become dependent on her parents once again. She decided she would need to resolve some of her fears before telling them. She knew it would be hard for her mother not being the first to know, but she decided to wait anyway.

HOW TO TELL

Charlene called her parents in another state. She knew they would be worried, so she prefaced the statement with, "Mom, I want you to know I'm all right now. I'm home, I wasn't badly hurt, and there are people here with me to help me. But I also want you to know my apartment was broken into. I was assaulted. I was raped." Charlene knew it would be easier for her mother if she gave her some reassurance that she had survived without severe physical injuries. The reassurance that she was safe now made it easier for her mother to deal with the fact that she had been raped.

It is important to give those people you tell as much information as you can about what is going well. People typically anticipate the worst. If they're not right there, as Charlene's parents were not, it is more difficult for them. Charlene was wise to tell them she was essentially okay before she told them she had been raped, because they didn't really "hear" what she told them afterward. They called her the next day when the shock had subsided and asked her to repeat much of the conversation.

You may pick a "good time" to tell, or there may never be a "good time." You may be glad you told some people or you may wonder why you even considered telling them. The process may go smoothly, or it may be awkward and uncomfortable, not at all as you planned or anticipated. You cannot know these results ahead of time, but you can be prepared for various possibilities. Most important, you need to feel comfortable with having done what you felt was right. If they don't understand, it is their problem. Don't let it become yours.

■ ■ ■

To the Significant Other

Not every rape survivor feels comfortable telling other people about the assault and seeking help. However, comfort, acceptance, and understanding from the people with whom you interact are at the heart of social support. You too may be uncomfortable about her telling other people. The largest single reason women state they do not report incidents of sexual assault is pressure from other family members not to tell anyone. In 1981 Binder reported that more than one-third of the women raped as children who did not report indicated that the decision not to tell was based on family pressure. Since 89 percent of women sexually assaulted when children do not report the incident, family pressure not to tell is indeed significant. Sometimes they wanted to tell, and at other times the survivor too was uncomfortable or uncertain about telling. The incident then becomes a family secret, a secret with considerable power, to be covered up and hidden. It's also possible that she hasn't told you. If so, what do you do? What can you say?

WHAT IF SHE DIDN'T TELL YOU?

You may hear about the rape from someone other than the survivor. Perhaps she doesn't want you to know, or she just hasn't been able to tell you yet. But now you know, so now what do you do?

If the rape is general information, she knows that. In this case it is probably best to acknowledge that it is indeed general information. If everyone is talking about the rape, it's best to talk with her rather than about her. She probably can use the support. Don't be afraid to bring it up. If she doesn't want to talk about it, she need not do so. However, if she would like to talk about the rape but doesn't know how to bring it up, this gives her the opportunity. A good opener may be simple statements such as "I heard you were raped. I feel really bad, and I was wondering how you are doing now." She's free to say nothing more than "Fine, thanks," or to go into greater detail.

If someone close to her told you and made you promise not to tell, then you have a special problem. While it is, of course, best to avoid making such promises, you may need to weigh the importance of breaking the confidence against the importance of talking with the survivor about the incident. That will depend on other factors in your relationship and her circumstances. If she has had the opportunity to tell you but has not done so, and if she has an adequate support system, you may want to forget about the incident unless she decides to bring it up.

You may make it easier for her to mention by being more sensitive to her moods and openly recognizing any change. Statements like "You seem nervous. Is there something bothering you?" may make it easier for her to tell you what is on her mind. Be careful not to push. It's important that she choose when and with whom she wants to talk.

You may be angry and hurt that she didn't tell you. Her not telling you does not mean that she doesn't like you or trust you or need and want your support. She may be trying to protect you from the terrors she went through, which now seem too horrible to even talk about. It may be that your acceptance of her is so important, so crucial to her, that she is unwilling to risk the possibility of your rejecting her or blaming her. Perhaps she does not want you to be worried or fear for her or yourself. It is also possible that she just can't ask for what she needs yet, especially if she is depressed. Just keep letting her know that you are and still will be there when she is ready to talk.

You don't know why she didn't tell you or hasn't told you yet. You can only guess. Perhaps she assumes you know and you don't want to talk about it. She has enough stress to deal with now. Your anger at her or withdrawal from her will only add to that stress. If the secret she is keeping from you is affecting your relationship—and it may well be—then by all means bring it up. Talk about what is going on. Both of you probably will feel much better.

WHAT WILL OTHER PEOPLE THINK?

People May Treat Her Differently

One of the reasons you too may not want anyone to know is a fear that if others know they will treat her differently. You may fear others will see her in all the stereotypic ways as devalued, tainted, or used. You may want to protect her from exposure to any or all of the myths and biases associated with rape.

It can also sometimes be hard to deal with other people who are always around wanting to help when you want to relax and be alone. Your privacy is important, and you have a right to protect and insist on it. Their need to do something could take power from her and make it more difficult for her to regain her independence and sense of control. This oversolicitousness can make you feel indebted. If you have insufficient opportunity or resources to reciprocate, you may feel uncomfortable and reject help that is offered even when you too could use the additional support.

Although it is certainly a personal decision, it is important to evaluate your reasons for not wanting others involved. If it is due to a fear of indebtedness with the inability to reciprocate, evaluate your concern well. It may not be necessary to refuse the help offered, though you may want to share your feelings with these people. Being able to help someone in a crisis is rewarding in and of itself. They may benefit as much from giving help and support as you do in receiving it. There are times when it is best to accept help graciously without feeling any obligation in return.

Neighbors May Be Afraid

Many neighborhoods, especially the quiet suburbs or university campuses, attempt to project an image of safety and security to

the residents. Many people choose to live in these areas specifically because of that image. They may not want to know that
rape occurs in their safe, secure, quiet refuge, and you may not
want to upset or frighten them.

But are you really doing them a favor? Perhaps not. If they are
willing to hear and accept reality, they may be more careful and
less likely to become victims themselves. If multiple assaults
have been occurring in your area, it will be even more important for people to know so they can be more cautious.

People May Blame You

If you're hesitant for others to know because you are afraid they
will blame you for not having protected her and prevented the
rape, this is more likely guilt you are feeling. In some way you
feel responsible because you weren't with her, were out of
town, didn't lock the door, et cetera. You need to resolve these
feelings.

Other people may blame you for the same reason they may
blame the survivor, in order to maintain their illusions of invulnerability. They want to believe their child or wife will be safe
because they will protect her, unlike you. No matter how unreasonable such blame may be, it can hurt. If you have allevi-
ated your own conscience you will deal with these insinuations
much better. Don't place other opinions above what you know
to be true.

Remember, because it is different from most crises, it is hard
to tell other people about something as devastating as rape.
There are circumstances that make openness safer, although no
one can guarantee what response will be encountered when the
story is told.

CONDITIONS THAT ENCOURAGE OPENNESS

By revealing your feelings and fears to another person, you
become much more vulnerable to disapproval and rejection.
Therefore, you must begin by letting the survivor know she can
trust you. If you accept what she has told you without judging
her, no matter how poor you feel her judgment may have been,

she will be more open with you in the future. You may not like what she did, because in some way it may have led to the rape, but it is important to tell her that her actions did not affect your acceptance of and high regard for her.

Maintain a reciprocal relationship. If there are things she can do for you, she may feel more comfortable asking you to do things for her. Another important dimension of any relationship is the balance maintained by each person between dependence and independence. When one person becomes overly dependent on another, losing the sense of independence, an insecure attachment develops. This is a result of the dependent person's feelings of anxiety and apprehension that should the relationship end, he or she would be unable to cope. The natural desire for closeness with the other person is thus accompanied by an intense insecurity and fear of losing that person. This dependence and exaggerated need may threaten the relationship.

When one person experiences anxiety resulting from insecurity, the other person is likely to withdraw from the relationship. As the dependency grows, it becomes more and more of a burden. The dependent person may hold on even tighter. Disaster often results when a relationship is held on to that tightly. To maintain a healthy relationship, we must each maintain our own sense of separateness, our own sense of responsibility for solutions to our problems, and of control over our lives.

6

THE FIRST ANNIVERSARY
AND BEYOND

Only those who dare truly live.
—Ruth P. Freedman, Each Day A New
Beginning

To the Survivor

Anniversary dates are extremely important in our culture.
While we all recognize and celebrate birthdays and wedding an-
niversaries, we often attempt to discount the importance of the
anniversary date of traumatic events. However, these anniversary dates have been found to have a significant impact on our
behavior and emotional well-being, often reawakening concerns we thought we had put to rest.

WHEN YOU ARE NOT "OVER IT"

The way you feel on or around the anniversary of the rape
depends on how well you have recovered from the assault, emotionally and physically. Some survivors may not have read-
justed by the end of the first year. For instance, they may not be
able to enjoy sexual intercourse yet, or they still may be afraid
to go out alone. They continue to experience considerable pain
and anguish, which is magnified by the arrival of the anniversary, making it an especially traumatic time.

135

Many of these women resort to heavy drug or alcohol use as a means of escape, or sleep most of the anniversary day away. Sometimes thoughts of death surface and she may say things like "I wish he had killed me. It would be so much easier." Thoughts of suicide may become intense on the anniversary date.

Anger that has been tolerable can turn into rage. While often directed toward men in general, homicidal thoughts toward the rapist may be experienced once again. Anger turned inward can result in severe depression lasting several days around the anniversary date.

If a year has passed and you still are unable to face the events of the assault, you may want to find a counselor or therapist, if you have not already done so. If you have been working with a counselor since the rape but are still having problems readjusting, don't worry. It takes many women more than a year to recover emotionally. Just keep working on your areas of concern and eventually they will be resolved.

WHEN YOU HAVE ESSENTIALLY RECOVERED

Unlike those who have not recovered, if you have essentially resolved the crisis you may spend considerable time thinking about "the day." On the anniversary, instead of avoiding thoughts of the assault, you may go to great lengths to face the events of the rape, reviewing and reliving the day hour by hour, watching the clock carefully. Many survivors return to the scene of the crime. One woman who was raped in her basement spent much of the anniversary day in the basement "putzing around, being in that space." Another woman used a lamp that the rapist had used in her home—a lamp she had seldom used before or since the rape.

Reviewing the changes you have made and the problems you have overcome makes you more acutely aware of your progress. Feel good about the inner strength you found and developed— strength you didn't know you had. It's important to acknowledge and feel good about yourself and the progress you have made. Although it was a painful experience, you survived—an entire year has passed. You can turn your back on that chapter of your life.

Do something special in recognition of the anniversary. One woman called and registered for a self-defense course on the anniversary date. Another quit a job that had been unsatisfying. She had survived a year and was now ready to move onward and face new challenges.

SURVIVORS WHO DON'T REMEMBER THEIR ANNIVERSARIES

Not every survivor will take notice of the anniversary date. You may have spent the whole year trying not to think about the rape, putting it aside. Perhaps you don't remember the exact date.

Even if you do not take particular notice of the date the assault occurred, around that particular time of year you could become anxious. If you were raped in the winter when it was cold and snowy, you may experience renewed anxiety the following year with the first snow. If you were assaulted in the summer, when it's once again warm and you are outside without your coat, you might be ill at ease. The resulting anxiety is seldom of the intensity of the panic attacks immediately following the rape. More likely it will be a general sense of discomfort, with the expectation of some unidentified danger lurking around the corner. The seasonal changes have brought back memories of the assault. This is a normal response and soon will pass.

You may not relate changes in your feelings or behavior around or just preceding the anniversary to the assault. Increased casual sexual activity, such as one night stands, in otherwise monogamous or sexually inactive women is not uncommon. One survivor recalled, "It was so unlike me. I started going out to bars and going home with men I met. I don't know why I did it. I slept with six different men in two weeks, more men than I'd slept with in the previous two years."

THINGS THAT FACILITATE OR DELAY RECOVERY

Reviewing the preceding year and noting the things that you or others have done that helped or delayed your recovery is beneficial. This may enable you to direct your energy in the year to come.

The efforts of supportive friends, both male and female, will probably head your list. These people were willing to listen, seemed to understand, and helped you sort out your feelings. However, you may have found out that your family and friends seemed so proud of how "strong" you were that it became difficult for you to express the pain you were actually feeling. They may have needed you to be strong because they were unable or unwilling to face your pain. Although being strong—being able to cope with daily life—has its place, to recover fully you need to recognize and deal with the pain. Remember, no one can feel "good" all of the time, no matter how well they handle the stresses of everyday living.

When you decided to address problems directly and took back control of your life you made the greatest progress. The changes you made in your job—where you live, who your friends are, and activities you participate in—made you feel more safe and removed unpleasant memories. They were steps you took to facilitate your recovery. Keeping busy with friends, hobbies, clubs, or counseling may also have helped.

When you stopped accepting the blame, you took an important step toward recovery. At the very least, you realized that you don't need to waste energy deciding where to place the blame for something that happened in the past. The task now is to put your life back in order and take control of your feelings about the rape today, and of the things you do or do not do today.

The most difficult event survivors report facing during the first year is having the assailant go to trial and be found not guilty. It's bad enough when he's not caught or not charged, but having to go through the experience of court only to see him found innocent and set free can be devastating. While many survivors express some satisfaction in having at least had the chance to tell their side of the story, they find an acquittal very difficult to deal with.

However, no matter what happens to the rapist, you survived the rape, and now you have survived another year. Give yourself credit for your progress even if you have not completed your journey yet.

The Special Fears

Many survivors are still afraid to go out alone a year after the assault, and some for years after that.

> There was a beautiful path through the trees down to the lake, but since the rape, each time Edith had gotten to the edge of the path her overwhelming fears stopped her. She changed her route to a much less pleasant, longer, busier road. One evening, she and her boyfriend decided to take the more scenic path again. As they approached the dark wooded area, Edith felt the fear and anxiety begin to rise as usual. Her muscles tensed, she started looking around her, and her breathing became more shallow and rapid. She noticed that her boyfriend, six feet five inches tall and muscular, continued walking, oblivious to what she was experiencing. Fear of a dark quiet area was not even part of his world. It did not need to be. Her fear turned to anger at the inequity. He, by virtue of his size and strength, was in control of his world. She was not in control of hers.

Special fears that remain for years are most typically associated with the circumstances surrounding the rape. Many survivors express panic when someone walks up behind them. Others continue to be afraid at home alone. One survivor who was raped by a man she invited to her apartment becomes tense and afraid more than a year later whenever her roommate brings a man home.

Many women are embarrassed to admit their fears to family or friends, feeling that, "It's been so long. I should be over it by now." Unfortunately, fear has no time limit. That does not mean, however, that you must continue to live with it. If you have not yet tried the techniques suggested in chapter 4, "Your

Recovery: Taking Back Control," you may want to do so now. If you've tried to deal with the fears yourself and they have remained, you may want to seek professional help.

Safety

Concerns about safety continue for years after an assault or an attempted assault. Many women report that they are just more careful now, because it makes sense to be more careful. They keep their house and car doors locked, even when inside, and are more aware of what is going on around them. Some carry Mace or whistles, and some take self-defense classes. They no longer trust strangers, accept rides from acquaintances they have recently met, nor do they offer rides to people they do not know well. As Rita said, "I'm more careful when I'm out, and more selective about who my friends are now. I don't trust just anyone. I guess I'm less naïve." She has learned to be careful, because rape can happen to anyone, anytime.

Rather than decide to distrust everyone, however, it is important to be more selective about whom you trust or you may close yourself off unnecessarily from interesting, sincere people whom you really can trust and with whom you would enjoy being. Learn to be less vulnerable without building a wide wall around yourself. Don't become afraid to trust again.

Talk to your children about your concerns and about the risks they may or may not want to take, but let them maintain control and make their own choices based on the information you have provided. The best you can do for your children is to help them learn to think for themselves and be responsible for their own choices.

CHANGE FOR THE BETTER

While rape itself is never a positive encounter, nearly half of all survivors report experiencing some beneficial results from the incident. This does not mean that the impact was not initially disruptive, traumatic, and painful. It means that they were able to mobilize their resources and overcome the turmoil.

At the end of the first year following her rape, one survivor described the assault as "a door open to set me free." She had made many positive changes in her life since the assault. She decided she no longer needed to conform to the expectations of others but rather had to decide what was best for her. She terminated an abusive relationship, quit a job she never liked, and started an eighteen-month course in a trade school. She and many other survivors report feeling stronger, more self-reliant, more serious, introspective, and thoughtful than they did before being raped. They have learned to trust and rely on themselves.

A crisis can and does bring people together. It may foster the growth of individual strength, as well as strengthening the bond between people. Many survivors have realized how dangerous it can be to rely completely on one person for support, and as a result have extended their circle of friends. Many also become more aware of the plight of women in our society and become more aware of women's issues in general. Some become active in feminist and other organizations.

Drug and alcohol abuse is a very serious and very important problem to face and resolve. Many women who had been denying the problem for years were able to stop as a result of their assaults. In most of these cases professional assistance was necessary. The assault was the impetus they needed to recognize drug or alcohol problems that had negative effects on their lives and that they needed help resolving.

By realizing each individual step toward recovery that they had taken successfully, they gained the strength and confidence to risk more, try more, and to attain success they had not believed possible. They had, one step at a time, put the rape in the past and taken control back from the rapist. They had learned to live in the present and make constructive plans for the future.

■ ■ ■

To the Significant Other

YOUR ANNIVERSARY CONCERNS

You may or may not be aware of a change in the rape survivor's behavior as the anniversary of the assault approaches. If you do note a change, don't be afraid to mention it to her, but avoid sounding critical or judgmental when you do. Instead, tell her what you observe to be different. You simply may say, "You seem to be staying home more and you look sadder to me lately. Is something bothering you? Could it be the fact that it's almost one year since you were raped?" She may be concerned but feel uncomfortable bringing it up again. This gives her an opening to talk about any anniversary concerns that exist. Perhaps she noted a difference in her behavior but did not connect it with the assault.

It is important not to assume your evaluation is accurate. Although she may act differently, something other than the assault may be the cause. If so, talk to her about these other concerns at this time.

If she still has not resolved the crisis but continues to be very angry and upset, she will probably avoid your attempts to discuss the rape. Her energy will be directed at avoiding the issue and escaping her memories of the assault. If she becomes more angry and depressed as the day approaches, don't take her anger personally. You may become the target, but remember that the rapist is the cause of her anger. Remind her that you're on her side. "You seem really angry. I don't want to make things more difficult for you. I'd like to help. Do you want to talk about the rape?" If she doesn't, she'll let you know. Respect her decision.

If she isn't ready to review the rape, do not try to force her to do so. Let her know that you care about her and would like to see her get the help she deserves, when she's ready. Let her know that, if she would like, you will help her locate a therapist or counselor.

Even though all the fears and anxieties may not have been resolved completely, you should recognize the progress she has made in the past year. This is a good time to tell her the things you think she has done well and how good you feel about her having found the strength to do them. Some survivors, usually those who have completed a large part of the process of resolution, want to take some time on the anniversary to review the experience and the progress they have made. She may want to do this alone or she may want to discuss her feelings with you. She may want to keep busy and distracted, or she may prefer not to recognize the day in any special way. Ask her what she would like to do on the anniversary day. Once again it's important to respect her wishes. Only she knows what will make the passage of the day the easiest for her, or the most beneficial.

This is a good time for you both to evaluate the changes that have occurred in the past year. Consider the ways your relationship has grown, the ways it is stronger. Are there things you know about yourself or about her now that you did not know before? Do you feel different about yourself or about her now from the way you felt last year? What have you learned?

This is also a good time to consider your goals for the year to come, both together and individually. If she is not ready to review the past year and you are, by all means do so on your own. What else would you like to change? How would you like to do things differently? How would you go about making these changes?

You too have survived the rape and the year that followed. You too have discovered strengths in yourself and in her of which you were not previously aware. Share these discoveries with her. You have come a long way, even if the crisis has not been entirely resolved. You are continually changing and growing. It's important to take time to recognize, evaluate, and appreciate your progress, whatever its magnitude.

IS SHE REALLY "OVER IT"?

Surviving rape is a long-term process. While a few women will continue to be dysfunctional years after the assault, and a few will recover "completely" without emotional scars remaining from the trauma, by far the large majority will return once again to their daily routines, and for the most part they will have successfully integrated the experience into their lives. They will have adjusted. However, one or two problems are likely to remain—fears, concerns, or instances of maladaptive coping, unnoticed by most people with whom they come into contact.

You may or may not be aware of these fears and anxieties. You too may continue to have some concerns beyond the first year that have not been resolved. As the years pass, the maladaptive patterns of coping will become more deeply imbedded and more difficult to resolve. How can you know if the survivor has really recovered? If she hasn't, what can you do to help? How can you tell if *you* are "over it"?

Sit down together and write out the things in your life and her life that are different, evaluating each as positive or negative. You may want to consider further changes now or at some future time. For instance, if you've been spending all your time together, you may decide to set some limits on this, diversify your interests, and both of you develop new friendships. If she quit working, or took a job with much less responsibility and stress, perhaps she is ready to look for something more challenging again. If she stopped any or all extra activities because of her fears, perhaps it's time to consider resuming them. Maybe you want to do this together. If you don't miss the old activities, there is no need to resume the same type of participation. There are other activities to choose from.

Some specific fears, anxieties, and concerns may bother you more than they do her. As long as she feels comfortable with the situation, she will have no motivation to change. It is important to let her know how you feel. Maybe she isn't aware of how she directly affects you. If you can talk about it, you may be able to reach a decision on how better to deal with these issues. You may need to stop meeting her needs before she will develop a more appropriate method of coping. You may decide to get help from a counselor in resolving the more difficult issues or areas about which you cannot agree.

She still may be continually sad, having lost interest in life, and not seeming to enjoy the things she does or the things you do together. This lack of interest and enjoyment in life is most likely the result of a low-level depression. It may get much worse at times. Depression is infectious. Being around someone who is depressed can make you feel blue too, as well as helpless to do anything for her. Before it gets to that point, and preferably as soon as you recognize what is happening, talk with her about the situation. Try to figure out how you both can feel better.

Remember that while she may look fine on the outside and may have returned to her usual routine, if she still harbors fears and concerns she is not functioning at her optimum level of ability. Before deciding on your course of action, be sure to evaluate the reality of your concerns in relation to your newfound sense of vulnerability. If either of you is in doubt about how adequately you have resolved your feelings, talk with a competent therapist.

WHAT IF SHE WON'T GET HELP?

What are your options if she is still having difficulty coping with her life but refuses to seek help? If you are sexually involved and she is there "in body only," what can you do? What can you do if you are roommates and she won't allow you to bring home men whom she does not know, or gets angry and upset when you do? If you're her parent and she's moved back home, afraid to live on her own, what can you do?

Being aware of your own feelings is the first step. It's easy to blame your feelings of discomfort on the survivor, or conversely, to accept her bad feelings as your own. So be certain about the origin of any conflict between the two of you. The next step is letting her know how her behavior or feelings affect you. It is important to have your own boundaries and to communicate these boundaries clearly and respectfully, without sounding judgmental. You have a right to be concerned. Tell her what you think is wrong with her behavior and how you would like to see it change. She is probably dissatisfied as well but does not see or believe that change is possible.

Encourage her to seek help. Find resources with names and phone numbers that she can utilize. If the problems are serious, offer to go with her to see a counselor. If she's hesitant to get help, explore the reasons with her one by one. Did she have a bad experience in the past? Perhaps you know someone who had a good experience who can talk to her. Is she afraid or unwilling to face the problem?

If she won't get help and the problem is interfering with your life, consider doing things differently yourself. See a counselor to help you deal with your feelings. If you cannot change the situation, you may need to withdraw from the relationship. Let her know you are considering doing this. It could even serve as the impetus for her to seek counseling, since she will see how serious you are about her need for help.

If you are a parent and believe it inappropriate for her to continue living with you, ask her to find her own place. You have a right to live your life as you wish and she has the responsibility for hers. Her continued dependence beyond the crisis, and especially beyond the first year, is indicative of other problems. Family counseling would probably benefit all of you.

While it is important to honor our commitments and help other people, especially those we love, it is important to evaluate our help and keep the commitment at a level we can handle. Decide at what point you are no longer willing to forgo your own needs and desires to meet hers by adapting your life to her unresolved fears. By not taking action, you contribute to the problem. Remember, enabling destructive behavior to continue is not helpful in the long run. It makes change more difficult later on, perhaps destroying your relationship in the process.

7

OVERCOMING THE TRAUMA OF A CHILDHOOD SEXUAL ASSAULT

> . . . There is nothing in man or nature which would prevent us from taking some control of our destiny and making the world a saner place for our children.
>
> —Ernest Becker, *Escape from Evil*

To the Survivor

If you were sexually abused as a child, your experiences probably have affected the way you view men, sex, or your sexuality, especially if you have never discussed the assault with anyone. It is never too late to talk about it and to get professional help in dealing with whatever unresolved feelings you have. For instance, it is not uncommon to resent your parents for not protecting you from sexual abuse.

Sexual abuse of children includes all sexual contact or stimulation inappropriate for the child's age and level of psychosocial development that occurs through the use of intimidation, misrepresentation, or force by an adult. The National Center for Child Abuse and Neglect estimates at least 100,000 children under the age of eighteen are sexually abused each year. Estimates from other centers run as high as 360,000 children each year. According to FBI statistics, since 1976 we have witnessed a 500 percent increase in the number of reported cases of sexually abused children, and recent research indicates that only a small percentage of actual cases are ever reported.

For the most part, children are not sexually abused by strangers enticing them with candy. They are abused by people they know and trust, by family members, close family friends, baby-sitters, school-bus drivers, physicians, leaders of boys' and girls' activity groups, and neighbors.

While the majority of young girls report being molested by men, some are molested by adult women. More than half of the young boys who are sexually assaulted are victimized by women or older girls. Very often older children or teenagers, many of whom were sexual-assault victims themselves, become child abusers.

Kim, two and a half years old, was brought to the hospital by her mother because the area around her clitoris was red, swollen, and itching. When questioned by the nurse, Kim initially said she couldn't tell. When pressed and assured it was okay to tell, she told the nurse that Terry, an eleven-year-old neighbor, "puts his potty thing in my potty thing" when he baby-sits.

Jamie, five years old, told the nurse a seven-year-old neighbor boy told her, "I'll beat you up if you don't make sex with me." He then proceeded to force her to suck his penis.

Carl, five years old, told his mother that his sixteen-year-old baby-sitter "made me touch between her legs and put my pee pee there, too." The baby-sitter had been sexually assaulted by a neighbor when she was five years old.

Children are sexually abused in all kinds of neighborhoods. It is not a problem limited to certain ethnic or socioeconomic groups. Research indicates that approximately one third of American women admit to having been sexually assaulted as children by adult males.

A 1983 study done in San Francisco found that 31 percent of almost one thousand adult women had been sexually abused by a nonfamily adult male before they were eighteen years old (20 percent of these before their fourteenth birthday). When incest is included with sexual abuse by a nonfamily member, the figures jump even higher. And when encounters with exhibitionists were also included, well over half of the women reported being victimized as children, many of them more than once.

If as a young child you were the victim of a single incident of brief sexual contact, such as fondling, with no threats, rewards, or penetration, you may have experienced little or no significant trauma. If you were allowed to talk about the incident with a trusted adult who did not blame you, you may have put the incident aside quickly and resumed normal activities. The more hysterical your parents' or other adults' response was upon finding out, the more traumatic the experience probably was for you.

Incest or sexual assault by a trusted friend is often more devastating than sexual assault by a stranger. Not only is it more likely to involve an ongoing relationship in which the child must deal with the feelings of being a helpless captive of the abuser, but additionally she must deal with the violation of her trust and love. If you were the victim of incest, while feeling helpless and vulnerable, you also may have liked the extra attention from the loved one who forced you into a sexual relationship. The result was probably confusion, ambivalence, and emotional turmoil. Long-term sexual abuse is also more traumatic because of the fear of doom or disaster should anyone find out what you were told to keep secret. That was a heavy responsibility to carry, perhaps for years.

It's difficult to feel good about yourself when you must carry such a terrible secret. Your self-esteem may have remained low as an adult, and your coping skills few. As a result you may have become easy prey to other men later in your life who also chose to abuse you. You may even have found that you are only attracted to abusive men. This self-destructive behavior, the result of your low self-esteem or continued feelings of guilt, may make you feel deserving of continued punishment.

As the years pass, you may effectively block all memory of the incident, not associating your chronic depression, anger, resentment, or continued victimization with the assault. Love once was used against you in a destructive fashion. Now, while uncertain why, you may mistrust or even may fear any man who claims to love you.

In the more traumatic cases, the general psychosocial development of the child stops at that age and developmental level. Even though children continue to mature physically and intellectually, socially and sexually they may act and feel like little children. Overcoming these effects usually necessitates long-term therapy.

Sexual dysfunction in later life is a frequent sequel to the sexual abuse of a child. Picking unaffectionate men is one unconscious attempt to limit your sexual involvement. Gaining excessive amounts of weight to make yourself sexually unattractive is another. Sexual nonresponsiveness is the most common result, feeling "sexually dead" and participating in sex but never having orgasms. In the more extreme cases, sex is avoided completely as a result of fear or abhorrence toward the act. Still others, especially those who learned early on to accept rewards in exchange for sex, engage in prostitution. These women remain victims. They have learned to cope in a very self-destructive manner. Many of the hundreds of thousands of male and female prostitutes in the United States were sexually abused as children.

While anorexia nervosa has many causes, it too has been associated with previous sexual abuse of an ongoing nature. While we still know comparatively little about all the causes of this disease, it is clear that some of these women have indeed been child sexual-assault victims.

> At 16 Jan was admitted to a hospital because of a significant weight loss due to anorexia nervosa. Her older sister, eighteen, was involved in prostitution. In the course of therapy it was discovered that both she and her sister were repeatedly abused by a hired hand on their farm. Her anorexia began six months after the first incident of sexual abuse.

If you are still struggling with unresolved feelings stemming from having been sexually abused as a child, review earlier chapters, particularly the section in Chapter 3 entitled "Common Feelings and Responses," and in Chapter 6, "The First Anniversary and Beyond."

• • •

To the Significant Other

Our children are vulnerable to abuse by adults. There is a wide discrepancy between the power of a small child and that of an adult authority figure, someone the child has been taught to respect and obey. It's not surprising that this power, control, and status can be used so easily to exploit a child. However, it is often hard to imagine why someone would do so. This disbelief unfortunately contributes to the safety of the abuser and makes the child more vulnerable.

Long-term effects will vary with the child's age at the time of the incident, relationship to the assailant, number and type of contacts, reaction of the parents upon disclosure, and treatment received. The first step in dealing with the sexual abuse of children is learning to recognize symptoms and clues.

CLUES TO THE SEXUAL ABUSE OF CHILDREN

While some children immediately will tell one of their parents or a trusted friend about the incident, many more are so intimidated by the perpetrator or so confused by a complexity of feelings that they keep the event a secret. They usually blame themselves and fear discovery almost as much as they feared the assault.

Infants

Unfortunately no child is too young to be safe from sexual abuse. Infants less than one month old have been sexually abused by adult caretakers. The sexual abuse of infants is usually limited to manual genital manipulation and in some cases oral sex. It is usually discovered when the child develops a redness in the vaginal area or a vaginal infection, most often gonor-rhea. Any vaginal discharge apparent in an infant should immediately be brought to a physician's attention, and sex-ually-transmitted-disease testing should be completed.

Preschool Children

Sudden unexplained changes in behavior are important clues that something is different in a child's life. Regression to a pre-vious type of behavior once outgrown, for instance, clinging to a parent, thumb-sucking, or bed-wetting. Sometimes a sudden fear of men or of a particular person, or the avoidance of a par-ticular place or activity develops. Any change in behavior should be explored with the child in a nonthreatening, nonac-cusatory manner. It's important for the child to know that you noticed these changes and want him or her to feel safer and better about these problems. Tell your child that being touched anywhere or in any way that makes him or her feel uncomfort-able is not okay. You want them to tell you these things so that you can make sure they do not happen again.

Other important clues to look for include symptoms of de-pression such as sleep disturbance, withdrawal, listlessness, loss of appetite, and sadness. Physical symptoms include any vaginal discharge, genital rash, itching or soreness and swelling around the clitoris in girls, and in boys, a pusy discharge from the penis. An unexplained inability to gain weight also may be indicative of prolonged sexual abuse.

It is important to remember that these physical and behav-ioral symptoms can have other origins as well. The whole pic-ture is important. It is appropriate and important to question a child about any unexplained symptoms or behavior patterns.

A child can be easily coerced, manipulated, or intimidated into cooperating with a powerful adult. It is unlikely, therefore, that there will be any signs of violence, because physical force is seldom necessary. Most often the sexual assault of preschool children is limited to genital manipulation. However, this is still extremely frightening and threatening to the child and may have a significant emotional impact on him or her.

While vaginal-penile penetration is occasionally involved, it is, fortunately, the exception. If bleeding from vaginal tears results surgical repair may be required. The presence of blood in urine or stool is indicative of vaginal or anal penetration. In one exceptional case involving a five-year-old child, her assailant, an older family friend, attempted to sew up a vaginal tear with needle and thread. The incident came to her mother's attention only after an abscess resulted causing the child severe pain.

Preteens

Between the ages of six and twelve, children are also quite vulnerable to coercion, threats, intimidation, and bribes in exchange for sexual favors. As a result, physical force is once again seldom necessary, and physical trauma is unlikely. However, vaginal penetration is more likely when the child is more than ten years old. Since intercourse could cause vaginal tears and bleeding, any spotting or blood on a child's underwear should not be overlooked. The child should be calmly and matter-of-factly questioned.

Any symptoms that resemble those of a sexually transmitted disease, such as a vaginal discharge, should be thoroughly investigated. Other physical symptoms include skin rashes, gastric distress, hysterical convulsions or seizures. High levels of anxiety can bring these on. Genitourinary problems are also common and are the result of infections as well as psychological distress focused in the genital area.

Regressive behavior and phobias toward people or places frequently occur. The child may fear men and cling to her mother, or become precociously seductive toward men and reject her mother, who she now sees as sexual competition for their favors. She may become overly busy, attempting to fill every moment in order to block out the thoughts of the assault. Truancy often results, as the child attempts to hide from her peers, who she feels will somehow "know" the atrocities she has endured. This, in addition to the child's inability to concentrate, impairs schoolwork, causing grades to drop.

Teenagers

Sexual exploitation of the teenager is in many cases the most devastating. The teenage years, when the child's self-image changes, are difficult enough without this trauma. The self-doubt, self-blame, guilt, and feelings of worthlessness that often result from sexual abuse can be crushing to an already fragile ego.

Severe depression, sleep disturbance, eating problems, and nightmares often develop. Social withdrawal, truancy, and even running away from home are not uncommon. The fewer friends the survivor has, the easier it is to keep the secret and hide her feelings of separateness. Drugs and alcohol, often readily available to teenagers, become a form of escapism.

Since adolescence is a time of psychosexual development, it is likely that the survivor's attitudes toward sex will be affected. While she may fear and avoid men, as younger children often do, the teenager may become more curious about sex and even sexually promiscuous in the months and years to come.

WHAT TO DO IF YOU SUSPECT SEXUAL ABUSE

Children are often naïve, trusting, and gullible enough to believe even the most absurd ploys their assailants use to keep them silent. An eleven-year-old child was afraid to tell about her ongoing sexual assault by a seventeen-year-old friend of her brother's because he had told her he would be electrocuted if she told anyone. An eight-year-old girl remained silent because an older neighbor told her he would kill his ailing wife, who was confined to a wheelchair, if she told anyone. A twelve-year-old girl allowed a close family friend to give her weekly rubdowns "to release the tension, so you won't get pregnant like your older sister." When he began to rub her crotch more often and to have oral sex with her, she finally became uncomfortable enough to tell her mother.

These children were made to feel responsible for someone else's problems. When incest is the case, many sexually abused children also feel responsible for any family turmoil or breakup that occurs.

The eleven-year-old just described began to get severe headaches and stomachaches, and considerable tension developed between her and her mother. When she finally told what had happened, she expressed anger at her mother, who she felt should have somehow known and protected her. This is a common response and is often the origin of tensions that build up following the assault. The child may want to tell but may be afraid to tell. She may desperately want her mother or father to "know" or to ask, thus absolving her from the guilt and responsibility of telling. The mother or father may suspect that something is wrong, but, hoping desperately that it is not true, are afraid to ask. They may try to block the thought of such an atrocity from their minds, pretending not to think about it, hoping it isn't real.

Finding Out

A child will usually let you know that she has been sexually assaulted in one of three ways: spontaneously, accidentally, or intentionally. The small child is the most likely to make a spontaneous disclosure, when he or she first comes into contact with the parent or a trusted adult. However, the small child is also easily intimidated by threats and later may deny the incident, making prosecution very difficult.

You may find out accidentally by walking in during or just after the assault, or when someone comes across some evidence, such as the blood-stained underpants of a nonmenstruating child.

I frequently left my six-year-old daughter with Tom, a seventeen-year-old neighbor, when I went shopping. I would never have believed he could do such a thing if I hadn't seen it with my own eyes. I was almost at the store when I remembered leaving a receipt for an item I wanted to return, so I had to go back for it. When I went into the living room, there he was kneeling on the floor between my daughter's legs. She was looking scared to death, sitting in a chair without any pants on. It was probably the worst thing . . . the most appalling thing I've ever seen.

Sometimes when a seemingly unrelated problem is brought to the attention of a doctor, school nurse, teacher, or counselor, upon closer inspection or in the course of a routine social history they will discover the sexual abuse.

While a child may tell you about the assault shortly after the incident, she is more likely to do so months or even years later. Children who are intimidated into silence when young often bury the incident, but they do not forget it. Some women first talk about the assault around the time of a first date, their first consenting sexual encounter, an engagement, a marriage, the birth of a child, or after another assault. These events may cause them to reflect on the incident and its impact on them at the time, as well as the impact the assault still may have on their lives today.

Your Response

The reaction of the parent, brother, sister, or friend first told about the assault can have a significant impact on the child. It is important not to become hysterical. This will only frighten the child more or make her feel she has hurt and upset you and is thus responsible for the assault. Do not suggest that she just try to forget about it or not talk about it. Additionally, if you avoid discussing the incident the child is likely to interpret your silence as blame. Thus she is denied the help and support she needs in dealing with the psychological and psychosexual consequences of the assault.

You can help the most by believing her. Children, especially young, innocent children, do not make up stories about being sexually assaulted.

Doreen, fourteen years old, first told her older sister about her assault by a neighbor. Her sister encouraged her to tell their mother, which she did. Their father, a friend of the man who had assaulted her, did not believe her. "Tell me the truth. Who really did this? Who are you covering up for? Was it that guy you hang around with? I told you to stay away from him. Don't you realize what a serious matter this is? You shouldn't lie about something this serious." Although Doreen insisted it was the neighbor who had assaulted her, she could not convince her father that she was telling the truth.

Fortunately for everyone involved, once the case was under investigation, another neighborhood girl testified that this man had assaulted her the summer before. She hadn't told anyone until she heard about Doreen. She had known that it would be her word against his and had felt too ashamed and embarrassed. The man pleaded guilty.

Remember, some children, especially teenagers, may giggle or laugh inappropriately because of their anxiety, not because what they are saying isn't true or is funny to them.

HELPING THE CHILD

Your first concern should be ensuring that the child is safe from further sexual abuse. Unlike incest, which may continue for years, the sexual assault of a child by a nonrelative is more often a one-time or short-term event. If the assault involves someone with whom the child has continual contact, it may be ongoing, and the child may not have the power to protect herself. The best, safest way to protect the child is to report the incident to the police. It is unrealistic simply to tell the child to stay away from the person who assaulted her. The child has come to you for help and protection. Besides, if you just try and keep the child away from the assailant but make no further report, it is likely someone else will become his victim in your child's place.

If you know the assailant, this can be a difficult move for you to make. But remember, he has traumatized a child or children, perhaps seriously impairing their psychosexual functioning for the rest of their lives. He must be stopped. He also needs help himself. "Normal," healthy, well-functioning men do not engage in sex with children.

It is also important to reassure the child that however she was coerced or enticed to engage in sexual behavior, it was not her fault. The assailant is responsible. It is very common for children to fear being blamed no matter how good your relationship with them may be. They have heard the phrase *I told you not to do that*, so often in the past. They have seen you and other adults get angry at them so often when they got dirty playing, tore a new shirt, or even cut themselves while using a knife. They knew they didn't mean to do these things, and they may even have tried hard to avoid them, but they were scolded nonetheless.

Children who are threatened into participating in sex with adults actually experience fewer sexual problems later than those who are rewarded for their participation. The latter group often experiences more ambivalence and has more guilt about succumbing to the temptation without threat of physical force. They need more help, support, and reassurance to absolve themselves from guilt. They should not be held responsible or punished for poor judgment or bad decisions.

Just as when an adult is sexually assaulted, it is important for the child to have an evidentiary exam. No matter how long it has been since the assault, testing for sexually transmitted diseases should be completed, even if the assault was limited to oral contact or manual manipulation. While the chances of contracting VD are minimal, it's best to be safe. The same is true with pregnancy testing. Even if the child has not yet menstruated, if she is eleven or twelve years old, close to the age of menarche, pregnancy testing should be done. Children who never had a period have become pregnant. If vaginal or anal penetration was involved, it is important to determine whether genital trauma occurred.

Seek supportive counseling for the child. Crisis intervention, though often consisting of only three or four sessions, may prevent years of torment and turmoil. It is best for a professional therapist who has worked with child-assault victims to assess the impact of the assault on your child. Your local rape crisis center can help you find a knowledgeable individual. In the long run, it is much easier to deal with difficult issues immediately rather than to allow them to continue to affect you or the child for years to come. But at the same time, be aware that as the child matures, other related problems that you will also have to deal with may develop, even if you did everything possible when the assault occurred.

REMEMBER, IT'S NOT YOUR FAULT

However much you would like to be able to protect your child, in reality you can't be with her all the time. Nor can you anticipate all possible problems and prepare your child for all possible dangers ahead of time. The fact that your child was sexually assaulted does not reflect on your parenting skills. While you certainly will find the assault upsetting, you need not feel guilty.

Marie was visiting with a friend's child in the hospital. The child had been very seriously beaten by a man who attacked and raped her on her way home from the grocery store. They were uncertain if she would live. Suzette, another family friend, happened to come at the same time and left with Marie. She told Marie, "It just makes me so angry to think that anyone could do something like that to a child." Marie told her, "It makes me angry too, but it scares me even more. My daughter is the same age. I'm afraid it could happen to her so easily, too." Suzette said, "If you were a good mother, your daughter wouldn't be out at night alone."

Marie felt absolutely devastated. She felt helpless to counter this irrational remark, and yet she was very angry. She also experienced considerable empathy for the child's parents. "I can't imagine what they must be going through. Their daughter has been brutally raped and may die. And friends like Suzette must be blaming them. I wish I could help more."

HOW CAN YOU KEEP YOUR CHILD SAFE?

The first and probably most important step in keeping your children safe is recognizing that they are vulnerable to sexual abuse by people they know and trust as well as strangers. The next step is teaching your children, without frightening them, what sexual abuse is, what it may involve, and what to do should a family member, friend, or stranger make them feel uncomfortable.

To do this, of course, means you must discuss sex with your child. Sex is a taboo subject within most families, except perhaps when a mother warns her daughter to be careful not to get pregnant if unmarried.

A very effective program directed toward children of all ages has been developed by the Illusion Theatre in Minneapolis. The format focuses on various kinds of touch and teaches children that being touched can make them feel good or bad. Children know that some touches make them feel uncomfortable. What they don't always know is what it means when they get uncomfortable and what to do when that happens. Children need to talk about good and bad touches with their parents or in school with their teacher and peers. When discussing it, use their terms to refer to their genitals so they know what you are talking about. Using dolls may also be helpful, especially dolls with anatomical parts.

Your child should know that whenever she feels uncomfortable, or if someone touches her in a way that makes her feel uncomfortable, she is to tell the person to stop, and say she has to leave immediately. She should then go to a place where she feels safe. If she is at school unable to reach you, she can tell her teacher or some other trusted adult. Talk to her about a number of situations in which she might feel uncomfortable and help her solve possible problems by considering what she might do in each situation. Discuss who she might feel comfortable telling if you are not immediately available—a neighbor, cousin, or guidance counselor. Let her know that you want to know, too, and will not be angry at her, because, whatever happens, it is not her fault. Even if this person is someone you both know and thought you could trust, and even if he made your child promise not to tell, she should tell you, because a promise to hide something so bad and unfair to her should not be kept.

You can't protect your child from a sexual assault by not talking about it and pretending that it is something that happens only in other neighborhoods. That attitude might make her more vulnerable and less likely to seek help and protection from ongoing abuse. Remember, however, that you need not frighten her or make her afraid to be touched by a male. Be sure to stress that hugs and cuddling feel good and are an important part of growing up feeling safe and secure. Hugs and cuddling feel different from sexual abuse, just like rape feels completely different from making love. Children know the difference, but they will need your assurance, permission, and encouragement to talk about uncomfortable feelings should they arise.

8

CONVICTING THE RAPIST

The mood and temper with regard to treatment of crime and criminals is, in any country, one of the most unfailing tests of its civilization.

—Winston Churchill

To the Survivor

In order to better understand the chance your case may have in court, you need to be aware of the factors about you, the assailant, and the circumstances surrounding the rape that, while they may not be fair or right, are likely to have an effect on the case. The following information is not meant to discourage reporting but to let you know what to expect. While the process may seem futile, it is not. Cases that go to court that are thought unlikely to be won, sometimes do result in convictions. However, it is sometimes necessary for the survivor, and in some cases her family as well, to push and continually insist that her case be heard.

All cases do not get the same thorough, unbiased investigative attention. You may need to convince the individuals within the system of the merits of your case and your credibility as a witness. The police officers, the attorneys, and the judges involved in your case may be wonderful and understanding, or terribly biased. Dealt with one at a time, these people probably will be more willing to reevaluate their biases and more willing to change than would the system as a whole. Your efforts today, combined with the efforts of other survivors and those fighting to change the system, are what will make change possible in the future.

THE PROBLEMS IN PROSECUTING

There are two primary strategies within the legal system for prosecuting this crime. The first is to arrest as many suspected rapists as possible and let the courts decide on their guilt or innocence. To a great extent, this occurred during the mid-1970s with the push for the reform of rape laws. The result was that it took hours of police time to gather evidence and do a thorough and complete investigation for each case. It then took the prosecuting attorney considerable thought and effort to build a good case and go to trial, and it was an emotionally trying time for the survivor as well. Then despite all this effort, only a small percentage of these men were found guilty by a jury and actually served time. In the large majority of the cases, the survivor, the police, and the prosecuting attorney expended a great deal of time and effort only to see the assailant go free. There was a considerable burden placed on the criminal-justice system with minimal payoffs in convictions.

Out of frustration, many prosecuting attorneys and police departments have opted for the alternate strategy of carefully screening cases before making an arrest. Today they are less likely to take a marginal case to court. Current cases are compared with past cases that have been won in court. "Good" cases with "good" witnesses are won more often than "bad" cases with "bad" witnesses. It is very frustrating and for attorneys it can be professionally detrimental to lose too many cases. The more "good" cases they lose, the more carefully they screen cases and the more selective they are about issuing warrants and taking people to court.

Their caution is then passed on to the police in the next rape case they investigate. The police may have spent days or weeks investigating an earlier case only to have the now-cautious prosecuting attorney refuse to charge the suspect for the assault. As a result they become more selective themselves about the cases they spend long hours investigating. Frustrations and feelings of futility and helplessness then "trickle down" one step further to the survivor. The police may discourage her from even making a report when they don't believe it will result in a guilty plea or conviction. They don't want to see her subjected needlessly to the emotional stress.

The end result of this caution and frustration is that it becomes a safer system for the criminal. A lot of "good" cases are not reported by survivors, investigated by police, or prosecuted by attorneys. More rapists go free, having learned that rape, although illegal, is socially "sanctioned" by the system.

To a great extent the progress of your case and the response you get from the police and the prosecuting attorney will depend upon how similar or dissimilar it is, and you are, to other cases they have won. What happens to your case will also depend on the stereotypes they believe about "good" and "bad" rape cases, and "good" and "bad" witnesses.

While progress has been made, there are still a multitude of problems within our criminal-justice system that makes prosecution of rape difficult. As Burt and Arbin reported in 1981, fewer than 10 percent of all rape cases ever go before a jury. It is important that you understand the system and the process involved, along with the problems and road blocks you may encounter along the way. There are points at which you can express your opinion and have an effect on the outcome of your case. However, you most likely will not be asked to do so and perhaps not even be made aware of that possibility. You may find that it isn't necessary to fight for your rights within the system. You may not have the energy to fight. Either way you have a right to know the other possible courses of action. With a better understanding of the system and a broader perspective with which you can evaluate the progress of your case, you can make more informed decisions.

A SUCCESSFUL CASE IN REVIEW

You are one of the lucky ones. You called the police right after the assault and you had a good description of the assailant. The police took you to the hospital, a detective came down and took your statement after the evidentiary exam, then you went home and waited.

The next day you got a phone call from the police. They had picked up a man who fit your description. Although he, of course, denied that he had been involved in the rape, the police asked if you would come down and identify him in a lineup. Being a little nervous, you called the rape crisis counselor who had been with you at the hospital and asked her to accompany you. You were certain he was the man. You told the police about an abdominal scar, which was present on the man you identified. A positive identification was made and the man was charged with the rape.

The suspect was arraigned in court. You were not required to attend. He pleaded guilty, so you did not need to go through a jury trial. He was sentenced a little later and went to a prison that has a respected program for sex offenders.

Most cases are not this simple. Problems occur with police investigations or prosecuting attorneys. At a number of points along the way someone could decide that your case should not be prosecuted. While it seems as though there is nothing else you can do if this occurs, there are a number of avenues within the legal system to pursue. Unless your area has a legal advocate or victim-and-witness-assistance program, you may not be made aware of these options. At first, the legal system and its language may seem intimidating and overwhelming. However, you will soon see that, taken step by step, the legal system is manageable and recourse is possible.

SURVIVOR ATTRIBUTES THAT MAY AFFECT YOUR CASE

It is not circumstantial evidence but rather the survivor's background—specifically, any alleged past nonconformist behavior or "misconduct" on her part—that is found to have the greatest impact on the outcome of the case. Misconduct and nonconformist behavior include such things as having an illegitimate child, sleeping with a boyfriend, a past record of criminal behavior, suspicion or allegations of prostitution, working as a topless dancer, involvement with drugs, or being seen getting inebriated (especially drinking in a bar alone).

Juries, as well as personnel within the criminal-justice system, often have minimal corroborative evidence to use in evaluating the testimonies of the survivor and the accused. There is seldom a witness to the assault, unless an accomplice was present. Therefore, decisions are often based on other factors, primarily other people's perceptions of you and the accused—your honesty and credibility. Their opinions depend on their often stereotypic beliefs about which rape accounts are "real," and which ones are fabricated, what type of person gets raped, and what type of man rapes.

No one says openly that men have a right to rape women. However, individuals on juries, attorneys, police, and perhaps even your friends and neighbors have come to tolerate rape when it involves a woman who does not act the way a woman—or "lady"—is expected to act.

Streetwise men are aware of these biases and use them in selecting their victims. Runaways are especially vulnerable. They are usually young, often naïve, have no resources, often nowhere to spend the night, and thus are dependent upon help from strangers for their subsistence. One rapist told the young girl he raped, "I know you're a runaway, so you won't go to the police."

On the other hand, a 1979 report by LaFree indicates that if the woman is living with her parents or husband, instead of alone (especially if divorced or widowed) or is living with another man, it is more likely that the case will get to court and that a conviction will result. By our social standards, she is more respectable and less likely to lie or consent to having sex with a man other than her husband. Furthermore, if the suspect is of a different race than the survivor, the jury is also less likely to believe it was consenting intercourse and more likely to convict the accused of rape.

Some studies have found that carelessness on the part of the survivor prior to the assault is more likely to result in an acquittal. Carelessness involves such things as leaving the door unlocked, being out walking alone at night, or accepting a ride from a stranger. It may be that these are important factors in determining which cases get to court, but once in court, other factors become more important. Hitchhiking has been treated very harshly by the courts. In 1978, a California judge reversed a rape conviction, explaining that unless there was an emergency, a female hitchhiker is inviting trouble. "It would not be unreasonable for a man in the position of the defendant here to believe that the female would consent to sexual relations."

Another major determining factor is how rapidly the woman reported the crime. The case is more likely to be won if the report was made immediately, which is seen as an indication of sincerity and lack of consent. Even a few hours' delay, unfortunately, may negatively affect the credibility of the survivor and raise doubts about her motives. People may assume that "she got angry the next day when he didn't call, so cried rape to get even." In a 1977 study of cases won, not one case reported later than twenty-four hours after the assault resulted in a conviction. As discussed earlier (see chapter 2, "Your Next Move Can Make a Difference"), a delay in reporting severely limits the investigation because evidence is so quickly lost.

Cases involving adult women under thirty years of age are more likely to result in acquittals, even though most rape victims fall in this age category. When the woman is older or white, it is more likely that the man will plead guilty and the case will not need to go to trial. This could be because the defense attorney does not feel that he or she has a great chance of winning in court, or as LaFree suggests because older women are more aware of the stress of court on them and more anxious to avoid it. They or the prosecuting attorney may thus be more willing to accept a guilty plea for a less serious crime, such as second degree rather than first degree criminal sexual conduct, or a less harsh sentence in order to avoid the additional stress of court.

While the laws in many states define rape as more traumatic and deserving of more severe punishment if a pregnancy results, juries seem to disagree. Most jurors do not see pregnancy as a factor aggravating the traumatic nature of the assault, but rather a factor that raises doubts as to the survivor's motives. As a result, attorneys often counsel women not to testify about a pregnancy that occurred or an abortion that was needed.

If the survivor is black, it is less likely that the accused rapist will plead guilty regardless of his race. And it is also less likely that the case will be won in court regardless of his race. Studies indicate that there is a prejudice against black women. It is no wonder that so many black women choose not to report to the police, even though they may go to the hospital to have injuries treated and for VD and pregnancy tests. "My brothers will take care of him. The police won't do anything anyway," one black woman said. One assailant chose to go with the police, whom he had called, instead of facing the survivor's three brothers, who were patiently waiting outside his door with baseball bats.

According to a Wisconsin judge, just being female is sufficient reason to be blamed for rape and for the accused to be set free. He refused to sentence a fifteen-year-old rapist, saying, "Women are sex objects. God did that, I didn't."

OFFENDER ATTRIBUTES THAT MAY AFFECT YOUR CASE

The outcome in rape cases is also significantly affected by attributes and the assumed character of the offender. The respectability of the assailant and his physical and social attractiveness have been found to be significant factors in assumptions made about his honesty. Even the most disheveled assailant will turn up in court clean-shaven, with a haircut, and often wearing a suit and tie. He does not appear to be the type of man who would rape. He is likely to have his wife, mother, father, and even older children accompany him and sit behind him—the picture-perfect middle-class American family unit. The more he can look like the police, the judge, or members of the jury, the more likely they are to empathize with him, and the less likely they are to find him guilty.

Married assailants are less likely to be arrested and charged with assault. They arouse the empathy of the police, who feel that "they have more to lose than the victim if the case is charged." However, single assailants who are younger than twenty-five are more likely to be arrested and convicted. If the suspect has a previous criminal record of any kind, the police

are more likely to arrest and charge him. If the past record includes sexual offenses and if this information is allowed in
court, he is also more likely to be convicted. However, if the
defendant does not take the witness stand, he cannot be asked
about his past sex-offense record and the prosecuting attorney
cannot bring it up. The jury then would not know about past
convictions. The exception is if special permission of the judge
can be obtained to call another woman raped by the same man,
and of course, if she agrees to testify.

> Ulana had been held captive for more than thirty hours by a
> man who had come to look at a car she was selling. He knew a
> friend of hers. Once in the car he had driven to a deserted location,
> where he raped her. He then took her to a friend's house, where he
> repeatedly raped her. She finally convinced him she would be
> missed if he did not release her. Once free, she reported the rape to
> the police. He was arrested and claimed she had consented.
> The court case was going badly until Vera, a fifty-five-year-old
> schoolteacher, took the stand. Tearfully, experiencing the pain
> and horror once again, she told of her rape five years earlier by the
> same man. She too had advertised a car for sale and he had raped
> her during the test drive. He had been sentenced to prison and was
> released only four days before raping Ulana. He was found guilty
> and returned to prison.

The assailant's race has been found not to be nearly as important a factor in the court outcome as the victim's race. While
black men make up a large percentage of the prison population,
a thorough review of court rape cases found they were less
likely than white men to be convicted of rape. This is thought
to occur because they are more likely to rape black women. As
mentioned earlier, cases involving black survivors are less
likely to result in convictions. Once the data is controlled to
account for the race of the survivor, black men are convicted at
the same rate as white men. The system is biased more against
black women than against black men.

When more than one assailant is involved, the case is more
likely to result in a conviction. Consent here is less likely to be
accepted by juries as a believable defense. It is also more likely

that the police will find discrepancies between the stories of two or more men, especially when they are quickly separated before being interviewed. Sometimes one decides to cooperate and testify against the others in return for a more favorable charge and sentence.

CIRCUMSTANCES OF THE ASSAULT

Circumstances inconsistent with common consenting sexual encounters are more likely to result in convictions. For instance, if the rape occurred in conjunction with another crime, such as robbery, the woman will probably be believed. However, since police are often biased about what they think women should and shouldn't do, where they should and shouldn't go, and how they should and shouldn't dress, this is not always the case.

> Dolores returned to her car after a late evening of drinking. She was wearing a tight, short skirt, and she was quite inebriated. Two men she had never seen before jumped her as she opened the door and threw her into the backseat. They each raped her, then dumped her out and drove away in her car. She stumbled into the street to stop a passing police car. A high-speed chase resulted, with the two men running stoplights, signs, and eventually wrecking her car. They told police she was the girlfriend of one of the men and that she often let him borrow the car. The police let them go and told Dolores, "It's your word against theirs." The assailants, while questioned by the police, were not even issued a traffic violation.

In a similar much-publicized case of the gang rape of a thirty-nine-year-old woman by five men, after three and a half years they were finally punished for damaging her car but not for the rape. They had damaged her car by beating it and jumping on it as they took turns beating and raping her. Both the woman and the car were left for dead on a cold January night. A sixth man, who even testified against his friends, returned to the scene and drove her to a safe location, probably saving her life. While they claimed the woman consented, they could not claim the car consented and so were convicted of damaging the car and each had to pay a fine of five hundred dollars in five-dollar weekly installments.

Another factor having a considerable impact on the outcome of the case is the relationship of the woman to the assailant. In many states there is still a marital exception in the rape laws. As a result, a husband cannot be charged with rape because a man cannot be charged for taking what is already his. This problem is discussed in greater detail in the next section, on rape laws. Beyond that problem, the courts, legal personnel, and juries are suspicious of complaints made against people with whom the survivor was previously acquainted. The establishment of a prior relationship with the survivor, especially a sexual relationship, casts doubt on her story and motives, regardless of her behavior just prior to the rape. A Kent State University study by Emmert and Koss also found that there was a direct relationship between the extent of a woman's relationship with the assailant and the steps she was likely to take to report. The better she knew him, the less likely she would take the measures required to report and prosecute. If women are less likely to report rape by an acquaintance, and the system makes it more difficult to prosecute an acquaintance-rape situation, these cases are indeed underrepresented within the court system.

If anal sex was involved, it is less likely that the jury will believe she consented, and a conviction is more probable. If the woman was injured, and especially if she was badly injured, it is probable that the case will end in a conviction if it gets to court. Her injuries are proof that she resisted. It is more likely that she will be believed in an attempted rape case than when she actually is raped. This is because too many people still believe the myth that a woman can only be raped if she wants to be. If the survivor went to her own home with the assailant willingly, was seen drinking with him, agreed to leave a bar with him, or accepted an invitation to his home, an acquittal is common.

The response you encounter within the legal system will depend to a large extent on how well you and the circumstances of the rape fit the stereotypic "good" or "bad" case. It is important to remember that the decision of the prosecuting attorney not to charge a case does not necessarily mean that the police or the prosecuting attorney do not believe you were raped. It reflects their knowledge of what kinds of cases will be won in court, and thus which cases are worth their effort and your effort in trying to win. While most of the factors cannot be controlled, there are things you can do to facilitate a positive response to your case, and to exert more control over the outcome.

The next section will review the process, the road blocks you may encounter, and suggestions on how you can deal with the road blocks.

RAPE LAWS

The average survivor does not realize that the criminal case is not her case. It is the state's case, because rape, like other criminal charges, is a crime against the state. While a very important one, the survivor is merely a witness. The prosecuting attorney is thus not her attorney but the state's attorney, and she is acting in the interest of the state. Should a conflict arise, the needs and desires of the state come before the survivor's. The survivor has no real rights in the decision process, although out of common sense and courtesy most prosecuting attorneys will involve the survivor as much as possible.

Rape laws originally come from the Roman law of *raptus*. *Raptus* was a violent theft that could apply to any kind of property that belonged to a man, including his slaves, children, or wife. It referred to abduction and theft, not to sexual violation. If a sexual assault occurred, it was still the abduction, *raptus*, that was charged. From their beginning, rape laws have been designed to protect a man's property, not to protect women.

Acceptance of the concept of women as the property of fathers or husbands is the reason why, until recently, a husband who raped his wife was legally protected by a spousal exclusion. Lord Hale, a British jurist, asserted that a husband could not be guilty of raping his wife, because, by their mutual matrimonial contract, the wife had given herself to her husband and she therefore had no right to deny her husband sexual access to her body. Her feelings or consent were irrelevant. In some states this exception also included people living together or in common-law marriages.

The National Organization of Women (NOW) National Task Force on Rape was active in lobbying for rape-law reform. A small victory was won by women in the mid-1970s when separated husbands were first removed from the spousal exclusion and could thus be charged with rape. Now the spousal-exclusion clause has been completely removed from rape laws in some states. Major victories have been won in rape-law reform, though many problems remain. Rape laws still vary from state to state. You can obtain a copy of your state's rape laws by calling your local prosecuting attorney's office, by going to any law library, or by calling your state documents registrar.

In most states the offense is considered most serious when penetration occurs; the victim is legally a child; weapons are involved; personal injury or pregnancy results; or when another felony, such as kidnapping, is also committed.

Now, in most states, penetration need not occur for the crime to be considered rape. Any nonconsenting contact with the sexual organs, including the breasts or buttocks, is considered rape. Revised laws also make it explicit that "sexual intercourse," in addition to vaginal penetration, includes penetration of the vagina or anus by an object (except for medical purposes) and by a person of the same or opposite sex.

The change in the sentencing structure is another important point of reform. In the states where rape conviction could result in death, castration, or life in prison, women were less willing to report, police and attorneys were less willing to charge, and juries were unlikely to convict. With more reasonable shorter sentences, conviction is more likely.

The determination of consent is an especially important issue. Many state laws require the woman to prove she resisted— by screaming, fighting back, kicking, or trying to run away. When weapons are not used and physical resistance is not apparent, some states do not consider the assault rape. In other states, the analysis of consent is based on the woman's character, reputation, and chastity, as discussed earlier. She is on trial instead of the assailant. This is an especially difficult problem because of the sexist stereotypes that must be eliminated for true justice to occur. The most progressive laws now recognize that the lack of the use of force is different from consent. The assailant should not be acquitted because he "believed in his mind" that the woman wanted sexual intercourse even though she said otherwise. More laws must specifically include coerced submission as rape.

THE POLICE INVESTIGATION

As we have seen, the police investigation and report is limited by the laws in your state defining what is and is not rape, as well as by personal biases the police have about what represents a "good" or a "bad" case.

A police investigation can have one of five outcomes. It may be *redlined; unfounded; exceptionally cleared; inactive, not cleared;* or *cleared by arrest.* Use of these categories may vary somewhat from precinct to precinct, so it is important to check with your police department as to their use of the categories and definitions of terms. Don't be afraid to ask.

Cases are redlined, not investigated, infrequently and only in the most unusual circumstances. The women involved in these cases include those who are thought to be psychotic, for example. Though a report may be made, no officer will be assigned to the case, so no investigation will occur.

The most controversial cases are those labeled "unfounded." Cases that are unfounded include those that the police have decided are not "real" rapes, or in which the legal criteria have not been met. In states that still have a spousal exclusion, rapes by a husband will be included in this category. This category also includes cases in which the suspect claims the survivor consented and the officer does not feel there is enough evidence to prove that rape occurred.

There is considerable police discretion allowed in determining which cases are included in this category, as clearly written criteria are absent. As a result, the myths and stereotypes that police believe become major factors in deciding which rapes are "real." Usually the police assigned to sex-offense cases have resolved most of their own biases. However, no matter how fair and unbiased the officers may try to be, biases are involved. Some officers make no attempt at hiding their biases.

The third category includes cases that are "exceptionally cleared." For the most part, these are cases the survivor wants dropped. She will simply miss her appointments with the police or won't answer her phone. She really may want the case dropped or she may just not have the energy to see it through. In a few unfortunate instances, a misunderstanding occurred. She expected the police to contact her again, while they thought she did not want to prosecute and were waiting for her to contact them if she changed her mind.

The fourth category includes inactive cases—cases pending, not closed, but not actively being investigated. The length of time a case can remain inactive is dependent upon the state's statutes of limitations. For adult sex offenses it is usually three years, and for cases involving children, seven years. This category includes cases in which there is a good description of the assailant but he cannot be found. It includes cases in which the prosecuting attorney would not issue a warrant due to a lack of sufficient evidence. They are kept open in hopes of obtaining additional evidence so the case can be resubmitted in the future, or of apprehending a suspect before the time limit runs out.

It is also possible that while a case is inactive, another similar assault will occur. If a likely suspect is apprehended for another rape, the first survivor may be asked to identify him as well. In a 1983 case in Minneapolis, four women were asked to make an identification in a lineup. Two were able to identify one man who had raped them both.

In the last instance, in which the case is cleared by arrest, the police have enough evidence to make an arrest. To do this they must take the case to the prosecutor. If the prosecutor also believes that the police have provided sufficient evidence for the state to prosecute, a complaint or a warrant for the assailant's arrest is issued. Now the police can make an arrest.

The time during the investigation prior to the arrest may be a very frustrating period for you, especially if you know the assailant. You may live near him or go to the same school he attends. Unfortunately, there are risks involved in arresting someone immediately. Sometimes a suspect is arrested right away on "probable-cause evidence." This means that the police have good reason to believe he is responsible but do not yet have sufficient evidence for a warrant. The police may make a probable-cause arrest if they catch the man at or near the scene of the crime or if they know who he is and are afraid he may leave the area.

When the suspect is arrested on probable-cause evidence, he can only be held for thirty-six hours without a complaint being issued by the county attorney. This means that if sufficient evidence is not obtained within that time, he must be set free. In only the most extreme cases will the suspect be held for another thirty-six hours by the prosecuting attorney.

Before the complaint can be issued, the police must gather the necessary evidence, and you must go down to the police station and make a formal statement. You may and should ask for a copy. If you do not return phone calls or go in to make this statement when you are supposed to, the suspect will be set free. It is essential that you maintain continual contact with the police during these initial stages of the investigation. It is disappointing and difficult for everyone to see the assailant walk free because you could not be contacted. This is one more of the many reasons only 2 to 3 percent of rapists are ever convicted and serve time.

There is also another factor that may prevent the police from arresting a suspect.

I was so angry that the police did not arrest him. After the man who abducted me raped me, his two friends raped me in his garage. I thought they were going to kill me. They called him by name. There were even tracks in the snow from the garage to his house when the police went back. I still don't understand why he's home, safe, and I'm here in fear for my life.

He was safe because the Supreme Court has ruled that a person cannot be arrested in his own home on probable-cause evidence. The only exception is when the police are in "hot pursuit," a reason challenged in court as well. A "man's home is his castle," even if he is suspected of rape. Any evidence obtained under these circumstances, without a search warrant, no matter how conclusive, could and probably would be thrown out of court.

It is also possible that you will go home expecting to hear from the police and not be called. If that occurs, do not hesitate to call and ask to talk with the officer who has been assigned to your case. Ask him what the status of your case is and what else you can do to help. Let him know you're interested. He probably gets one hundred cases or more each year. That's a lot of work. Realistically, the more likely he feels you are to follow through with the case rather than change your mind and ask to have the charges dropped, the more willing he may be to spend the extra time and energy trying to get the evidence necessary to make an arrest.

Once the suspect is arrested, you may need to go down to the police station to view a lineup. What this involves is viewing the suspect in addition to four or five other men through one-way glass. They will not be able to see you. The purpose is to see if you can pick him out and make a positive identification. You can have them repeat something said during the assault so that you can make a voice identification. If you think you see the man, even if you are not positive, mark the piece of paper the police have given you. If there are any scars or other marks that you feel would help identify him, let the police know if you have not told them earlier.

After the lineup is over you can talk with the police about any concerns you have about your identification. If the rapist had a beard or moustache before, tell the police. If he has gained or lost weight, tell them that too. They can then check with neighbors or employers. Corroboration of this type may even make the case a better one.

It can be frightening to see the assailant again. If you have a rape crisis counselor, you may want to ask her to accompany you to the police station. She will not be able to be present during the actual lineup, but she can provide support before and after. If you are not working with anyone, you may want to ask a friend to go with you.

A lineup will not be necessary if you knew the man. Even if you did not know him, a photo lineup may be possible instead of viewing him in person. If you do identify a suspect, from now on your primary contact will be with the office of the prosecuting attorney who is assigned to the case.

THE COURT SYSTEM

Most prosecuting attorneys do not have written criteria by which they judge how "good" a case is and whether or not they should issue a complaint or warrant. They essentially rely upon two criteria: the attorney must believe the case is "really" a rape, and that there is enough evidence to win the case in court. The attorney's judgment, based on personal biases, and experiences, thus plays an important role in the outcome of your case. Willingness to take the risk of charging a marginal case is also important.

If the attorney denies the case when the police initially present it, you have a right to meet and discuss the reasons for denial. At this time you may provide additional information and explain why you think a warrant should be issued. Do not assume the attorney has all the information. Information received thus far is only as good as the summary the police have submitted.

You will be the most important evidence should the attorney decide to take the case to court. Marginal cases initially denied have been taken to court because the survivor met with the attorney and convinced him or her that she would follow through with the case and make a good witness. Others have been less successful. It's the prosecutor's decision in the end, but you do have the right to have your feelings and concerns heard and to have any decision explained in terms you can understand.

You do have an alternative if the criminal charges are denied. You can press civil charges. To do this you must talk with a private attorney to see if you have a case. In a civil lawsuit you need not prove your case "beyond a reasonable doubt," as is required in criminal cases. Civil cases require "a preponderance of the evidence" be in your favor, so they are easier to win. Some survivors have pressed civil charges against the assailant; his place of employment, if the assault was in any way job related; the company in whose parking lot the rape occurred; or the apartment building or hotel that did not have sufficient security. You can press civil charges in addition to the criminal suit; it is not an either-or situation. Most typically you will sue for a dollar amount to cover physical and mental injury as well as any property damage. Unfortunately, the assailant will not be punished by prison as a result of a civil suit, and he will not have a felony on his record. However, it is an alternative more and more survivors are choosing today.

If you don't hear from anyone after a warrant has been issued, call and ask to talk to the attorney assigned to your case. Since the case is filed by the state, you may need to know the defendant's name to find out which attorney has the case. If you don't know his name, the police officer assigned to the case can give it to you. In some areas, usually the larger cities, there will be a legal advocate assigned to keep you posted as to the progress of your case. Some states now have a Victim's Bill of Rights. This requires that you be notified at important junctures, such as plea bargaining and sentencing. While you still do not have any decision-making rights, you are allowed to make your feelings and desires known and to be present if you like. You have a right to know what is happening and what the next step will be. It's also important for you to understand what unfamiliar terms mean; don't be embarrassed to ask to have them explained.

By now, you probably have been screened at least three times: by the police officer who took the initial report, the police investigator, and the prosecuting attorney. If you have made it this far, it is likely that they all believe a criminal rape occurred. The job at hand for the prosecuting attorney is to develop a strategy to show beyond a reasonable doubt in court that there was a rape and that the suspect is the man who raped you.

The Preliminary Hearing

The next court day or within thirty-six hours after the warrant has been issued and the suspect is arrested and charged, a preliminary hearing will take place. You do not need to be present. The suspect will be read the charges against him. If he does not have an attorney, a public defender will be assigned at this time and bail will be set.

The Arraignment

The next step is arraignment before a judge in the courthouse. You need not be present here either, though you may attend. The suspect's attorney will be present and he will enter his plea of guilty or not guilty at this time. If he pleads guilty, he will be asked to sign a formal sworn testimony of guilt and a date will be set for sentencing. While you probably will not be asked to do so, you may write to the judge or talk with a court service worker about the impact of the rape on your life and about your feelings regarding the sentence. If you think sentencing should be harsher than the sentencing guidelines suggest or if you really think he should be involved in a treatment program, this is the time to express your opinion to the judge or to the probation officer investigating the defendant's background and amenability to treatment. If he pleads not guilty, a date will be set for an omnibus hearing and for trial.

Plea Bargaining

The prosecuting attorney working with you will probably meet with the assailant's defense attorney prior to the trial to "plea bargain." What is involved here is a complex process. Each attorney evaluates the evidence available and determines his or her likelihood of winning the case. If the suspect pleads guilty as charged, his attorney will often have arranged that in return for his "cooperation" he will get a lighter sentence. It may also have been agreed that he can plead guilty to a less serious degree of sexual misconduct instead of standing trial for a more serious degree with a stiffer minimum sentence. If he does not have a strong defense, he is more likely to want to plea bargain. The option of going to trial, however, offers the assailant the possibility of complete exoneration. With a stronger defense, or if he believes you have little evidence, he may choose this option. If you do not want to go to court, you should push your attorney to accept a plea at this time.

The Omnibus Hearing

Shortly before the trial, there will be a preliminary, or omnibus, hearing. Once again you need not be present, although you may attend if you wish. The police will probably be present. The primary purpose of this hearing is to determine whether there is probable cause to believe a crime was committed by the suspect and to determine if any of his constitutional rights were violated. If probable cause exists and the defendant's constitutional rights were not violated, he may be held for trial. It is at this time that both attorneys tell the judge what evidence they wish to introduce to get qualified and accepted without wasting the time in court. For instance, if your attorney wants to introduce a torn, bloody blouse, he will say so. The other attorney may object, asking, "How do we know whose blouse or blood it is?" Your attorney would qualify the "chain of evidence" explaining that the blouse was taken in the emergency room by the nurse, given to the police officer, who gave it to him. Your name is on the bag containing the blouse.

The Pretrial Period

Typically it is two to three months before the trial occurs. During this time you can and probably should refuse to talk to the defense attorney or investigator unless your attorney is present. This includes phone conversations. Generally, the defense is contacting you only to try to find discrepancies between what you said in your statement and what you are saying now. It is not uncommon for you to remember something new, forget some details, or remember something differently. You probably won't want the defense to have access to this information. Be certain you know to whom you are speaking before giving out information about your case over the phone. If in doubt, refuse to speak to anyone until you can check with your attorney, even if the individual claims to be on your side.

Should you get any harassing letters or phone calls, report them to your attorney and the police immediately. Survivors have received letters and phone calls from assailants' mothers and wives begging them to drop the charges "or you will ruin all our lives." Remember: he is the one who decided to rape, not you, and you're probably not his first victim. Give these letters to your attorney.

Work closely with a victim advocate if one is available in the victim-witness program during this pretrial period. They are there to keep you informed of the progress of your case, to help you understand what is happening, and generally to make the process less trying for you. Don't hesitate to call them. If you work with an advocate, you may not meet with the attorney except once or twice before going to court.

Visit one of the courtrooms before a trial. Your advocate can show you where you and your attorney will sit, where the assailant will sit, and where you will be when you testify. Sit in on another case to see what it's like to be in court.

If uncertain, ask your advocate or attorney how you should dress for court. Be sure to wear something you like and in which you feel comfortable and good about yourself. Also remember that court is rather formal, so you may want to dress up somewhat. While slacks are fine in some areas, they are not in other areas. Blue jeans will probably not be a good choice. Don't wear clothes that may be interpreted as provocative. Avoid halter tops, low necklines, or extra short skirts. A simple suit, skirt and blouse, or dress will do nicely in most parts of the country.

Review your initial police statement just before going to court, paying particular attention to the details you may have forgotten over the past few months. Call the day before the trial is scheduled to ensure there are no postponements. Unfortunately, the trial may be postponed a number of times before it actually takes place due to the inability of a witness to be present, lack of an available judge, or illness, for instance. While delays may be necessary, sometimes the defense seems to be purposefully extending the process in the hope that you will give up and not be a witness against his client. It is difficult to get psychologically prepared for court over and over again just to have it delayed.

Jury Selection

The first day or two will be spent selecting the jury. Both attorneys ask each potential juror one or two questions and on the basis of their responses accept or disqualify them. Your attorney usually is allowed to excuse three people, and the defense attorney, seven people, without cause. After that they must state why they feel a particular person may be prejudiced against their client.

Many defense attorneys used to believe that they should avoid selecting young women if the survivor was young, because in other criminal cases they found the more the juror identified with the survivor, the more harsh they were with the offender. When more thoroughly investigated, this proved not to be true. Jurors, too, needed to believe in their own invulnerability. As a result, the more they were like the victim, the more they tended to blame her and find the defendant not guilty.

Though the evidence is often contradictory, for the most part studies have found that men are more likely to judge the assailant harshly, especially in recommending punishment. However, white males are more likely to assume that the survivor's actions were contributory. Men are most punitive toward the rapist and most likely to find him guilty when they themselves do not adhere strongly to sex-role stereotypes and are not coercive or violent in their own relationships with women. Women with daughters who are routinely in the same type of circumstances as the survivor was are likely to be more punitive toward the assailant. Women who know someone who has been raped are more likely to show empathy toward the survivor.

Older women are also more likely to be more punitive and suggest harsher sentencing for the assailant.

Your Day in Court

Opening statements will be made, then witnesses called and evidence introduced as your attorney builds your case and the defense attorney builds the defendant's. Though instructed to focus on facts, the defense attorney will attempt to develop the jury's empathy for the defendant. Neither you nor the assailant are required to take the stand to testify. You almost always will be called to testify, however, because your testimony is the most important part of the prosecution's case. When you do testify, your attorney will question you first. You will need to tell the events of the assault in detail. The courtroom is usually open to the public. You may find it difficult to retell the intimate details of the assault in court, especially with the assailant present. Don't be afraid to be emotional or cry. If you need more time, stop a moment, then continue.

When your attorney has finished, the defense attorney will cross-examine you. This may be an unpleasant experience. You may be asked seemingly insignificant details, such as a description of where all the furniture was in the room, in an attempt to find a small discrepancy or error to use to discredit the accuracy of your recall. Sound as confident and sure of yourself as you can when you do know the answers. If you are unsure, say so. "I don't know" or "I don't remember" are perfectly acceptable answers when true. If you did not hear the question or did not understand it, ask the attorney to repeat it. Your responsibility is to answer the questions to the best of your ability.

Try to be prepared for the unexpected. One defense attorney even "accidentally" called the survivor by her first name and the defendant's last name. The survivor corrected him. The defense attorney might ask you if you enjoyed the rape. One survivor responded, "If you really think I enjoyed being beaten, strangled, and raped, you're not very bright." You need not answer such a ridiculous question, however. Your attorney should object.

Most states do not allow the woman's past sexual history to

be brought into court *unless* she had a sexual relationship with the defendant prior to the rape; she had a sexual relationship with someone else just before the assault, so it could be his seminal fluid that was collected during the evidentiary exam; her past sexual relationships establish a pattern similar to the incident with the assailant; or she has a history of "false" rape reports, in which case the judge may rule that her sexual history is admissible evidence. Clever defense attorneys still asking leading questions, such as, "Isn't it true that on a number of occasions you have been known to meet men in bars and later willingly engage in sex with them?" Your attorney will object. The objection will be sustained, and the jury will be instructed to pretend they did not hear the statement—an impossible task, of course. Attacks on your character are especially painful to endure. Remember what you are there to do, and try to keep your composure so that you may be an effective witness.

If the assailant testifies, the prosecuting attorney may ask you not to be present for this part of the trial, feeling that your presence will distract the jury from what the defendant is saying. While it is certainly your decision to be present if he testifies, many survivors find it frustrating and infuriating to listen to the "stories" assailants present in court, even when the stories are so ridiculous that they are funny.

> Steve testified that "she came back to my apartment willingly to have sex. She wanted it too." When asked about the survivor's bruises and vaginal lacerations, he answered, "Well, while I was in the bathroom undressing, I peeked out the keyhole and saw her stealing my money. She stuck it up inside her. That's how she got the cuts there. I had to beat her and tear her clothes off to get my money back. She ran into the hall screaming."

The assailant will probably use one of two defenses: mistaken identity or consent. The first is by far the easiest on you in court. In this first instance, he will claim that while the rape may have occurred, he is not the person who did it. He may try to prove he was elsewhere or just that you cannot identify him beyond a reasonable doubt. He may have lost weight or gained weight, grown or shaved off facial hair. He certainly will be dressed very differently. One defense attorney had another man who looked very similar to the assailant sit beside him during the trial. The defendant sat in back of them with a hat pulled down over his forehead. Unfortunately, the survivor did not look closely and identified the wrong man. The case was lost. Fewer suspects use this plea because the medical evidence collected is so valuable in making an identification, even though it is not conclusive (see chapter 2, "Your Next Move").

If the assailant claims you consented to have sex with him, it will be your word against his, especially when there are no witnesses or signs of force. It is difficult to provide clear collaborative evidence showing a lack of consent. In this case his attorney will try to defame your character by implying that you asked for it or should have known what would happen, or in some manner are unconventional and do not conform to "normal" female behavior. The defense attorney might ask you where you live and if you have a male roommate, or may ask, "This wasn't the first time you were out drinking alone or left a bar with a strange man, is it? You asked him to dance first, didn't you?" One defense attorney even tried to make a survivor "look bad" through his condescending tone of voice when he asked her why she was wearing a plaid shirt "like men wear" and not carrying a purse.

One tactic the police try in cases where consent is the issue is to get both parties to agree to take a lie detector test and to announce the results in court before the defendant or survivor knows the outcome. However, few assailants and their attorneys will agree to this. While sometimes useful, lie detectors are not infallible. If you still believe you are at fault because you left your door unlocked or accepted a ride home from the rapist, you could appear to be lying.

At the end of the trial, in states that still require corroborating evidence, the judge warns the jury of the danger of convicting the defendant on the survivor's word alone, "because human experience has shown that girls and women do sometimes tell an entirely false story that is easy to make up, but extremely difficult to disprove." In no other criminal case is the jury warned in a similar way.

Unfortunately, juries are not instructed that it is still rape if the woman is married to the defendant or if she left a bar willingly with him. They are not warned of the danger of letting rapists back out on the streets, free to rape other women.

When the jury returns from deliberating its verdict, if the defendant is found guilty, a date will be set for sentencing. If he is found not guilty, he is released immediately. You must remember that even if he is acquitted, it does not necessarily mean that people don't believe he raped you. The whole jury must agree on his guilt to get a conviction.

Sentencing

In most areas a presentencing investigation will be completed by a parole officer, who should contact you to determine how you feel the rape has affected your life, and what you see as an acceptable outcome. This will be included in a report to the judge, who will decide on the sentence. If there is no investigation or you are not contacted, by all means write to the judge expressing your views. Your letter, the seriousness of the crime, and the assailant's past record will be used to set his sentence. Rape sentences have ranged from suspended sentences with no time in prison to 1,500 years in prison. In 1984, a Baltimore, Maryland grand jury recommended castration as the only effective deterrent for repeated offenders. A bill was introduced in the Georgia senate proposing castration of repeated sex offenders. It was defeated 33 to 19.

Many individuals feel sorry for the rapist and want to put him into treatment programs instead of prison. While it would be preferable to treat rapists and prevent their raping again, new treatment programs must first be developed. Treatment is being implemented as part of rehabilitation programs, but recidivism rates are high.

According to the Victim's Bill of Rights in some states, you should be notified when the sentencing will occur so, if you choose, you can be present. Check your state's policy. If you are not automatically notified, call and ask the date. If you don't want to be present, you can ask to be notified of the results.

Your case may proceed smoothly, your credibility and motives may not be challenged, and you may not need to fight for your rights within the court system. While only a small number of cases get to court, more of those taken to court are being won each year. The response of the criminal-justice system has been to screen the cases taken to court more thoroughly in the hope of winning a higher percentage of cases. Another more challenging solution, although one the legal system cannot accomplish alone, is better education of the public to dispel myths about rape.

The police, attorneys, judges, and future jurors must be better educated. There must be continued pressure for reform of the legal system and the law.

■ ■ ■

To the Significant Other

HELPING HER THROUGH THE LEGAL SYSTEM

It may be especially difficult for both you and the survivor when personnel within the legal system do not believe you or insinuate that somehow she deserved what happened. If this occurs, it is important for you to reassure her again that you believe her and she is not to blame. Your support will make the whole process easier.

If her case is not charged by the prosecuting attorney, or if the defendant is not found guilty in court, she will need your support in dealing with the disappointment. It is normal for her to feel angry, frustrated, helpless, and depressed. You too may experience these feelings. Allow her to go through that process without having to pretend that she feels better than she actually does. Remind her that his acquittal simply says something about the prejudices and continued injustice within our legal system.

You may want to discuss the possibility of a civil suit if the criminal case is won or lost. Consult an attorney to get advice on the wisdom of this alternative.

Instead of assuming you should attend the trial, ask the survivor if she wants you present. It may be more difficult for her to retell her story in full if you are there to hear the intimate details once again and to hear the defendant's lies. She may want you with her outside the courtroom only. Don't feel hurt or rejected if she doesn't want you there at all. Call your prosecuting attorney's office and ask if legal-advocacy services are available. A legal advocate could provide the support she needs at this time.

The stress of court will be draining. You will help her immensely if you can assume some of the responsibilities she normally carries, such as cooking, housework, and especially child care. If you cannot assume these responsibilities yourself, perhaps you can find someone else who can. If feasible, take some time off from work to be with her or plan some time to relax with her in the evening.

It probably is not a good time to plan activities with other people, unless they are very close friends. Ask her how she feels. If she is preoccupied with the court process and needs to talk about her concerns, social engagements and conversations with other people not involved could be too distracting or unnerving.

WHAT IF YOU KNOW THE ASSAILANT?

It may be especially difficult for you if the survivor was raped by an acquaintance you both know. You may have ambivalent feelings about the rape and wonder how much is true and how much she is to blame.

This is especially likely to occur if the assailant does not fit your stereotype of a rapist. Remember, even the least likely man could be a rapist. Looks can be deceiving. Ministers, successful businessmen, grandfathers, choir leaders, doctors, lawyers, the neighbor next door, the star quarterback, boys and men from all occupations and walks of life have committed and will commit rape. Estimates made by attorneys, the police, and rape crisis centers indicate that only 2 percent of the reported rapes are false. Therefore, if you believe her, you more likely will be right.

If you are experiencing a lot of ambivalence, talk with a rape crisis counselor. He or she may be able to help you resolve your concerns, and thus you will be better able to provide the survivor with the support she will need.

It is also possible that knowing the assailant and the type of person he is makes you doubt her less. You may wonder why she trusted him at all. But we all want to trust people and want to believe we are safe when out with friends.

You may never feel as though you really know for sure what happened. Maybe it doesn't matter. What really matters most now is that the survivor needs your support. You need to let her know how much you care about her. You don't need to judge her. There are enough people doing that.

PART 2

9

WHO RAPES?

I am my choices.

        —Sartre

Unfortunately, there is no easy answer to why men rape women, and in ever increasing numbers. The motivations are complex and hard to understand.

While police records indicate that the majority of reported rapists are between sixteen and twenty-five years old, the range is from ten to seventy. Those apprehended and imprisoned usually come from the lower socioeconomic groups, have little education, and frequently have criminal records, arrests, or convictions for other or similar crimes.

Apprehended rapists are, however, a select group as a result of many biases operating throughout our criminal-justice system. These biases largely determine which rapes are reported, which rapes the police believe and charge, and which men go to court and are found guilty. These biases are likely to result in an over-representation of poor, uneducated minorities among apprehended rapists compared to the number found in the general population. This also occurs with other categories of violent crimes. Ruth's case is a good example of how these biases operate.

Ruth, seventeen years old, was waiting for her girlfriend after classes at the university one evening, when a well-dressed man drove up and asked her for a light. As she approached his car he grabbed her and forced her inside. He drove her to a deserted area and raped her, after beating and strangling her. In the struggle, a card fell out of his shirt pocket onto the floor of the car. She grabbed it without his knowing. As he drove off, she also got his license plate number.

She ran home and told her mother, who immediately called the police and took her to the hospital for an evidentiary exam. Although she was not seriously hurt, she had several bruises on her neck. The card turned out to be his insurance card, complete with his name and address. They gave this to the police.

The mother became concerned when several days had passed without the police officer calling for further information, as he had said he would, so she called him. He told her that he had gone and talked with the man in question. However, he said, "He's a respectable salesman with a new baby. He's got a lot more to lose than your daughter. Besides, there are a lot of prostitutes working the area where your daughter was." He had decided not to proceed with the case.

BIOLOGICAL EXPLANATIONS OF RAPE

At one time it was believed that men with an extra male chromosome (XYY) were more aggressive and more likely to become violent than men without the extra Y chromosome. More sophisticated research later showed that this was not true. While there were indeed a large number of men with an extra Y chromosome in jails, there were many in the normal population as well. When these men committed crimes, they were not necessarily more violent. Biological factors such as a higher level of the male hormone testosterone have received attention recently as a possible explanation for why men rape. These men have been described as "sexually supercharged individuals," unable to control the biologically triggered sexual desires.

People who believe this theory then encourage treatment by the injection of a female hormone to lower their sex drive. Studies are currently underway at a number of centers in the United States to evaluate the effect of hormones on rapists. One such study was conducted in 1976 at the University of New Mexico.

This study found that the range and average levels of testosterone in convicted rapists is essentially the same as in men in the general population. They concluded that rape is not motivated by higher levels of testosterone and an uncontrollable sex urge but by a desire for dominance and control. They did find that the most violent rapists had higher testosterone levels than the less violent rapists, and they concluded that while men with higher levels of testosterone were not more likely to rape, they were more likely to use more violence when they raped.

Unfortunately some defense attorneys are now using this defense to keep their clients out of jail when they agree to take female hormone shots. No consistent relationship has been found between testosterone levels and sexual preference or sexual expression, however. The rapists report treatment works, but then they want to stay out of jail; they would be foolish to say anything else. The University of Texas Medical Branch in Galveston, Texas, recently refused to administer the drug Depo-Provera to a convicted rapist even though the drug treatment was listed as a condition of probation.

Rape is not biologically programmed. Rape-free societies do exist and will be considered in greater detail in chapter 10, "Preventing Rape." Rape is socially programmed in cultures such as ours where women are seen as unequal, in cultures that generally accept interpersonal violence and in which male dominance of women in social, business, and sexual encounters is expected and allowed. Rape is only an extension of the overall pattern of violence in interpersonal relationships in which women are expected to be submissive, to comply, and are often thought of as the property of men. To a great extent the rapist is only acting out the broader social script.

THE ROLE OF SEX AND AGGRESSION

During a rape, sex is used as a weapon to intimidate, control, and humiliate the victim. If rape were simply sexually motivated, Las Vegas, which is surrounded by legalized prostitution, would not have one of the highest rape rates in the nation, which, according to police statistics, it does.

There is clear evidence that at least one-third of rapists are sexually dysfunctional. Premature ejaculation or ejaculation immediately upon penetration are reported frequently, as is retarded ejaculation. Some survivors indicate that the rapist forced them to try numerous methods to get him to ejaculate. In a few cases, even after thirty minutes to an hour of steady penetration, he was unable to climax. The rapist often blames his inability to ejaculate on the survivor, on her inadequacy, as he probably has blamed it on his past sexual partners. Retarded ejaculation seems to occur in rapists with much greater frequency than in the population at large.

Rapists undergoing treatment often report encountering erective inadequacy. In these cases, the rapist experiences partial or complete failure to achieve and sustain an erection. This is sometimes resolved when he forces the victim to stimulate him manually or orally. Other rapists become sexually stimulated by their own violence or by the victim struggling to get away.

A 1974 study completed at the University of California confirmed a link between sex and aggression, though the association is still not well understood. They found that painful stimulation can evoke a sexual as well as aggressive response selectively in both men and women. Exposure to sexual stimuli was shown to increase aggressive as well as sexual responsiveness. There thus appears to be in some people a reciprocal relationship where anger may lead to sexual arousal, and sexual arousal to aggressiveness. The link may not be direct, however. Both forms of arousal may instead be the result of a rise in the general level of arousal of the individual.

THE ROLE OF PORNOGRAPHY

Pornography, like other social factors and conditions, contributes to the second-class status of women. It is naïve, at best, to assume that pornography entertains an individual without affecting his or her perceptions of sexuality and acceptable, appropriate behavior toward members of the opposite sex. While the 1970 President's Commission on Obscenity and Pornography concluded that there was no evidence of adverse effects of pornography, current research disputes this statement. Though the commission undertook a valuable review of a previously neglected area, it did not consider the impact of materials depicting violent or coercive portrayals of sexual relationships. Pornography today is much more explicit than in 1970 and includes more portrayals of coercive sexuality.

In the male fantasy world of pornography, the woman is presented as a sexual object—an anonymous, panting plaything. While she initially may object to the advances of the male, she soon invites the powerful, masterful man to use her sexually and appears to enjoy even the most gruesome torture. Pornography depicts forms of sexuality and aggression in which men derive pleasure at the expense of women, who are degraded and humiliated in the process.

There are many documented cases in which men have forced or coerced women to try assorted sexual techniques or activities that the men saw in pornographic films and magazines. Since women have been taught to be submissive and comply with male sexual demands, they may try to meet these sexual "needs" for fear of rejection. Otherwise he will feel justified in looking elsewhere for sex, and she may feel it is her fault because she did not meet his needs. Women often take the brunt of this porno-inspired experimentation, and perfectly sensitive women are then accused of being frigid when they, unlike the women in pornography, do not enjoy the roughness.

A research study completed in 1982 at Indiana University was designed to explore the consequences of continued exposure to pornography on beliefs about sexuality in general and dispositions toward women in particular. They found that those people who were frequently exposed to pornography perceived the popularity of unusual sexual practices in real life to be more common than did those *not* exposed, even though unusual sexual practices were not included in the films. The subjects exposed to pornography also greatly overestimated the numbers of people who are sexually active. Most disturbing, the research showed that both men and women in the former group later trivialized rape and were less compassionate toward rape victims. However, the women in each group still saw rape as more serious and acted more punitively toward rapists than the men in their group. The researchers found it interesting that people exposed to common sexual acts in erotic films would then come to view uncommon acts as occurring more frequently and rape as less serious. As this occurs, what impact does frequent exposure to sadomasochistic pornography have on people?

Another study conducted in 1981 in Canada by Malamuth found that exposure to rape movies resulted in more violent sexual fantasies. They questioned the potential role of such media in the development of antisocial attitudes and behavior.

Pornography is no longer limited to books, movies, and live sex acts on stage. Pornographic cartoons such as *The Rape of Sleeping Beauty* are now available on videotape for rental. Even cartoons on television show women to be pieces of property. In "Popeye," Popeye and Brutus constantly fight over Olive Oyl. In the process she is beaten over the head and dragged around screaming and protesting. She survives only by manipulating and pleading, a poor example for our sons and daughters. Now that we have moved into the computer age, so has pornography. Pornographic computer games are now available. One depicts a cowboy raping an American Indian woman tied to a post. When he rapes her, he "scores." Another depicts gang rapes and assaults. The longer the rape and assaults continue, the higher the "score." Once again, the victims smile while being assaulted.

As a society we cannot afford to treat rape and the degradation of women as a game. Like rape, pornography is antifemale, defamatory, and libelous to women who are depicted as compliant objects. Pornography is not an expression of sexual freedom; it is a powerful force undermining true sexual expression. Even nonviolent pornography, erotica, appears to promote sexual callousness toward women, a growing dissatisfaction with sexual reality, and the trivialization of rape. We cannot continue to legitimize a form of "entertainment" with such antisocial consequences.

MOTIVES FOR RAPE

Motives for rape are indeed complex, often overlapping, and difficult, at best, to understand. As a first step in preventing rape, we must try to determine not only who rapists are, so we can avoid them and lock them behind bars, but also why they rape. Rape is used as a form of social control by some men; it is a way men meet the social expectations of being "a man"; it is a form of revenge; and it is seen as a man's right.

Gang Rape

Studies indicate that a group situation can promote sex offenses in those who would not initiate this type of crime on their own. While these men are as likely to have criminal records as individuals who rape, it is unlikely that they will have a record of past sex offenses. Gang rape is thus not rape by a number of rapists but rather by a group that rapes. Psychologically, the man who rapes with a group of other men is reported to be more "normal" than the lone offender.

Neither sex nor injury is the motive or reward in gang rape. The group uses sex to demonstrate its power and to validate its strength through group conquest. It is a way for the group to interact, compete, develop camaraderie and cohesiveness. Group membership is strengthened by those participating. To refuse to join in would mean exclusion and the loss of esteem and peer recognition within the group. The rape may also be an expression of group hostility, frustration, or an attempt to compensate for feelings of inadequacy. Some fraternities and gangs actually consider rape a game, in which one member is charged with finding a woman and setting her up for the group.

Police reports indicate that approximately 10 to 20 percent of rapes involve more than one assailant. While there are usually two men involved in a group rape, it ranges from two to ten. Gang rape is most likely to occur on Friday or Saturday night. While the victim may be a stranger picked up off the street, more often she will have known or been acquainted with one member of the group, having met him that night at a party or a bar. The victim of gang rape is also more likely to have been drinking prior to the assault, making her more vulnerable. Gangs looking for a woman to rape generally look for a woman who appears to be more vulnerable. Similar to the lone assailant, men who rape in groups use alcohol or drugs about one-half of the time. Some violence, hitting, or kicking is likely to occur, resulting in minor injuries to the victim. Serious physical injury is uncommon.

Rape as a Form of Revenge

The man who rapes for revenge is motivated by anger. He feels as though he has been wronged, unjustly humiliated or degraded, and he intends to "get even." Sex is only the weapon; the goal is revenge. Rape may be the worst thing he feels he can do. Because of his distrust and disregard for the law and social structure he gets his revenge outside of the law rather than through the court system. He already may have a criminal record, and it is likely he has had it from the time he was a juvenile.

His anger and desire for revenge may be directed at a specific individual he feels wronged him, or it may be more generalized to an entire race. When the anger and desire for revenge is specific, the choice of victim becomes important. He may rape a woman because she terminated a relationship with him. Another man may choose to rape the woman's daughter, thinking this will hurt her more, "show her who's boss," and "end on my terms, not hers." In these cases, rape is the rapist's attempt to affirm his own worth by degrading another person, to make himself feel better by making the person who threatened his ego feel even worse, more powerless than himself. Men also rape women in order to get revenge at a man they feel has wronged them. The easiest target is "his" woman. Raping her is a way to get back at him by violating and damaging "his property."

In other instances, the identity of the victim is not important, though specific attributes, such as age, may make a woman a more likely candidate. The assailant may be angry at his wife or mother and feel unable to get back at her. During or after the assault he sometimes will tell the victim about the fight he had with this other woman. Some of these men have been victims of abuse themselves, physical, sexual, or both. They may be reenacting their own traumatic background. Men who are victims of abuse as children are more likely to become victimizers, while women who are victims as children are more likely to later become involved in abusive relationships in which they continue to be victimized. The most salient explanation revolves around culturally learned sex-role-appropriate behavior: young boys are taught (and later as men, continue) to strike back when hit or when angry; women are taught to be submissive and to turn the other cheek. Thus, issues are not resolved but rather perpetuate a cycle of violence that may continue through many generations of new victims and victimizers.

Unfortunately, racism and racial conflict have been part of American life since the country was founded. When minority group members rape white women, they may be striking back at the white man by asserting the little power they are allowed to have. Although their anger is directed at the dominant and controlling white race and primarily at the dominant white man, white women—"the white man's property"—are more accessible, vulnerable targets. Rapes may occur when members of minority populations are frustrated by a lack of control and are angered by an unjust society. Skin color thus becomes an important factor in the choice of the victim.

Contrary to popular belief, the greatest number of rapes occur between people of the same race. This is especially true with underreported acquaintance rapes. Interracial rapes usually involve strangers. The white woman is overrepresented in the population of reporting survivors of rape in relation to the general population figures, and the minority male is overrepresented in the category of reported offenders. Of course, many controversial factors and biases in reporting are involved, making it difficult to predict a pattern if all rapes were reported and recorded.

Marital Rape

If women are seen as the property of man—father or husband—then a man cannot be accused of taking what is already his. According to some, forced sex within marriage is thus not rape, but the right of the man.

"Damn it," Senator Jeremiah Denton, a Republican from Alabama, told the Senate Judiciary Committee, "when you get married, you kind of expect you're going to get a little sex, one way or the other." Using this line of reasoning, many states still have the marital exception as a part of their rape laws. A wife who is raped by her husband in one of these states has no legal recourse. Fortunately, these laws are slowly changing.

The Antisocial Rapist

Some men have routinely been able to get away with taking whatever they want. This type of person is self-centered and does not consider or care what other people do or do not want. He usually does not know his victim and tends to see her as an object, not a person. Some even depersonalize her so much that they are unable to describe her after the rape and would not recognize her in the future. He takes a woman much as he would take a car or radio. In many cases the rape is actually secondary to a robbery. The woman was there, so he raped her. He has poor impulse control and seeks immediate gratification. He may be frustrated by the demands of life, which he cannot face, and rely on sex as a means of overcoming distress by demonstrating mastery, conquest, dominance, and control.

He may equate sex with personal worth. He may ask his victim to evaluate his sexual performance, to affirm how "good" he is, and to tell him how much she enjoyed it. He may try to make her have an orgasm to better prove his prowess. He does not see himself as a rapist, let alone a criminal. He may even want to see her again. More than one rapist has been caught and imprisoned after calling back a survivor and asking to meet her again.

While the acquaintance rapist may be the most prevalent in the population at large, many studies have found that the rapist most likely to be reported and thus recognized within the legal system is the antisocial rapist who has complete disregard for the cultural and legal system within which most of us function. He may be a member of a subculture, and may or may not adhere to their norms and expectations. These men are likely to have long-term social adjustment problems, with few, if any, close friends. Their vocational and work history is often irregular, with sporadic employment in low-level jobs. Often they trust no one, exhibit poor judgment, and engage in self-defeating behavior.

MEN WHO ARE RAPED

It is impossible to estimate how many men are raped each year. While only one in ten women report rape, it is likely that many fewer men report being raped, not wanting to admit to the humiliation and degradation and not wanting to have their masculinity and sexuality questioned. The problem has been ignored for decades.

While men who are raped usually are raped by other men, some are also raped by women. Both are traumatic experiences.

Men Raped by Other Men

Many assume that only male children become rape victims or that male rape only occurs in prisons or among homosexuals. While male victims are often younger, the age range is as wide as that of female victims, a few months of age to over ninety. The primary difference seems to be in the number of assailants and the amount of force used in the cases reported.

It is likely for male rape victims to have been attacked by groups of men and to sustain more physical trauma than female victims. Those who come to the attention of the authorities may be a highly select group, however, since the physical trauma may be what precipitates their coming to a hospital. In a large number of cases, these men first came to the emergency room to get treatment for the nongenital trauma and did not report the sexual assault, which was discovered later.

Male rape is more common in settings where women are absent, such as male prisons. As with female rape, men are raped in an attempt to punish or control. Men in prisons have their own values and standards. For instance, inmates who have molested children are usually detested by other prisoners and may be raped as an "inside" form of punishment.

Male survivors face many of the same problems that female survivors face. Like the female survivor, the male survivor is often not believed or is accused of being a homosexual who was asking for it. An article published in the *Southern Medical Journal* in 1980 advised the physician examining a male rape survivor to "maintain a high level of suspicion, since in some cases the 'victim' may have an ulterior motive in reporting an alleged attack. Even if the survivor is a child, the story may be fabricated in a bid for attention."

The most difficult problem the male survivor faces is having his masculinity and sexual preferences questioned by other men. Most men protect their feelings of invulnerability by believing the male survivor wanted it, or "is not really a man anyway."

Men Raped by Women

Although it is highly unusual, women can and do rape men. The belief that it is impossible for a man to respond sexually when he does not choose to is incorrect. More recently, research has indicated that male sexual response can occur in a variety of emotional states, including anger and terror.

In reported and corroborated cases, men have been forced by a single woman or a group of women to participate in sexual activity, including intercourse under threat of physical violence. The men report being restrained physically, fearing not only for their safety but also for their lives. Despite their fear, anxiety, embarrassment, and terror, they report having had erections even though they felt no sexual desire. In some cases they repeatedly were stimulated manually by their female captors and even ejaculated a number of times.

These men, much like men and women raped by other men, experience significant emotional trauma, often for years following the rape. As they are more likely to try to hide the assault due to embarrassment, the problems are often aggravated. The most immediate impact is the disgrace and humiliation that makes the survivor feel that he is less of a man.

While these men usually come to the attention of therapists when seeking help for sexual dysfunction, the men initially may not have associated the dysfunction with the rape, especially since years have probably passed. Once in treatment, they may be involved with a therapist for years before divulging the assault.

Another major problem for men who responded sexually during an assault is that they later feel abnormal—any "normal" man would have been impotent. This adds to their feelings of inadequacy and may result in greater sexual-performance fears. These anxieties coupled with their sexual dysfunction may result in the fear that they are becoming homosexual. Other postrape trauma includes extreme depression, fear, and anxiety, as well as the initial shock, disbelief, and disorganization. These symptoms are similar to those seen in women.

While men are typically the aggressors, sometimes they too become the victims of assaults. If more men were aware that the possibility exists and that they are not invulnerable, perhaps they would be more understanding of the fear with which many women live their lives.

10

PREVENTING RAPE

*Experience has shown me that I am not
going to solve anything in one stroke, at
best I am only going to chip away at it.*

—Hugh Prather

Preventing rape means first knowing what this crime does not need to be. It is not an inherent factor of our existence with which we must learn to cope. Rape is not only an individual problem that each woman must work to solve, it is also a family problem, a social problem, and a national problem we all must work actively to resolve. Before we begin to prevent rape, we must first understand how we got to a point in our society where so many women are raped each year. We must understand what the threat of rape means, what its effects are, and what it reflects in our own and other cultures. We must understand how we differ from rape-free societies.

We must then determine our prevention strategies based on our understanding of the dynamics involved. There are measures you can take to make yourself less vulnerable to rape. There are also strategies your community, and our society, can employ to alter situations that facilitate, condone, or simply overlook rape. While you may choose, as an individual, to utilize avoidance or risk-reducing strategies to lower your vulnerability, in the long run, as a community, we must work toward removing the threat altogether. We must address and change those sociocultural factors that predispose us to be a rape-prone society.

Societies in which rape is absent or virtually unknown do exist. In 1982, Peggy Reeves Sandry, an anthropologist at the University of Pennsylvania, completed a review of data available on ninety-five tribal societies and found that half were rape free. The existence of these rape-free societies demonstrates that rape is not a biological force but a sociocultural force. It is the result of specific sociocultural factors, attitudes, and motivations of individuals within these societies. Among the factors that distinguish these societies are the status of women, attitudes about violence, and the parent-child relationship.

Women who live in rape-free cultures are respected, influential members of the community. They contribute equally with men to the well-being of the group and they have equal status with men. In most cases, no division of labor based on sex occurs. Women are economically independent and experience no limits on their mobility or the places they are permitted.

Dominance of others is not valued in rape-free societies, nor do these societies strive to dominate nature. Instead they take what they need from nature for food and shelter in the least violent, least aggressive manner possible. Their goal is to live harmoniously with each other and with their environment.

While there are certainly exceptions, for the most part the woman in a rape-prone society is mainly responsible for the nurturance of the children, and the husband is the head of the household. He provides for the family, protects them, and controls them. He is sometimes cold, distant, aloof, and stern. His main role in child care is to punish. In many American families, misbehaving children are told by their mothers, "You just wait till Daddy gets home." Many boys who grow up in rape-prone societies are taught to be tough and aggressive, not "sissies." Competition, often violent, is a way for them to demonstrate their superiority and dominance, the primary measure of their value and esteem. Rape serves as an illustration of this superiority.

PROTECTING YOURSELF

Some women remain safe by not going out of the house alone, especially at night; not going out without men to "protect" them; not making eye contact with passersby; never talking to strangers; only inviting men they know well to their homes; not living alone; and only wearing clothes that could not be considered "provocative."

These are passive instead of active measures. They limit your life and your activities. They may isolate you, limiting your access to people and activities that could benefit you in your social life or in your job. This passive resistance places the responsibility and burden for preventing rape solely on women.

In a 1982 report on dealing with urban crime, Riger indicated that this kind of avoidance behavior most often is used by people who see themselves as physically weak, helpless, and vulnerable. They are usually women or the elderly. They are also more likely to be poor, black, unemployed, and living in the inner city.

On the other hand, there are strategies that allow you to manage risk in the face of danger. You can learn to manipulate your environment instead of limit your life.

When you go out of the house alone, carry something that could be used as a weapon, such as keys, which can be held between your fingers. You can carry key rings that hold Mace containers or whistles that will attract attention. Since a knife or a gun can be taken away and used against you, carrying these weapons is not a good idea. Your local police department can tell you what weapons are legal to carry in your area.

It is helpful to look confident and as if you know where you are going whether or not you do when you walk down a street alone. Criminals often choose their victims by the way they carry themselves, not by their size, weight, or sex.

When driving alone, you should keep the doors locked, especially the passenger door. Have your keys ready when you approach your car, even in the daytime, and be aware of strangers near your car or people who may be following you. Keep your car locked when shopping and don't accept rides from strangers or give rides to strangers. Even the most innocent-appearing stranger may be dangerous.

> Sarah, sixteen years old, had stopped at a large chain store to shop on her way home from her girlfriend's. When she came back to her car, an old woman was sitting in it. She told Sarah she was tired. "I need a ride to my daughter's. Won't you please help me?" Sarah felt uncomfortable, but the woman was insistent. Her mother had specifically told her never to give a stranger a ride. Was this an exception? She told the woman she had to make a quick phone call first. Sarah called her mother, who told her to call the police so that they could give the woman a ride.
> When the police came they had difficulty extracting the old woman from Sarah's car. When they did, a knife fell out from under her skirt, and the "woman" turned out to be a man.

If you have to wait at a bus stop at night, you may want to wear shoes that are easy to run in. Always be alert. Know what is going on around you, and don't be afraid to run away before danger becomes acute.

Particularly if you want to live alone, your local police department will be able to tell you what parts of town have the lowest crime rates. You may decide not to live in a ground-floor apartment, especially with sliding glass doors, or if you do have sliding glass doors, you may want to use a bar to lock them. You should keep your ground-floor doors and windows locked at night with secure dead-bolt locks. You may even want to install a security system. Many good systems are now available, and with self-installation the price is reasonable. You may also decide to get a dog. It's also important to get to know your neighbors. You and your neighbors are much more aware than the police are of who is in your area and who does not belong. Call the police and then your neighbors if you see someone who looks suspicious, and ask them to do the same for you.

Even if you live alone, you need not identify yourself as a single woman. Instead of putting your full name on your mailbox, put only your first initial. Do the same in the telephone book. If you live in a secure building, never buzz someone in if you don't know who they are, and don't let a stranger walk in the locked door with you. More than one rapist has gained repeated access to locked buildings by using these two techniques. Insist that the entrance to the building and the parking area be well lit if it is not.

If someone comes to the door and wants to make a phone call, you can offer to make it. While there are certainly legitimate reasons for people to enter your home, you are the one who must decide whom to let inside. It is your right and responsibility to say no to people. If you did not call a repairman, don't let one inside. Before allowing him entrance, insist on talking with whoever called him. Even if a man is in a uniform, ask to see a picture ID before unlocking the chain lock.

> A fireman appeared in uniform at Suzanne's home and wanted to inspect her apartment. Even though he was insistent, she felt uncomfortable and would not let him inside. As soon as he left she called the police. They caught him as he was leaving the building. Three women in the area had been raped recently by a man posing as a fire marshal in order to gain entrance. All three made a positive identification.

Instead of being afraid to take a job where you need to work nights, come and go from the parking lot with a co-worker. Most businesses have escort services, although many women are hesitant to use them. If you don't like the idea of having to wait for a man to walk with you, ask a female co-worker to accompany you to your car, then drive her to hers. Don't drive off until she is safely inside with her car's motor running (cars don't always start).

If your car should stall on the road, you need not accept a ride from a stranger. If you feel uncomfortable, stay in your car with the doors locked, and ask the stranger to call the police. If you are on a major highway, the police will be along eventually. If you see someone stalled, instead of stopping, call the police and report the incident to them.

You may decide to take a self-defense course. Such courses are especially helpful in promoting the attitude that you are capable of taking care of yourself. They teach you that there are many ways to get out of situations safely before they become dangerous or threatening to you. Many women report that after taking self-defense courses, they feel stronger, braver, more in control, more cautious, and more confident. They have learned to assess the situation, and take control when attacked, without being too timid to make a move, if necessary. They have learned to get angry instead of freezing with fear. Your fear is an attacker's most powerful weapon.

Dealing with sexual harassment is another important part of prevention. Managing these situations before they escalate may prevent problems in the future. You must learn to distinguish between friendly behavior and behavior that is overly friendly. Go by your instincts. If it makes you uncomfortable, it is not okay. Even comments that appear to be compliments on the outside are harassment when too familiar. Tell the person, "It makes me uncomfortable when you say that. Please don't." Don't be intimidated. If you are uncomfortable, it is not a compliment. Not allowing behavior that makes you uncomfortable to continue is one way of maintaining control. Let people know your boundaries. If you do not really want to have coffee or go out with a man, tell him, "Thank you, but I'm not interested." If his response is "What's wrong? Don't you trust me?" A red flag should go up. You probably should not trust him. Don't be afraid to say no, or "That's not the point. I'm just not interested." Then don't feel guilty if he is hurt or upset that you would not do what he wanted you to do. What you want and your needs are equally important to his wants and needs.

If you don't like the way someone touches you or puts his arm around you, ask him politely not to do so. It is not rude to maintain your privacy. Learn to deal with sexual harassment yourself. If it is difficult, practice the things you want to say ahead of time alone in front of a mirror or with a friend. Don't smile when you ask someone not to touch you, or when you say no. It will make you look weak and may give a double message.

Instead of being afraid to talk to all strangers, choose the people you want to talk to and ignore the rest. Don't feel as though you have to say hi or talk with everyone who starts to talk to you.

It is extremely important to remember that every rape is different. Even if you were raped in a situation that sounds very similar to one in which someone else escaped being raped, it does not mean that you did anything wrong that caused your rape, or that you could have done anything differently to prevent it. Only you can judge what is possible and wise to risk in a particular situation at a particular time. The most important thing is living through the rape.

It is also important to remember that for the most part our information about resisters is quite biased. While many women successfully free themselves from a man intending on rape, most of these women do not make a police report. Many do call rape crisis centers or see counselors later as a result of the fear, anxiety, and anger they too experience. However, the numbers are still significantly lower than the actual number of attempted assaults. Most survivors of attempted rapes continue life as usual, feeling relief at their escape though aware of a newly gained sense of vulnerability. Some wonder later on, "Did he really plan to rape me? Maybe I overreacted and only imagined he was after me."

The resisters who do report are more likely those who were physically hurt while resisting. As a result, a common misbelief is that rape resisters are likely to get hurt. While women who decide to resist and fight off an intended rapist are sometimes badly hurt or even killed, many more are not hurt and successfully escape. We seldom hear from this latter group. In addition, women are often hurt who make no attempt to resist. Of the survivors interviewed in a 1984 Minneapolis study, approximately 25 percent of the women harmed did not resist in any way, and over 20 percent of those who resisted were not harmed.

In order to determine the situations in which resistance is most successful, researchers have compared information provided by survivors who escaped rape and survivors who were raped. However, this is not intended to provide general advice on how, when, or whom to resist. No one can tell if you will escape successfully, be seriously hurt, or be killed. You can only trust your senses.

A study completed in Chicago in 1981 found women who successfully resisted rapists were usually attacked by a stranger. They were more likely to be attacked outside, where both they and the rapist could flee more easily. Attacks that occur outside are also more likely to be interrupted by a passerby who may accidentally come upon the assault or hear screams or struggling. A young boy in St. Louis recently received national attention when he called the police, who then stopped two other boys who were raping a young girl in a city park. Shortly after that incident a group of women came to the rescue of another woman who had been stripped by a man intent on rape, during an early afternoon on a busy sidewalk of another large midwestern city.

Resisters were more likely to try a number of different strategies to get free. These women were also more likely to use active forms of resistance such as biting, kicking, hitting, struggling, and screaming. A 1977 Denver study found resisters were more likely to be younger, and victims older. Physical forms of resistance are more acceptable for children and teens than for older women. They have not yet learned to be passive and to submit to men and, as a result, they are more likely to kick, fight, and run away. The likelihood of physical resistance diminishes significantly among girls sixteen and older and is even less likely among those nearing twenty. Black women, however, were found in the Denver study to physically resist attackers at a somewhat older age than white women.

A study conducted in Israel in 1977 by Sebba and Cahan asked a group of convicted rapists what their victims could have done to make them stop the rape. The overwhelming response was to make them see her as a real person with real feelings and understand that what they were doing was going to ruin her life. These rapists reported that it was important for them to maintain an emotional distance from their victim, and to see her as a nameless, faceless object. They did not relate to her suffering. Over 50 percent denied harming the victim emotionally or physically and expressed no regret for the rape. They reported feeling emotions for their victims only in the cases they did not carry through. When they could not depersonalize the victim as insignificant, when she told them her problems or somehow aroused personal feelings in the assailants, they did not rape.

Talk alone won't necessarily prevent rape. The Chicago study also found that women who were raped were more likely to use fewer, and more passive, forms of resistance, such as pleading or talking their way out. They more likely knew the assailants and were attacked in their homes with fewer avenues of escape for themselves or the rapists. In some cases they were awakened from their sleep and were confused or disoriented. They were usually threatened with force and were afraid of being killed. Their initial response when attacked was fear rather than anger, and their primary concern was in staying alive and living through the experience without being mutilated.

The timing of the resistance appears to be an important factor in its success. So is maintaining control. It is always preferable to escape before the situation becomes physical. There is usually an ambiguous period during which you're really not sure what he wants and he is not really sure what his next move will be, either. This is your chance to take control. Don't wait until you "know" he plans to hurt you. Why give him the benefit of the doubt? If you feel uncomfortable, it is time to take action. Many women let this initial chance for escape pass by because they are afraid of looking silly or appearing rude when no real harm was meant. The alternative is too serious to worry about either of these. It is better to make a scene than to be raped. If you even think you hear someone following you, don't be afraid to run away, or turn and face the person if escape does not seem possible. One woman who had just taken her first self-defense lesson found herself in such a situation.

Carla started taking the self-defense course because she had been raped a year before in her home. One night while walking home from the bus, she heard footsteps behind her and was afraid someone was following her. "I crossed the street. He did too. He was getting closer. It was almost midnight, and the street was deserted. There was nowhere to run. My heart was pounding, and my knees weak from the fear. "No," I said to myself, "I will not let it happen again! No man is going to rape me again!" My fear turned to anger. I stopped, turned around, quickly yelled as I did so, and assumed a karate stance. Fortunately he turned and ran away, because that was as far as my first class had gone."

Carla had caught him off guard and thwarted a potential rape. Rapists, like other criminals, usually have one scenario that they repeat. This man's was probably to grab the woman from behind. He was afraid to attack a woman face-to-face, especially one who looked so strong and sure of herself. Although Carla's fear soon returned, she had been powerful and in control when necessary.

While on her first date with Andy, Lucy began to get uncomfortable as he drove back from the restaurant and became insistent that she accompany him to his apartment. The more angry and insistent he became, the more frightened she became. He locked the doors so she could not get out of the car. She pretended to change her attitude and affectionately moved over beside him as he stopped at a light. As she did so, she put her foot down hard on the accelerator and rammed into the car stopped in front of them. As the driver of the car they had hit came back to talk with her date, she unlocked her door and got out.

If a stranger enters your home uninvited, order him out—loudly. You'd be surprised how many leave. To maintain control of the situation, you need to react with authority and sound forceful and commanding—angry instead of afraid. You need to look self-assured and confident on the outside no matter how anxious you are. He is counting on your being afraid and doing what he wants.

Remember, only you can decide if attempts at resisting are appropriate. The most important thing is to stay in control and be alert for the right moment to resist, if it should come along. Your success will depend on the situation and the assailant, as well as on you. Not everyone has the opportunity to get away.

COMMUNITY PREVENTIVE STRATEGIES

Rape is a crime against the community, not just the individual. The community has both an opportunity and a responsibility to play an active role in effecting change through political, legal, and neighborhood organizations.

Politicization of Women

Individual women in positions of power and influence and groups of women must become more politically astute and active, demanding change. These concerned individuals need to develop public pressure groups with task forces, and initiate legislative lobbying efforts. They must demand accountability from public and private boards, businesses and organizations, and become familiar with the voting record of elected officials on women's-rights issues.

Uncooperative agencies and businesses, such as those selling rape video games, should be picketed, and press releases should be made, clearly stating the objections to those businesses. Political pressure was exerted by Women Against Pornography in New York City in outrage over the video game *Custer's Revenge*, in which the cowboy rapes the Indian maiden to "score." The end result, far from adequate, is that the video is still on the market, but the woman now smiles when raped and is not bound. Not giving up, activists are currently in the process of putting pressure on legislatures to pass ordinances banning the distribution of the game. Oklahoma City has done this.

Due to persistent efforts on the part of professional and citizen groups including both men and women, Congress mandated in 1976 the National Center for the Prevention and Control of Rape. Money was specifically allocated through NCPCR for funding rape crisis centers across the country and for rape research. This center has ever since performed a valuable function as a resource to assist individuals, institutions, and communities to understand, prevent, and control rape.

The legislature, as a result of political pressure and the entrance of more women into the legal profession, has also made changes in the laws relating to rape. As discussed earlier, these laws now make it easier to prosecute. The changes in these laws have not been sufficient. Laws alone won't stop rape. The laws are only as good as the people who enforce them.

Myths, biases, and stereotypes about rape held by individuals within the criminal-justice system and within the pool of prospective jurors limit the enforcement of these laws and the prosecution of rapists.

When the government decided it was time to stop litter, an active campaign was launched across the country and littering was essentially stopped in many areas. When a West Coast city elected a woman mayor who took an interest in stopping rape, there was significantly less rape. Perhaps when more women are sitting in the House and Senate, preventing rape will become as important as curtailing litter.

Neighborhood Activism

Neighborhood organizations can play an effective role in lowering the incidence of rape by establishing neighborhood watches. This program, introduced by the police in many areas, is an effective way people can watch out for each other by reporting any suspicious activities to the police. Participation in neighborhood organizations is also important. It is a good way to get to know the people in your community and enlist their help in dealing with the threat of rape. As a group, you may be able to remove signs of neighborhood decay and again improve the general feelings of safety.

Communities have held meetings in churches or schools to ensure that everyone is aware of a rapist working the area, so everyone can take extra precautions. Fliers may go out publicizing the assaults and speakers may be brought in to talk about preventive strategies. Some communities have begun "lights on campaigns" at night, keeping porch and yard lights on, and calling the police when suspicious-looking individuals are seen.

Safety-awareness programs should be targeted at the teenagers and women under thirty, who make up the large majority of rape survivors. Reporting should be encouraged to help catch rapists and spare other women from victimization. Education to dispel myths and stereotypes should be directed at people within the legal-justice system—police, attorneys, judges, clerks—who interact with survivors and who make decisions about which cases are prosecuted. Most important, this education must include the general population, the pool of potential jurors for cases that make it to court.

SOCIOCULTURAL PREVENTIVE STRATEGIES

In order to effectively stop rape, rather than deflect the rapist to another individual or another community, rape prevention must occur within the sociocultural context and include the assurance of equality for women, the nontolerance of interpersonal violence, and a change in our child-rearing practices.

Assurance of Equality for Women

Men and women do not need to share the same bathroom to be equal, though that was one of the scare tactics used to defeat the Equal Rights Amendment. Women and men can remain different though equal. But equality for women will only be achieved when sexual oppression is removed from our laws, our institutions, our family structure, and our psyches. Equal status means that the separation of jobs and decision making must occur on the basis of ability not sex. It means that sex-role stereotyping must be eliminated from the attitudes and perceptions of the expected and appropriate behavior of both men and women. It means that sex biases must be eliminated from hiring practices, from organizational boards of directors, from businesses, and from religious institutions.

Equal rights also means assuming equal responsibility and contributing equally to the social welfare. It means no longer devaluing women's work, as has been done for generations by both men and women. When the first woman climbed Mount Everest, a prominent male guest on a television talk show commented, "If a woman can do it, it must not be that hard." Women's work is devalued openly in the amount of money we are willing to pay her in comparison to a man.

Sex-role stereotypes and the women's dependence on men is a burden and limits men as well as women. Neither reaches full potential with so many expectations and limitations based solely on gender. Women must let go of the false security that dependence provides, and affirm their own worth independent of a man. Dependence on someone else only relieves fear and conflict for a brief period. It does not resolve it. Only self-reliance will do that. While men may act benevolently toward a woman who submits willingly to their control, some may quickly justify violence when the woman is not grateful. You cannot be "protected" and independent at the same time. As long as someone else is responsible for you, you are not in control.

It is possible to be feminine and still be independently successful, aggressive, and an equal to men. Yet many women who achieve career success and equality in the business world are insecure in their femininity in social relationships. It is also possible for men to be masculine and nurturing at the same time.

Instead of trying to stop rape through men's solutions, by restricting women's activities and thus further victimizing them, women must become more actively involved with the problem of rape and in deciding appropriate solutions. As Golda Meir proclaimed when the Israeli government suggested putting a curfew on women to "protect" them from rape: "Put a curfew on men."

Each of us must be a party to the resolution of this problem. Rape is an affront to the civilized standards of all members of humanity. It is a sociocultural problem of grave magnitude. It is not something that is going to be resolved overnight. To stop rape a sociocultural change must occur. The result must be a new social order, a new way of life—more fulfilling and rewarding—with a new freedom for all involved. In the process of bringing about this change, we must not establish a new adversary system pitting women against men. Both men and women must work together to stop rape. Women must assume their place as equals to men—strong, independent, self-reliant, and in control of their lives and bodies.

RAPE CRISIS CENTERS
IN THE UNITED STATES

In all the listings below, the first telephone number is a twenty-four-hour hotline, unless otherwise indicated.
* indicates not a twenty-four-hour hotline.

ALABAMA

BIRMINGHAM

Rape Response Program
3600 Eighth Ave. South
Birmingham, AL 35222
(205) 323-7273

DOTHAN

Wiregrass Comprehensive Mental
Health Center
104 Prevatt Rd., P.O. Drawer 1245
Dothan, AL 36302
(205) 794-0300; (205) 794-0731

MONTGOMERY

Council Against Rape—
Lighthouse
830 S. Court St.
Montgomery, AL 36104
(205) 264-7273; (205) 263-4481
(office)

ALASKA

ANCHORAGE

Standing Together Against Rape
111 E. Thirteenth St.
Anchorage, AK 99510
(907) 276-7273; (907) 276-7279
(weeknights, weekends)

FAIRBANKS

Women in Crisis—Counseling
and Assistance, Inc.
702 Tenth Ave.
Fairbanks, AK 99701
(907) 452-7273; (907) 452-2293
(office)

KENAI

Rape Intervention Program
Women's Resource Center
325 Spruce St.

Kenai, AK 99611
(907) 283-9479

NOME

Bering Sea Women's Group
P.O. Box 1596
Nome, AK 99762
(907) 443-5444

ARIZONA

PHOENIX

Center Against Sexual Assault
(CASA)
5555 N. Seventh Ave.
Phoenix, AZ 85013
(602) 257-8095

TUCSON

Tucson Rape Crisis Center, Inc.
P.O. Box 40306
Tucson, AZ 85719
(602) 623-7273; (602) 624-7273
(office)

ARKANSAS

FORT SMITH

Rape Crisis Service
P.O. Box 2887, Station A
3111 S. Seventieth St.
Fort Smith, AR 72913
(501) 452-6650

LITTLE ROCK

Rape Crisis, Inc.
P.O. Box 5181, Hillcrest Station
Little Rock, AR 72225
(501) 375-5181

CALIFORNIA

BAKERSFIELD

Rape Hotline Kern County
Kern Medical Center
Bakersfield, CA 93305
(805) 324-7273

BERKELEY

Bay Area Women Against Rape
1515 Webster
Oakland, CA 94612
(415) 845-7273; (415) 465-3890
(office)

CHICO

Rape Crisis Intervention
of North Central California
P.O. Box 423
Chico, CA 95927
(916) 342-7273

CLAREMONT

Project Sister Rape Crisis Service
520 N. Indian Hill Blvd.
Claremont, CA 91711
(714) 626-4357

CONCORD

Rape Crisis Service of Concord
1760 Clayton Rd.
Concord, CA 94523
(415) 798-7273

DAVIS

Yolo County Sexual Assault
Center
222 D St.
Davis, CA 95616
(916) 758-8400; (916) 662-1133
(Woodland Hotline);
(916) 371-1907 (E. Yolo Hotline);
(916) 758-0540 (office)

FAIRFIELD

Upper Solano County Rape Crisis
Service
P.O. Box 368
Fairfield, CA 94533
(707) 422-7273

FORT BRAGG

Community Assistance in Assault
and Rape Emergency (CAARE
Project, Inc.)
461 N. Franklin St.
Fort Bragg, CA 95437
(707) 964-4357

FRESNO

Rape Counseling Service of
Fresno, Inc.
3006 N. Fresno St.
Fresno, CA 93703
(209) 222-7273; (209) 227-1800
(office)

LAGUNA BEACH

Rape Crisis Unit
Laguna Beach Free Clinic
460 Ocean Ave.
Laguna Beach, CA 92651
(714) 494-0761 * (Mon.–Fri. 10:00
A.M.–10:00 P.M.)

LAKEWOOD

SuCasa
12305 E. 207th St.
Lakewood, CA 90715
(213) 868-3783

LOMPOC

Lompoc Rape Crisis Center
P.O. Box 148
Lompoc, CA 93438
(805) 736–8913; (805) 736-7273;
(805) 928-5818

LONG BEACH

Long Beach Rape Hotline
P.O. Box 14377
Long Beach, CA 90803
(213) 597-2002

LOS ANGELES

East Los Angeles Rape Hotline,
Inc.
P.O. Box 63245
Los Angeles, CA 90063
(213) 262-0944 (bilingual);
(213) 267-0771 (office)

Los Angeles Rape and Battering
Hotline
Los Angeles Commission on
Assaults
Against Women (LACAAW)
P.O. Box 48903-Z
Los Angeles, CA 90048
(213) 392-8381; (213) 655-4235
(office)

Rape Response Service
Thalians Community Mental
Health Center
Cedar-Sinai Medical Center
8730 Alden Dr.
Los Angeles, CA 90048
(213) 855-3506; (213) 855-3530
(office)

MERCED

People Against Rape
P.O. Box 2068
Merced, CA 95344
(209) 383-2818

MONTEREY

Rape Crisis Center of the
Monterey Peninsula
P.O. Box 862

Monterey, CA 93940
(408) 375-4357

ORANGE

Orange County Rape Crisis
Hotline
1107 E. Chapman
Orange, CA 92666
(714) 831-9110

PALO ALTO

Mid-Peninsula Rape Crisis Center
4161 Alma St.
Palo Alto, CA 94306
(415) 493-7273; (415) 494-0972
(office)

PASADENA

Rape Hotline Exchange
Pasadena–Foothill Valley YWCA
78 N. Marengo Ave.
Pasadena, CA 91101
(818) 793-3385

PLACENTIA

Alpha Center
117 N. Main St.
Placentia, CA 92670
(714) 993-4400; (714) 993-4403

RIVERSIDE

Riverside Area Rape Crisis Center
2060 University, Suite 101
Riverside, CA 92507
(714) 686-7273

SACRAMENTO

Sacramento Rape Crisis Center
2224 J St.
Sacramento, CA 95816
(916) 447-7273; (916) 447-3223
(office)

SAN BERNARDINO

San Bernardino Rape Crisis
Intervention Services
1875 N. D St.
San Bernardino, CA 92405
(714) 882-5291; (714) 883-8689
(office); (1-800) 222-7273

SAN DIEGO

Center for Women's Services and
Studies
2467 E St.
San Diego, CA 92101
(619) 233-3088

SAN FRANCISCO

San Francisco Women Against
Rape
3543 Eighteenth St.
San Francisco, CA 94110
(415) 647-7273

University of California Rape
Treatment Center
500 Parnassus Ave.
San Francisco, CA 94143
(415) 666-9000

SAN JOSE

YWCA
375 S. Third St.
San Jose, CA 95112
(408) 287-3000; (408) 295-4011
(office)

SAN LUIS REY

Women's Resource Center
4070 Mission Ave.
San Luis Rey, CA 92068
(619) 757-3500

SAN MATEO

San Mateo Women Against Rape
P.O. Box 6299
San Mateo, CA 94403
(415) 349-7273

SAN PABLO

Rape Crisis Center of West
Contra Costa
c/o Brookside Hospital
Vale Rd.
San Pablo, CA 94806
(415) 236-7273

SAN RAFAEL

Marin Rape Crisis Center
P.O. Box 392
San Rafael, CA 94902
(415) 924-2100

SANTA BARBARA

Santa Barbara Rape Crisis Center
700 N. Milpas St.
Santa Barbara, CA 93103
(805) 569-2255; (805) 963-6832
(office)

SANTA CRUZ

Santa Cruz Women Against Rape
P.O. Box 711
Santa Cruz, CA 95061
(408) 426-7273

SANTA MONICA

Rape Treatment Center
Santa Monica Hospital Medical
Center
1225 Fifteenth St.
Santa Monica, CA 90404
(213) 319-4000

SANTA ROSA

Sonoma County Women Against
Rape
P.O. Box 1426
Santa Rosa, CA 95402
(707) 545-7273; (707) 545-7270
(office)

STOCKTON

Sexual Assault Center of San
Joaquin County
930 N. Commerce
Stockton, CA 95202
(209) 465-4997; (209) 941-2611
(office)

COLORADO

ASPEN

Aspen Mental Health Clinic
P.O. Box 2330
Aspen, CO 81612
(303) 925-5400

BOULDER

Mental Health Center
Attn: Ronah Brodkin
Rape Crisis Team
1333 Iris
Boulder, CO 80302
(303) 443-7300

COLORADO SPRINGS

Rape Crisis Service
12 N. Meade St.
Colorado Springs, CO 80909
(303) 471-4357; (303) 633-4601
(office)

DURANGO

Rape Intervention Team
c/o Community Hospital

3801 N. Main Ave.
Durango, CO 81301
(303) 259-1110

FORT COLLINS

Crisis and Information Helpline
700 W. Mountain
Fort Collins, CO 80521
(303) 493-3888

GRAND JUNCTION

Rape Crisis Center
1129 Colorado Ave.
Grand Junction, CO 81501
(303) 243-0190

GREELEY

Weld County Sexual Assault
Support Team
Box 240
Greeley, CO 80632
(303) 352-7273

CONNECTICUT

BRIDGEPORT

Rape Crisis Service/YWCA
753 Fairfield Ave.
Bridgeport, CT 06604
(203) 333-2233; (203) 334-6154
(office)

HARTFORD

Sexual Assault Crisis Service
YWCA
135 Broad St.
Hartford, CT 06105
(203) 522-6666; (203) 525-1163,
ext. 205 (office)

MIDDLETOWN

SAFE, Middlesex County
Sexual Assault Crisis Service

Community Health Center
P.O. Box 1514
Middletown, CT 06457
(203) 346-7233

MILFORD

Milford Rape Crisis Center
P.O. Box 521
Milford, CT 06460
(203)878-1212

NEW HAVEN

Rape Counseling Team
Yale–New Haven Hospital
20 York St.
New Haven, CT 06504
(203) 785-2222

Rape Crisis Center
YWCA
48 Howe St.
New Haven, CT 06511
(203) 624-2273

NEW LONDON

Women's Center Rape Crisis
Service
120 Broad St.
New London, CT 06320
(203) 442-4357

STAMFORD

Rape Crisis Service of Stamford
c/o Stamford Hospital
Shelburn Rd.
Stamford, CT 06901
(203) 329-2929; (203) 348-9346
(office)

WATERBURY

Sexual Assault Crisis Service
of the Central Naugatuck Valley,
Inc.

YWCA
80 Prospect St.
Waterbury, CT 06702
(203) 753-3613

DELAWARE

WILMINGTON

Victim/Witness Service Unit
820 N. French St., 8th floor
State Office Building
Wilmington, DE 19801
(302) 571-2566

DISTRICT OF COLUMBIA

WASHINGTON, D. C.

D.C. Rape Crisis Center
P.O. Box 21005
Washington, DC 20009
(202) 232-0202

FLORIDA

GAINESVILLE

Rape/Crime Victim Advocate
Program
730 N. Waldo Rd., Building "B,"
Suite 100
Gainesville, FL 32601
(904) 377-6888; (904) 372-3659
(office)

MIAMI

Rape Treatment Center
1611 N.W. Twelfth Ave.
Miami, FL 33136
(305) 325-7273; (305) 549-6949
(office)

OCALA

Creative Services/Rape Crisis,
Spouse Abuse
P.O. Box 2193
Ocala, FL 32678
(904) 622-8495

ORLANDO

Victim Advocate
Orange County Sheriff's Office
2400 W. Thirty-third St.
Orlando, FL 32809
(305) 420-4029

PENSACOLA

Rape Crisis Center of West
Florida
Lakeview Center
1221 W. Lakeview Ave.
Pensacola, FL 32501
(904) 433-7273

SARASOTA

SPARCC—Safe Place and Rape
Crisis Center
of Sarasota, Inc.
P.O. Box 1675
Sarasota, FL 33579
(813) 365-1976; (813) 365-0208
(office)

TAMPA

Hillsborough County Crisis
Center
2214 E. Henry St.
Tampa, FL 33610
(813) 238-8411

Sexual Abuse Treatment Center
2214 E. Henry St.
Tampa, FL 33610
(813) 228-7273

WEST PALM BEACH

Sexual Assault Assistance Project
Pan-Am Bldg., Suite 400
307 N. Dixie Hwy.
West Palm Beach, FL 33401
(305) 833-7273; (305) 837-2073
(office)

GEORGIA

ATLANTA

Rape Crisis Center
Grady Memorial Hospital: P.O.
Box 26049
80 Butler St., SE
Atlanta, GA 30303
(404) 588-4861

AUGUSTA

Augusta Rape Crisis Line
1350 Walton Way
Augusta, GA 30904
(404) 724-5200

SAVANNAH

Rape Crisis Center of the Coastal
Empire, Inc.
P.O. Box 8492
Savannah, GA 31412
(912) 233-7273

HAWAII

HONOLULU

Sex Abuse Treatment Center
Kapiolani Children's Medical
Center
1319 Punahou St.
Honolulu, HI 96826
(808) 524-7273

IDAHO

BOISE

Rape Crisis Alliance
Boise, ID
(208) 345-7273

CALDWELL

Rape Crisis Center of Canyon
County
1717 Arlington South
Caldwell, ID 83605
(208) 454-0101

MOSCOW

Women's Center
University of Idaho
Moscow, ID 83843
(208) 885-6616* (8:00 A.M.–5:00
P.M.); (208) 882-4511 (nights)

POCATELLO

Pocatello Women's Advocates
454 N. Garfield
Pocatello, ID 83204
(208) 232-9169; (208) 232-0742
(YWCA)

TWIN FALLS

Volunteers Against Violence, Inc.
P.O. Box 2444
Twin Falls, ID 83301
(208) 733-0100

ILLINOIS

BELLEVILLE

Rape Team
Call for Help, Inc.
500 Wilshire Dr.
Belleville, IL 62223
(618) 397-0963

CHICAGO

Rape Hotline
Department of Human Services
510 N. Prestigo Ct.
Chicago, IL 60611
(312) 744-8418; (312) 744-5829

Rape Victim Advocate Program
8519 W. Catalpa
Chicago, IL 60656
(312) 942-7277

Chicago Women Against Rape
Loop YWCA—Women's Services
37 S. Wabash
Chicago, IL 60603
(312) 372-6600, ext. 301 * (9:00
A.M.—5:00 P.M.)

EDWARDSVILLE

Rape and Sexual Abuse Care
Center
Southern Illinois University at
Edwardsville
P.O. Box 154
Edwardsville, IL 62026
(618) 692-2197

JOLIET

Will County Rape Crisis Center
P.O. Box 2354
Joliet, IL 60434
(815) 722-3344; (815) 744-5280
(office)

LOMBARD

Dupage Women Against Rape
(DWAR)
26 W. St. Charles Rd.
Lombard, IL 60148
(312) 971-3927; (312) 629-0170
(office) (YWCA)

ROCK ISLAND

Rape/Sexual Assault Counseling
Center
of Scott and Rock Island Counties
King Center; 630 9th St.
Rock Island, IL 61201
(309) 793-4784

ROCKFORD

Rockford Rape Counseling
Center, Inc.
1358 4th Ave.
Rockford, IL 61108
(815) 964-4044; (815) 962-3268
(office)

SPRINGFIELD

Rape Information and Counseling
Service (RICS)
P.O. Box 2211
Springfield, IL 62705
(217) 753-8081; (217) 522-4520
(office)

INDIANA

COLUMBUS

Rape and Battered Spouse Crisis
Line
Quinco Consulting Center
2075 Lincoln Park Dr.
Columbus, IN 47201
(812) 376-7273; (800) 832-5442
(toll-free in Indiana only)

EVANSVILLE

Crisis Line
Youth Services Bureau
312 N. W. Seventh
Evansville, IN 47708
(812) 425-4355

FORT WAYNE

Rape Awareness
P.O. Box 10554
Fort Wayne, IN 46853
(219) 426-7273

WARSAW

Protective Services for Sexual
Assault
Otis R. Bowen Center for Human
Services
850 N. Harrison St.
Warsaw, IN 46580
(219) 267-7169

LAWRENCEBURG

Rape Crisis Intervention Team
Community Mental Health
Center
285 Bielby Rd.
Lawrenceburg, IN 47025
(812) 537-1302

IOWA

AMES

Story County Sexual Assault Care
Center
P.O. Box 1965, ISU Station
Ames, IA 50010
(515) 232-2303

CEDAR RAPIDS

Rape Crisis Services
YWCA
318 Fifth St., SE
Cedar Rapids, IA 52401
(319) 363-5490; (319) 365-1458
(YWCA)

DAVENPORT

Rape/Sexual Assault Counseling
Center
of Scott and Rock Island Counties
115 W. 6th St.
Davenport, IA 52803
(319) 326-9191

FORT DODGE

Rape/Sexual Assault Victim
Advocates
Trinity Regional Hospital
South Kenyon Rd.
Fort Dodge, IA 50501
(515) 573-8000

IOWA CITY

Rape Victim Advocacy Program
130 N. Madison St.
Iowa City, IA 52240
(319) 338-4800

KANSAS

HAYS

Helpline
P.O. Box 290
Hays, KS 67601
(913) 628-1041

HUMBOLDT

Rape Counseling
Southeast Kansas Mental Health
Center
1106 S. Ninth St.
Humboldt, KS 66748
(316) 473-2241

HUTCHINSON

Women's Crisis Center (Rape
Center)
Route 2, Box 37

Hutchinson, KS 67501
(316) 663-2522

JUNCTION CITY

Junction City–Geary County
Rape Crisis Team
Geary County Hospital
Box 490
Junction City, KS 66441
(913) 238-4131

LAWRENCE

Headquarters
1419 Massachusetts
Lawrence, KS 66044
(913) 841-2345

MANHATTAN

Crisis Center, Inc.
P.O. Box 164
Manhattan, KS 66502
(913) 539-2785

WICHITA

Wichita Area Sexual Assault
Center, Inc.
1801 E. Tenth St.
Wichita, KS 67214
(316) 263-3002; (316) 263-0185
(office)

KENTUCKY

LEXINGTON

Lexington Rape Crisis Center
P.O. Box 1603
Lexington, KY 40592
(606) 253-2511; (606) 252-8514
(office)

OWENSBORO

Green River Comprehensive Care
Center Crisis Line

Rape Victim Services Project
233 W. Ninth St.
Owensboro, KY 42301
or 1001 Frederick St.
Owensboro, KY 42301
(502) 684-9466

Rape Victims Services Project
1316 W. Fourth St.
Owensboro, KY 42301
(502) 926-7273

LOUISVILLE

RAPE Relief Center
604 S. Third St.
Louisville, KY 40202
(502) 581-7273

NEWPORT

Women's Crisis Center of
Northern Kentucky
321 York St.
Newport, KY 41071
(606) 491-3335

LOUISIANA

ALEXANDRIA

Work Against Rape—Sexual
Assault Care Service/HELPLINE
1404 Murray St., P.O. Box 1908
Alexandria, LA 71309
(318) 445-2022

BATON ROUGE

Stop Rape Crisis Center
East Baton Rouge Parish District
Attorney's Office
215 St. Louis St., #307
Baton Rouge, LA 70801
(504) 383-7273

NEW ORLEANS

YWCA Rape Crisis Service
601 S. Jefferson Davis Pkwy.
New Orleans, LA 70119
(504) 483-8888; (504) 488-2693
(office)

MAINE

PORTLAND

The Rape Crisis Center of Greater
Portland
P.O. Box 1371
Portland, ME 04104
(207) 774-3613

MARYLAND

ANNAPOLIS

Anne Arundel County Sexual
Offense Crisis Center
1127 West St.
Annapolis, MD 21401
(301) 224-1321

BALTIMORE

Baltimore Center for Victims of
Sexual Assault
1010 St. Paul's St., Suite 2A
Baltimore, MD 21202
(301) 366-7273; (301) 685-0937

BETHESDA

Community Crisis Center/Sexual
Assault Services
4910 Auburn Ave.
Bethesda, MD 20814
(301) 656-9420; (301) 656-9526
(office)

CHEVERLY

Prince George's County Sexual
Assault Center
Prince George's General Hospital
and Medical Center
One Hospital Dr.
Cheverly, MD 20785
(301) 341-4942; (301) 341-2005
(office)

COLUMBIA

Howard County Sexual Assault
Center
Harriet Tubman Center
8045 Rt. 32
Columbia, MD 21044
(301) 997-3292; (301) 531-6096
(office)

MASSACHUSETTS

AMHERST

Counselors/Advocates Against
Rape
Everywoman's Center
Wilder Hall, University of
Massachusetts
Amherst, MA 01003
(413) 545-0800; (413) 545-0883
(office)

BOSTON

Rape Crisis Intervention Program
Beth Israel Hospital
330 Brookline Ave.
Boston, MA 02215
(617) 735-3337; (617) 735-4645
(information)

CAMBRIDGE

Boston Area Rape Crisis Center
Women's Center
46 Pleasant St.

Cambridge, MA 02139
(617) 492-7273

DEDHAM

Norfork County Rape Unit
360 Washington St.
Dedham, MA 02026
(617) 326-1111

HYANNIS

Mid-Cape Rape Crisis Unit
78 Pleasant St.
Hyannis, MA 02601
(617) 771-1080

LYNN

Rape Crisis Intervention Services
Greater Lynn Community Mental
Health Program
Union Hospital
500 Lynnfield St.
Lynn, MA 01904
(617) 595-7273

SPRINGFIELD

Hotline to End Rape and Abuse
(HERA)
P.O. Box 80126
Springfield, MA 01138
(413) 733-2561

WORCESTER

Rape Crisis Program
1016 Main St.
Worcester, MA 01609
(617) 799-5700; (617) 791-9546
(office)

MICHIGAN

ANN ARBOR

Assault Crisis Center
2350 E. Stadium

Ann Arbor, MI 48104
(313) 994-1616; (313) 971-9780
(office)

BAY CITY

Bay County Women's Center for
Rape and Assault
P.O. Box 646
Bay City, MI 48707
(517) 893-4551

DETROIT

Rape Counseling Center
Detroit Police Department
4201 St. Antoine
Detroit, MI 48201
(313) 224-4487; (313) 832-2530
(office)

EAST LANSING

Sexual Assault Counseling of the
Listening Ear
547½ E. Grand River Ave.
East Lansing, MI 48823
(517) 337-1717

GRAND RAPIDS

Rape Crisis Team
240 Cherry St.
Grand Rapids, MI 49503
(616) 774-3535

KALAMAZOO

Kalamazoo Sexual Assault
Program
YWCA
211 S. Rose St.
Kalamazoo, MI 49007
(616) 345-3036

MUSKEGON

Rape/Spouse Assault Crisis

Center of EveryWoman's
Place, Inc.
1433 Clinton
Muskegon, MI 49442
(616) 722-3333; (616) 726-4493

PONTIAC

Oakland Crisis Center for Rape
and Sexual Abuse
YWCA of Pontiac–North Oakland
92 Whitmore St.
Pontiac, MI 48058
(313) 334-1274; (313) 334-1284

PORT HURON

St. Clair County Domestic
Assault and Rape Elimination
Services Task Force (DARES)
700 Fort St.
Port Huron, MI 48060
(313) 985-5538

SAGINAW

Saginaw County Sexual Assault
Center
1226 N. Michigan Ave.
Saginaw, MI 48602
(517) 755-6565

MINNESOTA

BRAINERD

Women's Center of Mid-
Minnesota, Inc.
P.O. Box 602
Brainerd, MN 56401
(218) 828-1216

DULUTH

Aid to Victims of Sexual Assault
2 E. Fifth St.
Duluth, MN 55805
(218) 727-4353

MINNEAPOLIS

Sexual Assault Resource Service
at Hennepin County Medical
Center
701 Park Ave.
Minneapolis, MN 55415
(612) 347-5832 (office)
24-hour on-call services through
Crisis Intervention Center
(612) 347-3161

Sexual Violence Center
1222 W. 31st Street
Minneapolis, MN 55408
(612) 842-5555; (612) 824-2864
(office)

Rape and Sexual Assault Center
2431 Hennepin Ave. South
Minneapolis, MN 55405
(612) 825-4357 * (9:00 A.M.–7:30
P.M.)

ROCHESTER

Rapeline Program
515 Second St. S.W.
Rochester, MN 55902
(507) 289-0636

ST. CLOUD

Central Minnesota Sexual Assault
Center
701½ Mall Germain St.
St. Cloud, MN 56301
(612) 251-4357

ST. PAUL

Sexual Offense Services of
Ramsey County (SOS)
529 Jackson
St. Paul, MN 55101
(612) 298-5898

WINONA

Women's Resource Center
14 Exchange Bldg.
Winona, MN 55987
(507) 452-4440

MISSOURI

COLUMBIA

The Shelter
800 N. Providence, Suite 2
Columbia, MO 65201
(314) 875-1370; (314) 875-1369
(office)

KANSAS CITY

MOCSA
106 E. 31st Terrace
Kansas City, MO 64111
(816) 531-0233; (816) 931-4527

SPRINGFIELD

Rape Crisis Assistance, Inc.
432 Market
Springfield, MO 65802
(417) 866-6665

MONTANA

BILLINGS

Billings Rape Task Force
1245 N. Twenty-ninth St.,
Rm. 218
Billings, MT 59101
(406) 259-6506

KALISPELL

Kalispell Rape Crisis Line
Box 1385
Kalispell, MT 59901
(406) 755-5067

NEBRASKA

LINCOLN

Rape/Spouse Abuse Crisis Center
1133 H St.
Lincoln, NE 68508
(402) 475-7273

OMAHA

Women Against Violence
YWCA
222 S. 29th St.
Omaha, NE 68131
(402) 345-7273

NEVADA

LAS VEGAS

Community Action Against Rape
749 Veterans Memorial Dr., Rm.
150
Las Vegas, NV 89101
(702) 366-1640; (702) 385-2153
(office)

NEW HAMPSHIRE

MANCHESTER

Women's Crisis Line for Rape
Victims and Battered Women
YWCA
72 Concord St.
Manchester, NH 03101
(603) 668-2299

NASHUA

Rape and Assault Support Services
10 Prospect St., P.O. Box 217
Nashua, NH 03061
(603) 883-3044

NEW JERSEY

FLEMINGTON

Women's Crisis Services
26 Main St.
Flemington, NJ 08822
(201) 788-4044

NEWARK

Sexual Assault Rape Analysis
Unit (SARA)
1 Lincoln Ave.
Newark, NJ 07104
(201) 733-7273

NEW MEXICO

ALAMOGORDO

HELPline Rape Crisis Team
Otero County Mental Health
Association
1408 Eighth St.
Alamogordo, NM 88310
(505) 437-8680; (505) 437-7407

ALBUQUERQUE

Albuquerque Rape Crisis Center
905 Vassar NE
Albuquerque, NM 87106
(505) 247-0707

ARTESIA

Artesia Rape Crisis Team
Artesia Council for Human
Services, Inc.
801 Bush Ave.
Artesia, NM 88210
(505) 746-6222

CARLSBAD

Carlsbad Area Rape Crisis Center
Carlsbad Area Counseling and
Resource Center

701 N. Canal
Carlsbad, NM 88220
(505) 885-8888; (505) 887-0493
(office)

DEMING

Rape Crisis Program
P.O. Box 1132
Deming, NM 88031
(505) 546-2174 (office)

FARMINGTON

Center Against Sexual Assault
(CASA)
724 W. Animas
Farmington, NM 87401
(505) 325-0238

GRANTS

Rape Crisis
The Resource Center, Inc.
P.O. Drawer 966
Grants, NM 87020
(505) 287-8504; (505) 287-7985
(office)

HOBBS

Rape Crisis Center
Lea County Crisis Center, Inc.
920 W. Broadway
Hobbs, NM 88240
(505) 393-6633

LAS VEGAS

Rape Crisis Services
Sangree De Cristo Mental Health
Service
116 Bridge St.
Las Vegas, NM 87701
(505) 454-1451 * (8:00 A.M.–5:00
P.M.)

PORTALES

Roosevelt County Rape Crisis
Advocacy
Mental Health Resources, Inc.
300 E. First St.
Portales, NM 88130
(505) 432-2159; (505) 359-1221
(office)

ROSWELL

Counseling Association
109 W. Bland
Roswell, NM 88201
(505) 623-1480

SANTA FE

Santa Fe Rape Crisis Center, Inc.
P.O. Box 2822
Santa Fe, NM 87504
(505) 982-4667

TAOS

Community Against Rape, Inc.
Box 3170
Taos, NM 87571
(505) 758-2910

NEW YORK

BINGHAMTON

Rape Crisis Center
56–58 Whitney Ave.
Binghamton, NY 13902
(607) 722-4256

BRONX

Mayor's Task Force on Rape
Borough Crisis Center
Lincoln Hospital
234 E. 149th St.
Bronx, NY 10451
(212) 579-5624

BROOKLYN

Kings County Hospital Rape
Victim Companion Program
451 Clarkson Ave.
Brooklyn, NY 11203
(718) 735-2424

BUFFALO

Volunteer Support
Rape Advocacy Program
Crisis Services, Inc.
3258 Main St.
Buffalo, NY 14214
(716) 834-3131

JAMAICA

Mayor's Task Force on Rape
Borough Crisis Center
Queens Hospital Center
82-68 164th St., Rm. A-124
Jamaica, NY 11432
(718) 990-3187, 990-3188, or
990-3189

NEW YORK CITY

Rape Crisis Program
Department of Community
Medicine
St. Vincent's Hospital
153 W. Eleventh St.
New York, NY 10011
(212) 790-8068 *; (212) 790-8000
(evenings, weekends)

Rape Intervention Program
St. Luke's/Roosevelt Hospital
Center
44 Morningside Dr., Apt. 1
New York, NY 10025
(212) 870-1875 * (9:00 A.M.–5:00
P.M.)

ONEONTA

Oneonta Rape Crisis Network
c/o Opportunities for Otsego
32 Main St.
Oneonta, NY 13820
(607) 432-8088

PLATTSBURGH

Rape Crisis Program/Plattsburgh
Community Crisis Center
29 Protection Ave.
Plattsburgh, NY 12901
(518) 561-2330

ROCHESTER

Rape Crisis Service of Planned
Parenthood
of Rochester and Monroe County
24 Windsor St.
Rochester, NY 14605
(716) 546-2595

SCHENECTADY

Rape Crisis Service of
Schenectady, Inc.
c/o Planned Parenthood
414 Union St.
Schenectady, NY 12305
(518) 346-2266

SYRACUSE

Rape Crisis Center of Syracuse,
Inc.
423 W. Onondaga St.
Syracuse, NY 13202
(315) 422-7273

NORTH CAROLINA

ASHEVILLE

Rape Crisis Center of Asheville
P.O. Box 7453

Asheville, NC 28807
(704) 255-7576

BURLINGTON

Rape Crisis Alliance of Alamance
County
Box 2573
Burlington, NC 27215
(919) 227-6220

CHAPEL HILL

Orange County Women's Center
406 W. Rosemary St.
Chapel Hill, NC 27514
(919) 967-7273; (919) 968-4646
(office)

CHARLOTTE

Charlotte-Mecklenburg Rape
Crisis Service
P.O. Box 34372
Charlotte, NC 28234
(704) 375-9900

CONCORD

Cabarrus Rape Crisis Council
c/o Help Line
P.O. Box 1761
Concord, NC 28025
(704) 788-1156 * (8:00 A.M.–5:00
P.M.
and 7:00 P.M.–11:00 P.M.)

GREENSBORO

Turning Point
1301 N. Elm St.
Greensboro, NC 27401
(919) 273-7273; (919) 373-1345
(office)

GREENVILLE

Rape Victim Companion Program
REAL Crisis Prevention, Inc.

312 E. Tenth St.
Greenville, NC 27834
(919) 758-4357

MORGANTON

Foothills Rape Crisis Service
Burke County Human Resources
Center
700 East Parker Rd.
Morganton, NC 28655
(704) 433-4200

RALEIGH

Interact/Rape Crisis Center
17 Glenwood Ave.
Raleigh, NC 27605
(919) 755-6661

SALISBURY

The Rape, Child and Family
Abuse Crises
Council of Salisbury-Rowan, Inc.
127 W. Council St.
Salisbury, NC 28144
(704) 636-9222; (704) 636-4718
(office)

STATESVILLE

Rape and Abuse Prevention Group
of Statesville/Iredell County, Inc.
906 Fifth St.
Statesville, NC 28677
(704) 872-7638

NORTH DAKOTA

FARGO

Rape and Abuse Crisis Center of
Fargo-Moorhead
P.O. Box 2984
Fargo, ND 58108
(701) 293-7273

GRAND FORKS

Grand Forks Rape Crisis Center
27½ S. Third
Grand Forks, ND 58201
(701) 746-8900

OHIO

AKRON

Akron Rape Crisis Center
146 S. High St.
Akron, OH 44308
(216) 434-7273

CANTON

Rape Crisis Center
American Red Cross
618 Second St., NW
Canton, OH 44703
(216) 452-1111

COLUMBUS

Rape Crisis Center
P.O. Box 02084
Columbus, OH 43202
(614) 221-4447

Women Against Rape
P.O. Box 02084
Columbus, OH 43202
(614) 221-4447 * (5:00 P.M.–9:00
A.M.);
(614) 291-9751 (information)

TOLEDO

Toledo United Against Rape
P.O. Box 4372
Toledo, OH 43609
(419) 241-0888

WARREN

Rape Crisis Team
P.O. Box 1325

Warren, OH 44482
(216) 393-1565

OKLAHOMA

ENID

Rape Crisis Center
525 S. Quincy, P.O. Box 3165
Enid, OK 73701
(405) 234-7644

NORMAN

Norman Shelter Crisis Center
P.O. Box 5089
Norman, OK 73070
(405) 360-0590

OKLAHOMA CITY

Rape Crisis
YWCA Women's Resource Center
129 N.W. 5th
Oklahoma City, OK 73102
(405) 524-7273

OREGON

CORVALLIS

Center Against Rape and
Domestic Violence
216 S.W. Madison, P.O. Box 914
Corvallis, OR 97339
(503) 754-0110

OREGON CITY

Victim Assistance Division
707 Main St., Suite 210
Oregon City, OR 97045
(503) 655-8616

PENNSYLVANIA

ALLENTOWN

Rape Crisis Council of Lehigh
Valley, Inc.
P.O. Box 1445
Allentown, PA 18105
(215) 437-6610

ALTOONA

Sexual Assault Volunteer Effort
Mental Health Center
Altoona Hospital
Howard Ave. and Seventh St.
Altoona, PA 16601
(814) 946-2141

BUTLER

Center on Rape and Assault
(CORA)
337 E. Penn St.
Butler, PA 16001
(412) 282-7273

Irene Stacy Community Mental
Health Center
112 Hillvue Dr.
Butler, PA 16001
(412) 287-0791

DOYLESTOWN

Doylestown Network of Victim
Assistance
8 W. Oakland Ave.
Doylestown, PA 18901
(215) 752-3596; (215) 348-5664
(office)

DU BOIS

Crisis Unit
Clearfield/Jefferson Community
Mental Health Center
102 Hospital Ave.

Du Bois, PA 15801
(814) 371-1105; (814) 371-1100

EAST STROUDSBURG

Women's Resources
Monroe St.
East Stroudsburg, PA 18360
(717) 421-4200; (717) 421-4000 (at night)

ERIE

Rape Crisis Center
4518 Peach St.
Erie, PA 16509
(814) 868-1001

HARRISBURG

Harrisburg Area Rape Crisis
Center
215 Market St.
Harrisburg, PA 17101
(717) 238-7273

LANCASTER

Lancaster Rape Aid and
Prevention
501 W. James St.
Lancaster, PA 17603
(717) 392-7273

MEADVILLE

Crisis Line
751 Liberty St.
Meadville, PA 16335
(814) 724-2732

MEDIA

Delaware County Women Against
Rape, Inc.
P.O. Box 211
Media, PA 19063
(215) 566-4342

NORRISTOWN

Rape Crisis Center
P.O. Box 1179
Norristown, PA 19404
(215) 277-5200

STATE COLLEGE

Women's Resource Center/Rape-
Abuse Services
111 Sowers St., Suite 210
State College, PA 16801
(814) 234-5050; (814) 234-5222
(information and referral)

WEST CHESTER

Rape Crisis Council of Chester
County
Box 738
West Chester, PA 19381
(215) 692-7273

WILKES-BARRE

Luzerne County Women
Organized Against Rape (WOAR)
132 S. Franklin St.
Wilkes-Barre, PA 18701
(717) 823-0765

YORK

Rape and Victim Assistance
Center of York
437 W. Market St.
York, PA 17404
(717) 854-3131

RHODE ISLAND

CRANSTON

Rhode Island Rape Crisis Center,
Inc.
1660 Broad St.

Cranston, RI 02905
(401) 941-2400

SOUTH CAROLINA

CHARLESTON

People Against Rape
701 E. Bay St.
Charleston, SC 29403
(803) 722-7273

GREENVILLE

Rape Crisis Council of Greenville,
Inc.
700 Augusta St.
Greenville, SC 29605
(803) 232-8633

SOUTH DAKOTA

ABERDEEN

Women's Resource Center
317 S. Kline
Aberdeen, SD 57401
(605) 226-1212

BROOKINGS

Brookings Women's Center
802 Eleventh Ave.
Brookings, SD 57006
(605) 688-4518

TENNESSEE

KNOXVILLE

Knoxville Rape Crisis Center
P.O. Box 9418
Knoxville, TN 37920
(615) 522-7273; (615) 522-4745
(office)

MEMPHIS

Comprehensive Rape Crisis
Program
260 Poplar St., Suite 300
Memphis, TN 38122
(901) 528-2161

NASHVILLE

Rape and Sexual Abuse Center of
Davidson County
P.O. Box 120831
Nashville, TN 37212
(615) 327-1110

TEXAS

ABILENE

Abilene Rape Crisis Center
P.O. Box 122
Abilene, TX 79604
(915) 677-7895

AMARILLO

Rape Crisis and Sexual Abuse
Service
804 S. Bryan, Suite 207
Amarillo, TX 79106
(806) 373-8022

BEAUMONT

Rape Crisis Center of Southeast
Texas, Inc.
P.O. Box 5011
Beaumont, TX 77706
(409) 835-3355

DALLAS

Dallas County Rape Crisis Center
P.O. Box 35728
Dallas, TX 75235
(214) 521-1020

EL PASO

Rape Crisis Services
El Paso Mental Health
5250 El Paso Dr.
El Paso, TX 79905
(915) 779-1800

FORT WORTH

Rape Crisis Support of Tarrant
County
1203 Lake St.
Fort Worth, TX 76102
(817) 335-7273

KILLEEN

Families-in-Crisis Center
P.O. Box 25
Killeen, TX 76540
(817) 526-6111

LUBBOCK

Lubbock Rape Crisis Center
P.O. Box 2000
Lubbock, TX 79457
(806) 763-7273; (806) 763-3232

ROUND ROCK

Rape Crisis Center
2109 N. Mays
Round Rock, TX 78664
(512) 255-1212

SAN ANTONIO

Rape Crisis Line
P.O. Box 27802
San Antonio, TX 78227
(512) 349-7273

TYLER

Rape Crisis Center
1314 South Fleishel
Tyler, TX 75701
(214) 595-5591

UTAH

PROVO

Utah County Rape Crisis Line
P.O. Box 1375
Provo, UT 84601
(801) 226-8989

VERMONT

BURLINGTON

Women's Rape Crisis Center
P.O. Box 92
Burlington, VT 05401
(802) 863-1236

RUTLAND

Rutland County Rape Crisis
Team
Box 121
Rutland, VT 05701
(802) 775-1000

VIRGINIA

ARLINGTON

Rape Victim Companion Service
1725 N. George Mason Dr.
Arlington, VA 22205
(703) 558-2048

CHARLOTTESVILLE

Charlottesville Rape Crisis Group
214 Rugby Rd., P.O. Box 6705
Charlottesville, VA 22906
(804) 977-7273; (804) 295-7273

NORFOLK

Tidewater Rape Information
Service, Inc. (TRIS)
253 W. Freemason St.

Norfolk, VA 23510
(804) 622-4300

RICHMOND

Crisis Intervention Program
501 N. Ninth St.
Richmond, VA 23219
(804) 648-9224

WASHINGTON

BELLINGHAM

Whatcom County Rape Relief
Whatcom County Crisis Service
Mason Bldg., 124 E. Holly, Rm.
209
Bellingham, WA 98225
(206) 676-1175; (206) 384-1485
(office)

BREMERTON

Rape Response
920 Park Ave., P.O. Box 1327
Bremerton, WA 98310
(206) 479-8500

EVERETT

Sexual Assault Center
1103 Pacific
Everett, WA 98201
(206) 258-7780

OLYMPIA

Safe Place
P.O. Box 1605
Olympia, WA 98507
(206) 754-6300

PULLMAN

For Pullman, see Moscow, Idaho,
or call (509) 332-4357

RENTON

King County Rape Relief
305 S. Forty-third St.
Renton, WA 98055
(206) 226-7273; (206) 226-5062
(office)

RICHLAND

Benton Franklin Rape Relief and
Sexual Assault Program
P.O. Box 9
Richland, WA 99352
(509) 943-9104

SEATTLE

Seattle Rape Relief
1825 S. Jackson
Seattle, WA 98144
(206) 632-7273

Sexual Assault Center
Harborview Medical Center
325 Ninth Ave.
Seattle, WA 98104
(206) 223-3047 (days); (206)
223-3010
(nights, weekends: ask for social
worker)

SPOKANE

Rape Crisis Network
N. 1226 Howard St.
Spokane, WA 99201
(509) 624-7273

TACOMA

Pierce County Rape Relief
Allenmore Medical Center
Bldg. "B," Suite 2002
Nineteenth & Union
Tacoma, WA 98405
(206) 474-7273; (206) 597-6424
(office)

WENATCHEE

Wenatchee Rape Crisis Center
Chelan County Special Services
Center
1630 North Wenatchee Ave.
Wenatchee, WA 98801
(509) 663-7446

YAKIMA

Rape Relief Program
Central Washington
Comprehensive
Mental Health Center
Great Western Bldg.
321 E. Yakima Ave.
Yakima, WA 98901
(509) 575-4200

WEST VIRGINIA

MORGANTOWN

Rape and Domestic Violence
Information Center
P.O. Box 4228
Morgantown, WV 26505
(304) 292-5100

WISCONSIN

GREEN BAY

Green Bay Rape Crisis Center,
Ltd.
131 S. Madison
Green Bay, WI 54301
(414) 433-0584

MADISON

Dane County Project on Rape
312 E. Wilson St.
Madison, WI 53703
(608) 251-7273 (7:00 P.M.–7:00
A.M.)

Rape Crisis Center, Inc.
P.O. Box 1312
Madison, WI 53701
(608) 251-2345 (daytime Crisis
Intervention Service; 7:00 A.M.–
5:00 P.M.)

OSHKOSH

Winnebago County Rape Crisis
Center
660 Oak St.
Oshkosh, WI 54901
(414) 426-1460 (office)

KENOSHA

Kenoshans Sexual Assault
Treatment Program
St. Catherine's Hospital
3556 Seventh Ave.
Kenosha, WI 53140
(414) 658-1717

WYOMING

ROCKSPRINGS

Sweetwater County Task Force on
Sexual Assault
450 S. Main
Rocksprings, WY 82901
(307) 382-4381

SUGGESTED ADDITIONAL READINGS

GENERAL

Dowling, Colette. *The Cinderella Complex*. New York: Pocket Books, 1981.

Lovelace, Linda. *Ordeal*. New York: Berkley Books, 1980.

Schaef, Anne Wilson. *Women's Reality*. Minneapolis: Winston Press, 1981.

RAPE

Beneke, Timothy. *Men on Rape*. New York: St. Martin's Press, 1982.

Brownmiller, Susan. *Against Our Will*. New York: Simon and Schuster, 1975.

Griffin, Susan. *Rape: The Power of Consciousness*. San Francisco: Harper & Row, 1979.

Groth, A. Nicholas. *Men Who Rape*. New York: Plenum Press, 1979.

Hilberman, Elaine. *The Rape Victim*. Washington, D. C.: American Psychiatric Association, 1976.

Hursch, Carolyn J. *The Trouble with Rape*. Chicago: Nelson-Hall, 1977.

Medea, Andra, and Kathleen Thompson. *Against Rape*. New York: Farrar, Straus and Giroux, 1974.

Russell, Diana E. H. *Politics of Rape*. New York: Stein and Day, 1975.

Schwendinger, Julia R. and Herman. *Rape and Inequality*. Beverly Hills, Calif.: Sage Publications, 1983.

Warner, Carmen Germaine. *Rape and Sexual Assault*. Germantown, Md.: Aspen Systems Corporation, 1980.

CHILDREN

Brady, Katherine. *Father's Day*. New York: Dell, 1979.

Geiser, Robert L. *Hidden Victims: The Sexual Abuse of Children*. Boston: Beacon Press, 1979.

INDEX